Social-Emotional Prevention Programs for Preschool Children's Behavior Problems

Catrinel Alice Ştefan

Social-Emotional Prevention Programs for Preschool Children's Behavior Problems

A Multi-level Efficacy Assessment of Classroom, Risk Group, and Individual Level

palgrave
macmillan

Catrinel Alice Ştefan
Babeş-Bolyai University
Cluj-Napoca, Cluj, Romania

ISBN 978-3-030-09068-5 ISBN 978-3-319-74751-4 (eBook)
https://doi.org/10.1007/978-3-319-74751-4

Softcover re-print of the Hardcover 1st edition 2018

Cover Design by Thomas Howey

Printed on acid-free paper

This Palgrave Macmillan imprint is published by Springer Nature
The registered company is Springer International Publishing AG
The registered company address is: Gewerbestrasse 11, 6330 Cham, Switzerland

Preface

This book approaches preschool children's social-emotional development from both a theoretical and an applied perspective. It is intended to offer a step-by-step description of the process involved in translating theoretical knowledge about children's social-emotional competencies into an effective intervention tool for school-based interventions. Such an undertaking is important due to several reasons. First, in spite of numerous research outcomes supporting the relevance of children's social-emotional competencies for their mental health and school adjustment, interventions aiming to develop social-emotional skills are not yet part of systematic school-based prevention efforts. Second, a relatively large proportion of preventive interventions in schools are not developed by considering scientific evidence, nor do they rely on systematic assessment of their outcomes. And third, specifically for Romania, while the reforms within the educational system placed an emphasis on social-emotional learning, they did not provide an appropriate set of tools which would have enabled teachers to address the building of such skills in the classroom.

Taken together, these arguments would suggest that researchers should not only provide empirical evidence concerning the efficacy of a particular intervention, but they might consider offering an insight into how research can actually inform the development of interventions in schools. Therefore, this book was written with the intention of bridging an academic perspective grounded in empirical evidence concerning an intervention's efficacy with the practitioner's perspective emphasizing its content and sustainability in ecological contexts.

Thus, this book covers each step involved in the development and efficacy assessment of a multifocused (child, parent, and teacher) prevention program for preschool children's behavior problems. The book is organized in six chapters, and contains three appendices. Chapter 1 focuses on introducing the reader to the relevance of social-emotional development for children's mental health and school adjustment. Furthermore, the chapter provides definitions of emotional and social competencies, as well as descriptions of corresponding child behaviors. Also, children's skills are discussed within the context of protective and risk factors for behavior problems, while also offering an integrative perspective on how different risk factors pertaining to the child, the parent, or the educational environment can enhance the risk of such difficulties. An analysis of strengths and weakenesses of prevention programs is offered considering the manner in which evidence-based interventions aim to address different types of risk sources.

Drawing from the concluding remarks of the previous chapter, Chap. 2 is aimed at describing the theoretical framework of the Social-Emotional Prevention Program (SEP). Thus considering some of the limitations of previous prevention programs, the SEP is defined as a hybrid prevention program including a universal (for low-risk children) and an indicated (for high-risk children) intervention. A comparison between SEP and other evidence-based prevention programs is offered together with a description of each intervention component: the classroom curriculum, the teacher training, and the parent training.

The next three chapters discuss results from the SEP efficacy assessment at different levels. More precisely, Chap. 3 presents results from the efficacy testing at the classroom level; Chap. 4 focuses on results from comparisons of outcomes related to separate measures of social and emotional competence screening at two intervention levels: universal intervention targeting high-risk children, and universal intervention targeting moderate- and low-risk children; and Chap. 5 presents the outcomes for classroom observed behaviors in a single-subject experiment. Thus, these chapters contain results obtained across different informants (i.e., child, parent, teacher) and different assessment methods (i.e., child report, questionnaire, classroom observation) employing a variety of research designs from partially randomized controlled trials to multiple baseline designs and corresponding statistical procedures. Results of SEP efficacy are discussed not only in relation to extant evidence-based interventions, but also in relation to specific implications of the findings for practice in schools.

Chapter 6 summarizes the theoretical, methodological, and empirical contributions of the studies presented in the previous three chapters. It also covers an in-depth discussion of the limitations of these studies and presents corresponding future directions of research, while the final section of the chapter discusses how findings on SEP efficacy could influence policy making in the field of early education.

In addition to the chapters, the book also includes three appendices. These contain the treatment planner for each SEP component of the classroom curriculum, the teacher training and the parent training. Each treatment planner consists of a detailed description of the objectives, activities and methods employed in SEP. These provide a helpful insight into how intervention principles described in Chap. 2 were employed in the actual intervention.

Cluj-Napoca, Romania Catrinel Alice Ştefan

Acknowledgments

This book includes research presented in a doctoral thesis defended on 15 October 2010 at Babeş-Bolyai University in Romania and therefore it is important to acknowledge the contribution of all those who have supported this project. I am grateful to my Ph.D. supervisor Professor Mircea Miclea Ph.D. (Babeş-Bolyai University). His belief that we as researchers must not only seek to uncover knowledge, but also need to give something worthwhile and life-changing back to the people from our communities, has been a true inspiration. Also, I am thankful to Professor Oana Benga, Ph.D. (Babeş-Bolyai University) whose guidance was instrumental in taking the first step in developing what was later to become the Social-Emotional Prevention Program (SEP). In addition, my thoughts turn to the school headmasters and teachers who agreed to get involved in this project without any expectation of reward, to the parents who welcomed this undertaking, and to the students who have helped with different data collection procedures.

Contents

1 **Introduction: Principles Underlying the Development of Social-Emotional Prevention Programs for Preschoolers' Behavior Problems and Characteristics of Evidence-Based Interventions** 1
Defining Social-Emotional Competencies in Preschool Children 2
Protective and Risk Factors Involved in the Development and Maintenance of Behavior Problems 8
Characteristics of Evidence-Based Prevention Programs for Preschoolers' Behavior Problems 16
References 25

2 **The Conceptual Framework of the Social-Emotional Prevention Program** 41
Underlying Assumptions of SEP Development 42
The SEP Framework in the Context of Evidence-Based Preventive Programs from the Field of Early Education 45
Objectives, Structure, and Contents of the SEP Program 48
Parent Training 55
References 59

3 Assessing SEP Efficacy at the Classroom Level: Effects on Children's Social-Emotional Competencies and Behavior Problems 67
Introduction 67
The Current Study 70
Method 70
Results 78
Discussion 84
Conclusions and Implications for Practice 88
References 89

4 Assessing SEP Efficacy as a Function of Children's Risk Status: A Separate Evaluation of Indicated and Universal Intervention Levels 95
Introduction 95
The Current Study 99
Method 101
Results 107
Discussion 144
Conclusions and Implications for Practice 154
References 155

5 Assessing SEP Efficacy at the Individual Level: A Multiple Baseline Evaluation of Changes in Observed Classroom Behaviors 163
Introduction 163
The Current Study 166
Method 167
Results 173
Discussion 184
Conclusions and Implications for Practice 186
References 188

6 Conclusion: Contributions of Research on SEP Efficacy to the Field of Early Education Programs, Limitations, and Future Directions 195
Theoretical, Methodological and Empirical Contributions to Advancing Knowledge About Preventive Programs for Preschoolers 195
Limitations and Future Directions of Research 204
Implications for Practice and Policy Makers in the Field of Early Education 209
References 213

Appendix 1 221

Appendix 2 237

Appendix 3 253

Index 269

List of Figures

Fig. 1.1	Interactions between intrapersonal and interpersonal risk factors involved in increasing risk of early onset conduct problems	14
Fig. 5.1	Observation of compliance across 3 participants in a non-concurrent MBD	180
Fig. 5.2	Observation of frustration tolerance across 3 participants in a non-concurrent MBD	181
Fig. 5.3	Observation of prosocial behaviors across 3 participants in a non-concurrent MBD	182
Fig. 5.4	Observation of cooperative behaviors across 3 participants in a non-concurrent MBD	183

List of Tables

Table 1.1	Emotional and social competencies in preschoolers and their corresponding skills and behaviors	3
Table 1.2	Empirically validated preventive interventions targeting social-emotional competencies	18
Table 3.1	Risk status and demographic factors for dropout and non-dropout participants from the intervention and control groups	71
Table 3.2	Means and standard deviations for intervention and control groups	79
Table 3.3	Student-classroom hierarchical linear modeling analyses: the effects of SEP on experimental task performance controlling for gender, age, and preintervention score	81
Table 3.4	Student-classroom hierarchical linear modeling analyses: the effects of SEP on teacher's ratings controlling for gender, age, and preintervention score	82
Table 3.5	Student-classroom hierarchical linear modeling analyses: the effects of SEP on parent's ratings controlling for gender, age, and pretest score	83
Table 4.1	SEP mechanisms underlying the universal and the indicated prevention strategies	96
Table 4.2	Demographic characteristics and risk status of intervention and control group children as a function of risk status and type of competence screening performed by teachers	102
Table 4.3	Demographic characteristics and risk status of intervention and control group children as a function of risk status and type of competence screening performed by parents	103

Table 4.4 Intervention effects on children's classroom behaviors and declarative knowledge for the high-risk social competence groups 110
Table 4.5 Intervention effects on children's classroom behaviors and declarative knowledge for high risk emotional competence groups 113
Table 4.6 Intervention effects on children's classroom behaviors and declarative knowledge for moderate-risk social competence groups 115
Table 4.7 Intervention effects on children's classroom behaviors and declarative knowledge for low-risk social competence groups 118
Table 4.8 Intervention effects on children's classroom behaviors and declarative knowledge for moderate-risk emotional competence groups 121
Table 4.9 Intervention effects on children's classroom behaviors and declarative knowledge for low-risk emotional competence groups 124
Table 4.10 Intervention effects on children's behaviors at home and declarative knowledge for high-risk social competence groups 127
Table 4.11 Intervention effects on discipline and stress for children's parents from the high-risk social competence groups 129
Table 4.12 Intervention effects on children's behaviors at home and declarative knowledge for high-risk emotional competence groups 131
Table 4.13 Intervention effects on discipline and stress for children's parents from the high-risk emotional competence groups 132
Table 4.14 Intervention effects on children's behaviors at home and declarative knowledge for moderate-risk social competence groups 134
Table 4.15 Intervention effects on discipline and stress for children's parents from the moderate-risk social competence groups 135
Table 4.16 Intervention effects on children's behaviors at home and declarative knowledge for low-risk social competence groups 137
Table 4.17 Intervention effects on discipline and stress for children's parents from the low-risk social competence groups 138
Table 4.18 Intervention effects on children's behaviors at home and declarative knowledge for moderate-risk emotional competence groups 139

Table 4.19	Intervention effects on discipline and stress for children's parents from the moderate-risk emotional competence groups	140
Table 4.20	Intervention effects on children's behaviors at home and declarative knowledge for low-risk emotional competence groups	142
Table 4.21	Intervention effects on discipline and stress for children's parents from the low-risk emotional competence groups	143
Table 5.1	Participant risk assessments based on teacher evaluations	168
Table 5.2	Description of positive and negative child behaviors observed in the classroom	171
Table 5.3	Means, standard deviations, mean shift, variability changes, level changes, and autocorrelations for observed behaviors	175
Table 5.4	*Z* scores derived from the *C* statistic and its standard deviations for observed classroom behaviors	177
Table 6.1	Theoretical, methodological, and empirical contributions	196

CHAPTER 1

Introduction: Principles Underlying the Development of Social-Emotional Prevention Programs for Preschoolers' Behavior Problems and Characteristics of Evidence-Based Interventions

Several epidemiological studies indicate that incidence rates for early onset behavior disorders are rapidly increasing, and behavioral markers of such disorders can be identified in 5–25% of preschool children (Snyder 2001). Also, about 50% of children with moderate to severe symptoms of externalizing problems at this age continue to manifest similar problems after entering school (Webster-Stratton 1996; Webster-Stratton and Taylor 2001). Among those with continuing problems the most frequent diagnoses are oppositional defiant disorder (ODD), conduct disorder (CD), and attention-deficit hyperactivity disorder (ADHD) (Webster-Stratton 1996). This raised significant concerns as behaviors problems stemming from early childhood seem to be associated with long-term social adjustment problems such as peers' rejection, delinquency, or substance abuse, as well as school related difficulties such as school dropout (Moffitt and Caspi 2001; Snyder 2001). One potential strategy for decreasing children's risk for maladaptive behaviors is through implementing preventive strategies in school settings. Schools offer an invaluable opportunity to address the mental health needs of a large category of children, as research data suggest that 1 in 3 preschoolers is likely to manifest some sort of difficult behavior during preschool (Prinz and Sanders 2007).

C. A. Ştefan, *Social-Emotional Prevention Programs for Preschool Children's Behavior Problems*,
https://doi.org/10.1007/978-3-319-74751-4_1

Preventive programs delivered in schools are aimed at developing social-emotional competencies, as research has shown that children's difficulties in this domain are associated with increased levels of aggression and non-compliance, behavioral markers of externalizing problems (Eisenberg et al. 2005a, b; Hastings et al. 2000). Additionally, some longitudinal studies have emphasized the relative stability of these competencies from preschool to adolescence (Abe and Izard 1999; Eisenberg et al. 2003), meaning that maladaptive interaction patterns become more resistant to intervention if they are reinforced over time. Given the burden which mental health problems place on children, their families, and society, as well as the compelling empirical evidence supporting the notion that early intervention programs targeting social-emotional development may be effective in preventing the escalation of maladaptive behaviors, it is important to investigate the underlying principles of developing these programs in order to understand how their efficacy could be enhanced (Nation et al. 2003; Nelson et al. 2003).

Defining Social-Emotional Competencies in Preschool Children

A large body of empirical evidence suggests that low levels of social-emotional competencies place children at increased risk of developing externalizing problems (Eisenberg et al. 2005b; Hastings et al. 2000). However, in order to understand how interventions target social-emotional development in preschool children, one must first define this set of competencies. Broadly stated, social-emotional competencies encompass a set of declarative and procedural knowledge which is necessary to understand and manage emotions, feel and show empathy towards others, as well as establish and maintain positive relationships with others (Mayer and Salovey 1997). Although social and emotional competencies are highly related, recent research has suggested that they are interconnected abilities, encompassing different knowledge and skills (Halberstadt et al. 2001). Therefore, in the following sections these competencies are described separately as emotional competencies and social competencies.

Emotional Competencies

A working definition of emotional competence states that it is the ability to effectively manage emotions which are elicited during social transactions (Buckley et al. 2003; Saarni 2001). In order to achieve competence in this respect, 3 types of abilities should be acquired: emotion recognition, emotional expressiveness, and emotion regulation, which are presented in Table 1.1 (Denham 2006). *Emotion recognition* involves 2 sets of abilities: (1) expressive recognition meaning the ability to accurately label an emotion; and (2) receptive recognition involving the ability to identify an emotion based on facial cues (Denham 2006). Children who exhibit difficulties in recognizing their own emotions as well as other emotions are more likely to manifest difficulties in accurately decoding emotional cues (Dunn and Cutting 1999; Halberstadt et al. 2001). This is of particular importance during social interactions, in which mistakingly decoding a facial response as anger instead of sadness, could elicit negative interpretations about the other child's intentions ("he does not want to share the toy"). Increased ability to recognize emotions is mostly predictive of children's ability to manage emotions (Eisenberg et al. 2005a, b; Schultz et al. 2001). Conversely, research confirmed that children who are less accurate in recognizing emotions are also likely to act aggressively, which in turn increases the probability of being at risk of externalizing problems (Denham et al. 2001, 2002). Development of children's emotion knowledge is mostly grounded in their learning experiences emphasizing the use of words describing emotions and discussions about emotions mainly during parent-child conversations (Eisenberg et al. 2003; Martin and Green 2005). These strategies were shown to elicit positive effects on children's ability to effectively regulate emotions and display prosocial behaviors (Denham et al. 2000; Izard et al. 2001).

Table 1.1 Emotional and social competencies in preschoolers and their corresponding skills and behaviors

Competence		*Skill*	*Behavior*
Emotional competence		1. Emotion knowledge	Expressive/receptive recognition
		2. Emotion expressiveness	Predominantly positive expression
		3. Emotion regulation	Adaptive self-regulatory strategies
Social competence	1. Interpersonal	Problem-solving	Turn taking, sharing, waiting, etc.
		Peer relations	Involvement in cooperative play
	2. Intrapersonal	Compliance with rules	Active compliance
		Frustration tolerance	Delaying rewards

The second component of emotional competence, *emotional expressiveness*, refers to the ability to convey messages containing features of emotions (i.e., mostly facial expressions) in a socially acceptable manner (Denham 2007). Emotional expressiveness is generally equated in the field of developmental psychology to a tendency to manifest predominantly positive or negative emotions. Positive emotional expressiveness has been linked to increased levels of prosocial behavior, peer acceptance, and higher parent and teacher rated social competence (Denham et al. 2001; Eisenberg et al. 2000; Roberts and Strayer 1996). In turn, negative emotional expressiveness characterized by predominant expressions of anger seems to be associated with lower levels of empathy and higher rates of aggressive behavior (Eisenberg et al. 2000; Strayer and Roberts 2004). Children who predominantly express anger during their play interactions with peers are more likely to exhibit symptoms associated with externalizing problems (Cole et al. 1996; Eisenberg et al. 2005b; Kochanska et al. 2000). Emotional expressiveness is associated with certain temperamental characteristics, but it is also influenced by caregivers' emotion socialization strategies (Eisenberg et al. 1998). More precisely, preschoolers who are expected to suppress negative emotions are deprived of learning contexts in which they can be taught how to effectively manage such emotional reactions. In contrast, children who are encouraged to express their emotions are more likely to acquire and internalize rules for socially acceptable emotional displays (Chaplin et al. 2005; Eisenberg et al. 2003), and manifest more prosocial behaviors in relation to other children (Roberts 1999).

The last component of emotional competence is *emotion regulation*. Emotion regulation refers to "the intrinsic and extrinsic processes involved in evaluating, monitoring and modifying emotional reactions [...] in order to accomplish one's goals" (Thompson 1994; Stansbury and Sigman 2000). According to Stansbury and Sigman (2000) children progress during this developmental stage from mainly coregulatory (i.e., controlled by adults) to more self-regulatory (i.e., self-controlled) strategies. Research on children's emotion regulatory abilities has established that preschoolers are able to understand and perform a relatively wide range of self-regulatory strategies which include: attention disengagement (i.e., thinking about something else), behavioral disengagement (i.e., doing something else), problem-solving (i.e., finding and implementing a solution to a problem), or cognitive reappraisal (i.e., reinterpreting a given situation) (Cole et al. 2003, 2009; Compas et al. 2001).

Children's emotion regulatory abilities seem to be influenced by both temperamental and parent related childrearing practices. Research on children's emotional regulation abilities uncovered that they are tightly related to the concept of effortful control, the ability to inhibit a dominant response in order to perform a subdominant response (Eisenberg et al. 2004; Rothbart and Bates 1998). More precisely, children low on attention focusing and inhibitory control, are more likely to exhibit high levels of externalizing problems (Eisenberg et al. 2005b; Hill et al. 2006; Spinrad et al. 2006). Moreover, emotion regulation processes are related to emotional expressiveness, as children with poor regulatory abilities are more likely to express negative emotions such as anger (Calkins and Dedmon 2000; Gilliom et al. 2002; Eisenberg et al. 2005a). Therefore, difficulties with anger regulation are most often associated with increased levels of aggression and impaired social functioning (Eisenberg et al. 1999; Rydell et al. 2003; Spinrad et al. 2006). Temperamental influence on children's emotion regulation abilities interplays with parental strategies which can either contribute or interfere with effective emotion regulation. Self-regulatory skills also develop as children internalize other's evaluations about their own emotions. Therefore, parents who respond to children's emotions by accepting and being supportive are actually increasing the probability that their child is able to effectively use adaptive self-regulatory strategies such as behavioral and attentional disengagement or problem-solving, whereas parents that are dismissive, punitive, or exhibit high levels of distress as a result of children's negative emotions harbor more avoidant or aggressive strategies in managing emotions (Berlin et al. 2008; Eisenberg et al. 1999, 2005b).

Social Competencies

Social competence is defined as the capacity to manifest goal oriented, socially acceptable behaviors, which have positive consequences for the individual or the group (Merrell and Gimpel 1998). Whereas skills associated with emotional competence are relatively straightforward to identify in the literature on children's early development, deriving a taxonomy of social competence related skills seems to be more challenging. More precisely, factor analysis methods extracted 5 dimensions of social competence: peer relations, self-management, academic, compliance, and assertion (Merrell and Gimpel 1998). Another approach proposed the distinction between problem-solving abilities and interpersonal abilities (Denham 2006). Based on these classifications, a hybrid model of social competencies can be derived, which is depicted in Table 1.1: (1) social interpersonal competence including problem-solving abilities and peer relations (e.g., prosocial behavior, play cooperation); and (2) intrapersonal skills related to self-management abilities (e.g., compliance with rules, reward delay).

Interpersonal skills refer to a child's ability to interact with peers during play. The first category of interpersonal skills is *problem-solving*, namely the ability to find constructive solutions to conflicts during play (Howe et al. 2002). During this developmental stage, the following types of play related conflicts seem to occur most often: (1) conflicts about continuing a play scenario; (2) conflicts related to play space; and (3) conflicts related to play activities (Howe et al. 2002). In such circumstances children can choose between constructive, aggressive, or avoidant strategies to manage conflicts (Ricaud-Droisy and Zaouche-Gaudron 2003). Constructive strategies mean that children resort to the so-called prosocial behaviors as a means of solving the conflict. Prosocial behaviors are defined as a category of voluntary actions directed to other people's benefit (Krueger et al. 2001). Preschoolers' prosocial behaviors include sharing toys, asking and providing help, or turn-taking (Caldarella and Merrell 1997; Warnes et al. 2005). Prosocial behaviors play a catalyst role in developing and maintaining friendships with other children, as children who employ such problem-solving strategies are perceived positively by their peers and are easily accepted in play groups (Zanolli et al. 1997).

Conversely, children who resort to destructive, aggressive strategies are more likely to be rejected by their peers (Romano et al. 2005; Sebanc 2003). The risk faced by children who are rejected by their peers is that their aggressive behavior patterns are consolidated and may become a potential symptom of conduct problems (Eisenberg et al. 1999). It is also apparent that these types of socially unacceptable solutions are more often employed by preschoolers compared with older children (Crick et al. 1997, 1999). It seems that this constitutes a developmental trend which subsides in a large category of preschoolers by the age of 5, as children are exposed through modeling to more prosocial problem-solving. However, research also highlights the negative long-term consequences of consolidating such strategies on accurate information processing (Crick and Dodge 1994; Lemerise and Arsenio 2000). In a model of social behavior proposed by Lemerise and Arsenio (2000) based on Crick and Dodge's (1994) model, it is apparent that the mechanism underlying aggressive behavior is related to misattributing hostile intentions to others' behaviors even when such inferences are not supported by actual social cues.

The second category of interpersonal skills is related to children's ability to establish friendships through involvement in *cooperative play*. During preschool, children learn to interact in larger groups, predominantly with same-sex peers (Colwell and Lindsay 2005; Fabes et al. 2003). Gradually they are able to control more complex interactions, and one prerequisite for such abilities is pretend play (Wilburn 2000). Children engaging more frequently in pretend play have positive interactions with their peers and are perceived by teachers as more socially competent (Sebanc 2003). Pretend play abilities also represent an important acquisition in children's behavioral repertoire, as it is an ability exploited in group interactions. More precisely, cooperative play evolves during preschool from isolated play, which requires minimal verbal exchanges to a more complex form of play in which children put together scenarios requiring extensive verbal exchanges (Haight et al. 1999; Maguire and Dunn 1997). Thus, during this developmental stage children learn about reciprocity, namely about the fact that their ability to elaborate on other children's play initiatives is key to maintaining interactions and provides the context for developing friendships (Cutting and Dunn 2006; Haight et al. 1999). Unsurprisingly, children who are more skilled at initiating play or answering adequately to other children's requests are more popular among their peers (Howe et al. 2005; Mendez et al. 2002a, b). On the other hand, children lacking cooperation skills are rejected by their peers, and consequently, are more likely to avoid social interactions due to negative feedback (Hay et al. 2004; Mendez et al. 2002a, b).

The second type of social competence, namely intrapersonal competence can be defined as children's ability to manifest socially acceptable behavior as a result of their capacity to effectively manage emotions. A first type of intrapersonal social competence is *compliance with rules*, a set of behaviors enacted in order to adapt to parent or teacher expectations concerning a given behavior (Wahler 1997). As opposed to compliance, non-compliance takes different forms, but research suggests that only direct non-compliace defined as the tendency to say "no" to adults' requests is actually associated with increased levels of externalizing problems (Kochanska 2002; Kochanska et al. 2000). Furthermore, direct non-compliance is associated with more frequent anger outbursts, thus offering further support to the notion that difficulties with anger regulation impact children's social behaviors (Lee et al. 2004, 2008).

The second type of intrapersonal social competence is related to *reward delay*. The experimental paradigm which evaluates this behavior is called the "marshmallow experiment" (Wulfert et al. 2002). The initial experimental paradigm proposed by Mischel (1974) required children to make a choice between a smaller, but immediate reward and a larger, but delayed reward. It was also apparent that children who chose the lager, delayed reward were more successful in managing their emotions. This ability has important consequences for children's ability to adapt to environmental demands (Wulfert et al. 2002). For example, children who are able to delay rewards are more apt to tolerate frustration, and therefore, less inclined to react aggressively when frustrated (Eigisti et al. 2006; Wulfert et al. 2002). Also, one long-term effect of low frustration tolerance is decreased academic performance (Bembenutty and Karabenick 2004), as children are less equipped to ignore distractors and focus their attention on learning tasks (Cemore and Herwig 2005).

Protective and Risk Factors Involved in the Development and Maintenance of Behavior Problems

Children's risk of behavior problems is the result of complex interactions between different risk factors (Fabes et al. 2006). Hence, in order to gain a better understanding of the behaviors targeted by community-based preventive interventions, it is important to describe developmental pathways which might lead to children's behavior problems. In the following sections, several protective/risk factors are reviewed: (1) child related factors; (2) parent related factors; (3) educational environment related factors; and (4) context related factors.

Child Related Factors

As consistently pointed out throughout the current chapter, social-emotional skills are predictive of positive outcomes ranging from children's mental health to their school adjustment and performance. Overall, children with better developed competencies are less likely to be rated high on measures of externalizing problems; conversely, children who are rated by their teachers and parents as low on social-emotional skills tend to score higher on measures of aggressive and non-compliant behaviors (Denham et al. 2001, 2002). The mechanisms involved in increasing children's risk can be ascribed to a cascade of interactions. Most of the currently available research data on social-emotional development are derived from correlational studies, which suggest that the relationship between emotional and social competencies is bidirectional. However, some research supports the notion that emotional competence could precede, and represents a pathway for social competence development (Denham et al. 2003a; Lemerise and Arsenio 2000).

A closer look at how these competencies are interrelated, would suggest that such a scenario is plausible. For instance, difficulties in recognizing emotions have been associated with difficulties in emotion regulation (Denham et al. 2003b; Eisenberg et al. 2005a; Schultz et al. 2001). Additionally, predominantly negative emotion expressiveness is related to more difficulties in emotion regulation, and such difficulties were shown to increase the likelihood of aggressive behaviors (Eisenberg et al. 2002, 2005b). Also, children who display maladaptive emotion regulation strategies are less likely to resolve conflict by eliciting prosocial behaviors, and are more likely to respond non-compliantly to adults' requests (Lee et al. 2004, 2008). In sum, these results would suggest that to some extent gains children make in their emotional competencies are important prerequisites for improved adjustment, as children who exhibit adaptive emotion regualtion strategies and prosocial behaviors are more popular among their peers and are more easily accepted by them (Denham et al. 2001; Eisenberg et al. 2000; Roberts and Strayer 1996).

Parent Related Factors

The most often parent related factor addressed by research on children's risk of externalizing problems is parenting style, which is a relatively broad concept encompassing behaviors that shape parent-child interactions such as parental knowledge about children's development, discipline style, and child monitoring (Sanders and Morawska 2005). Research on parenting style indicated that it is a reliable predictor of children's continued patterns of behavior problems from preschool to first grade (Kilgore et al. 2000; Snyder et al. 2005b).

Parental knowledge about child development, the first component of parenting style discussed, is relevant because parental understanding of their child's ability helps them set age-appropriate expectations (Sanders and Morawska 2005). When parents are insufficiently informed or lack altogether such knowledge, they tend to either expect too much or too little from their children. In the first case, expecting too much exposes children to failure because high expectations mean that they do not have the necessary skills to perform according to parents' standards. This in turn, can lead to non-compliance as a self-protective mechanism which children put in place in order to shield their self-esteem from repeated failure (Hess et al. 2004; Stoiber 1992). On the other hand, expectations that are too low often signal overprotective parenting, which can lead to children's sense of reduced self-efficacy, decreased autonomy, and difficulties in social adjustment (Gutermuth-Anthony et al. 2005; Hess et al. 2004).

Concerning the second component of parenting style, the literature from the field of developmental psychology differentiates between positive discipline and harsh/inconsistent discipline. Positive discipline is described as an effective form of parenting which relies on emphasizing children's positive behaviors through use of praise, while employing non-punitive, constructive strategies to manage misbehaviors (Sanders and Morawska 2005). Opposed to this discipline style, harsh discipline refers to the excessive use of punishment, including corporal punishment, and a tendency to criticize children for their misbehaviors, which enhances children's risk of externalizing problems (Bradley and Corwyn 2007; Curtner-Smith et al. 2006). Harsh parenting practices are thought to model children's aggressive behaviors, which are consequently enacted in interactions with peers or other adults (Bor and Sanders 2004; Sanders and Morawska 2005; Snyder et al. 2005a). Therefore, children manifesting such behaviors are rejected by their peers and are perceived as less socially competent (Chang et al. 2003; Dennis 2006). On other hand, besides harsh discipline, another parenting style associated with risk for externalizing problems is inconsistent discipline, characterized by parent's inability to react consistently to children's behaviors (Sanders and Morawska 2005). As a result, children learn that no predictable associations can be established between a particular behavior and its consequences, which can impact their response to adult authority figures by increasing non-compliance and, implicitly, risk of conduct problems (Nelson et al. 2007; Stanger et al. 2004).

The last component of parenting style refers to *parental monitoring*, defined as a set of parental behaviors employed for the purpose of structuring the children's environment through supervision of their activities and location (Dishion and McMahon 1998). Parental monitoring and supervision have been consistently inversely associated with risk of externalizing problems, whereas low levels of monitoring have been related to higher rates of misbehavior, as well as increased persistence in misbehavior (Ceballo et al. 2003). Furthermore, research comparing children who are supervised by their parents with those unsupervised, suggested that those from the latter category are more prone to developing externalizing type behaviors (Ceballo et al. 2003; Kilgore et al. 2000).

Educational Environment Related Factors

Parents are not the only adults responsible for shaping the children's environment and behaviors, as teacher-child interactions in the classroom might be as important for children's healthy development as parent-child interactions. Among the factors pertaining to the educational environment, several are noteworthy: teachers' classroom management strategies, the teacher-parent partnership, and peer interactions in the classroom.

Similar to parenting style, teachers exhibit *classroom management style*. This concept is related to the teachers' beliefs about the amount of control which should be exercised in managing misbehavior (Vitaro et al. 2005). These beliefs can be conceptualized on a continuum from teachers who actively support the development of children's self-control and autonomy through guidance, to teachers who place an increased emphasis on applying rules in an overly directive and rigid manner (Erdena and Wolfgang 2004; Filcheck et al. 2004). The former attitude has been shown to actually encourage children's non-compliance as a response to the psychological control imposed by teachers (Birch and Ladd 1997).

Concerning teachers' discipline style, one widely accepted view is that similarly to parental strategies, resorting to more punitive and/or inconsistent discipline strategies in the classroom results in adding to children's risk for behavior problems (Vitaro et al. 2005). More precisely, children interact during their school years with multiple teachers, each employing a variety of discipline strategies. Some research suggests that consistent use of harsh and/or inconsistent discipline strategies by teachers, especially when the same type of strategies are employed at home by parents, can result in additional risk of long-term negative consequences such as increasing the risk of school dropout and absenteeism during adolescence (Di Lalla et al. 2004). However, at this moment more empirical evidence is needed to better understand the independent effects of these classroom management strategies on children's mental health. It is also important to note that the use of proactive discipline strategies centered on praising rather than punishing children are conducive to a positive classroom climate which promotes on-task behaviors and significantly reduces misbehaviors (Babkie 2006).

Some empirical evidence supports the notion that *teacher-parent partnerships*, which enhance parental engagement in children's education, are associated with lower levels of behavior problems, as well as increased later academic success (Ryan and Stiller 1994; Vickers and Minke 1995). It is hypothesized that appropriate teacher-parent communication encourages parents to take on more responsibility and involvement in their children's education, as opposed to situations in which a gap is created between teachers' and parents' expectations (Knopf and Swick 2007). Furthermore, difficulties in teacher-parent communication often result in teachers' hardships in tackling behavior problems, which require parental involvement and cooperation between adults (Swick 2004; Swick and Hooks 2005).

Children interact in the classroom with both teachers and with other children. Thus, not only the quality of the adult-child relationship is important, but also the quality of peer interactions. Research focusing on children's peer play patterns suggests that children low on emotion regulation skills and who interact aggressively with their peers tend to be rejected by other children (Vaughan et al. 2007). Once these children are confronted with repeated peer rejection, they end up establishing friendships with children who exhibit similar behavior problems, thus reinforcing and consolidating aggressive interaction styles (Birch and Ladd 1998; Snyder et al. 2005b). Moreover, some research posits that when teachers must manage a larger number of children with disruptive behaviors, this increases the likelihood that they will employ more harsh and/or inconsistent discipline strategies, which further contributes to increased risk of behavior problems (Howes et al. 1994).

Context Related Factors

The final category of risk factors described pertains to the context in which the child is raised, and includes external factors that influence family interactions. Research examining the influence of *socio-economic status* (SES) on early childhood development suggests that children whose parents have not graduated from high-school and have low income levels are more likely to show some sort of difficulty in social-emotional development (Denham et al. 2000; Masten and Coatesworth 1998), as well as difficulties in school adjustment (Fantuzzo and McWayne 2002; Mendez et al. 2002a, b). The mechanism through which low SES influences children's social-emotional development is related to the lower levels of parental involvement in children's daily activities, when they are also required to manage economical hardships (Sanders 2003).

More precisely, parents from disadvantaged SES backgrounds are more likely to employ more harsh discipline strategies, to monitor their children's activities to a lower extent, and to spend less time engaged in parent-child activities such as playing or reading compared to parents from moderate or high SES backgrounds (Gutermuth-Anthony et al. 2005). There is also some evidence supporting the notion that SES is a moderator between inappropriate discipline and externalizing problems, suggesting that the strongest positive association between harsh/inconsistent discipline style and behavior problems occurs for low SES children (Curtner-Smith et al. 2006; Gutermuth-Anthony et al. 2005).

Besides socio-economic background, one widely cited adverse context is *parental mental illness*. Among the investigated effects of parental mental health issues on children's social-emotional development most have dealt with the impact of maternal depression (Trapolini et al. 2007), antisocial personality disorder (APD) (Chronis et al. 2007), and substance abuse (Burstein et al. 2006) on children's outcomes. The results seem to suggest that irrespective of the type of parental psychopathology, mental health problems result in 2 negative outcomes: (1) parents are more likely to establish insecure attachment relations with their children, as children cannot rely on prompt and consistent parental support when distressed (Chronis et al. 2007; Elgar et al. 2004; Trapolini et al. 2007); and (2) parents are more likely to use harsh and/or inconsistent discipline strategies, as well as less likely to monitor their child's behavior (Burstein et al. 2006; Merikangas et al. 1998; Nelson et al. 2007).

And finally, contextual risk factors include children's exposure to *family conflict*. Research suggests that the most deleterious effects on children's behaviors do not reside in mere exposure to conflict, but rather from exposure to inappropriate adult conflict resolution strategies and high levels of negative emotionality. These affect children's sense of trust in adults and perceptions of control (Kitzman 2000). Furthermore, negative problem-solving can be modeled and used by children when interacting with others, whereas parents are more likely to resort to harsh discipline and are less likely to exhibit emotional availability for their children, both of which increase the risk of externalizing problems (Kitzman 2000; Sturge-Apple et al. 2006). Research posits that especially parental emotional availability might be essential for children's learning about adaptive emotion regulation strategies, and for preventing the use of aggressive strategies in peer conflict (Cummings et al. 2007).

A Descriptive Model of Developmental Pathways Involved in Risk of Early Onset Conduct Problems

Empirical findings reviewed in the previous sections support the notion that child, parent, educational environment and context related factors have both an interactive, as well as an additive, effect on children's risk of early onset conduct problems. A modified version of the developmental pathways involved in the risk of behavior problems developed by Webster-Stratton and Taylor (2001) is presented in Fig. 1.1.

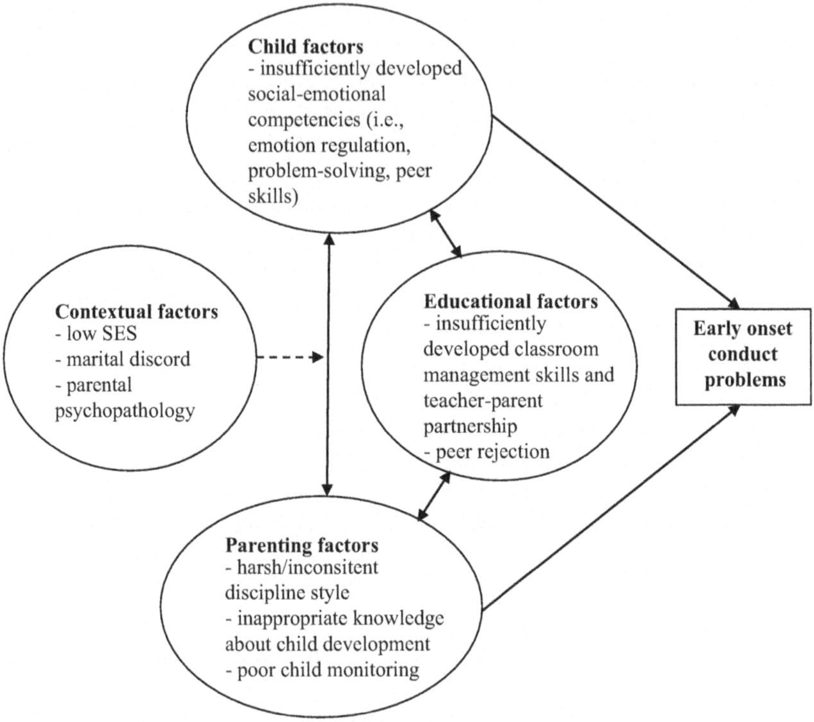

Fig. 1.1 Interactions between intrapersonal and interpersonal risk factors involved in increasing risk of early onset conduct problems

The proposed model first suggests that children develop both emotional and social competencies, and that difficulties in these domains which might take the form of deficient emotion regulation skills, aggressive interactions, and difficulties in establishing positive peer relationships are associated with increased risk of behavior problems (Denham et al. 2001; Eisenberg et al. 2005b; Hastings et al. 2000). Children's challenging behaviors often result in negative attributions elicited by parents (Nicholson et al. 2005; Snyder et al. 2005a). These negative perceptions about children are associated with more frequent use of harsh and inconsistent discipline strategies, which were also shown to increase behaviors consistent with externalizing type problems (Bradley and Corwyn 2007; Cole et al. 2003; Denham et al. 2000). However, unlike the original model of Webster-Stratton and Taylor (2001), the current version of the model acknowledges the fact that the relationship between child and parental risk factors is bidirectional. Children's behaviors might influence parents' choice of discipline strategies, but it is also possible that parental expectations, discipline strategies, and level of monitoring affect children's social-emotional development.

Both child and parent related risk factors can interact with contextual risk factors. Low SES, parents' mental health issues, or family conflict result in increased parental stress, which is in turn associated with more inappropriate parenting strategies. Conversely, these parenting strategies are linked to children's difficulties in terms of social-emotional development (Curtner-Smith et al. 2006; Sturge-Apple et al. 2006). Hence, it can be inferred that parent and child risk factors are potentiated by context related risk factors, and as suggested by the dotted line in Fig. 1.1, these risk factors have a moderator effect on the relationship between parenting practices and children's social-emotional skills.

The educational environment can also contribute to reinforcing children's negative behavior patterns, foremost because aggressive children are rejected by their peers, and thus they tend to interact with children who share similar adjustment difficulties (Maguire and Dunn 1997; Snyder et al. 2005b; Vaughan et al. 2007). Moreover, if teachers encounter difficulties in managing such behaviors, research has uncovered that they are more likely to be more directive in their discipline strategies (Lewis 1999). Given such findings, a second way in which the model depicted in Fig. 1.1 departs from the original Webster-Stratton and Taylor (2001) model is that it proposes that not only child related risk factors interact with those from the educational setting, but also teachers' choices concerning discipline and their attitudes towards children with behavior problems can further reinforce maladaptive behavior patterns (Snyder et al. 2005a).

In a similar vein, risk factors pertaining to the educational environment can actually enhance parental risk factors, as harsh and inconsistent parenting practices elicited by frequent misbehavior at home, can be also elicited in the classroom. Furthermore, there is evidence suggesting that parents whose children exhibit adjustment problems are less likely to interact with teachers, whereas teachers have difficulties in establishing cooperative partnerships with parents (Knopf and Swick 2007; Vickers and Minke 1995). This evidence further supports the notion that parent related and educational environment related risk factors have both an interactive and additive effect on children's risk of early onset conduct problems.

Characteristics of Evidence-Based Prevention Programs for Preschoolers' Behavior Problems

Identifying developmental pathways involved in preschoolers risk of behavior disorders is a required step in understanding how preventive interventions are supposed to elicit changes in children's behaviors. Prevention programs differ in terms of their target population, and types of activities involved. Depending on children's risk there are several types of interventions: (1) universal interventions, also known as primary prevention, which are designed for all children; (2) indicated or selective interventions, also known as secondary prevention programs, which are designed for children who are either at risk of externalizing problems or are deemed as at risk due to some contextual factors (e.g., low SES communities, high juvenile delinquency rates, etc.); and (3) early intervention or tertiary prevention programs targeting children already exhibiting specific symptoms of a conduct problem, in order to decrease the possible negative effects associated with mental health problems (Durlak and Wells 1998).

In spite of data showing that preschool competencies impact children's later emotional, social, and cognitive adjustment, there are only a limited number of evidence-based interventions targeting preschoolers (Izard 2002; Nelson et al. 2003). Additionally, only some of these interventions directed at children's social-emotional competence development meet the criteria for well-established interventions, meaning that at least 2 independent replication studies based on the intervention manual have shown the program's efficacy (Chambless and Hollon 1998). In the following sections of this chapter, universal, indicated, and selective interventions for preventing children's behavior problems are discussed by outlining the strengths and limitations of each approach.

Child Focused Interventions

Universal interventions are designed to target all children irrespective of whether they exhibit risk of behavior problems or not. This type of intervention is classroom delivered and consists of a set of activities included in a curriculum for social-emotional development implemented by teachers or mental health professionals working in schools (Lochman and Wells 2002; Sheffield et al. 2006).

The underlying assumption of such interventions is that classrooms represent an appropriate context in which children can be taught about properly interacting with others (van Lier et al. 2005; Webster-Stratton and Hammond 1997). In terms of their content, as it can be seen from Table 1.2, empirically validated universal interventions include interventions covering in particular social skills development by teaching rule compliance, problem-solving and how to establish and maintain friendships (Domitrovich et al. 2007; Kellam et al. 1998; Shure and Spivak 1982). Apart from intervention modules targeting social skills, there is also a trend to include units devoted to emotional competencies such as emotion understanding and emotion regulation (Domitrovich et al. 2007; Kellam et al. 1998; Webster-Stratton et al. 2001). This is largely the consequence of research suggesting that specific emotion related skills have important implications for the development of socially acceptable behavior (Blair 2002; Izard 2002; Witherington and Crichton 2007).

Evidence concerning universal intervention's efficacy suggests that participation in such prevention programs was associated with gains in children's social-emotional skills, but they showed little positive effects on reducing aggressive and non-compliant behaviors (Domitrovich et al. 2007; Kellam et al. 1998). A potential solution to this shortcoming was partially addressed through the inclusion of teacher training in universal intervention programs (Kam et al. 2003; Webster-Stratton et al. 2001). In fact addressing teachers' ability to manage misbehavior in the classroom, as well as offering them extended support in implementing classroom activities, have been associated with more positive results in terms of reducing levels of externalizing problems (Kam et al. 2004). However, it is noteworthy that in general universal interventions are more effective for children with moderate levels of behaviors consistent with externalizing problems rather than children who are already at risk, which leads to the conclusion that children who are at risk require more complex intervention strategies (Stoolmiller et al. 2000).

Parent Focused Interventions

The second major intervention method for children with behavior problems is parent training. Parent training is rooted in the assumption that children's difficult behavior is learned within inadequate parent-child interactions (Bradley and Corwyn 2007; Cole et al. 2003; Curtner-Smith et al. 2006; Sanders and Morawska 2005). However, it should be noted that parent training is mainly delivered in 2 contexts: (1) indicated/selective interventions; and (2) early interventions for children with already diagnosed conduct disorders (Hinshaw et al. 2000). A further difference between these programs is represented by the training format: group interventions are

Table 1.2 Empirically validated preventive interventions targeting social-emotional competencies

Target group	*Program name*	*Age*	*Intervention format*	*Intervention content*	*Type of prevention*
Child focused	I Can Problem-Solve (ICPS; Shure and Spivak 1982)	4–5 years	Classroom activities	Problem-solving skills, prosocial behavior, peer skills	U
	Good Behavior Game (GBG; Kellam et al. 1998)	6–7 years	1. Classrooom activities 2. Teacher training	1. Peer skills, rule compliance, reading and writing skills 2. Classroom management skills	U
	Promoting Alternative Thinking Strategies (PATHS; Domitrovich et al. 2007; Kam et al. 2003)	6–8 years	1. Classrooom activities 2. Teacher training + weekly consultations	1. Emotional regulation, emotion understanding, interpersonal skills, self-esteem, problem-solving skills 2. Classroom management skills	U
Parent focused	Living with Children (Patterson et al. 1982)	3–12 years	Individual parent training	Positive discipline strategies, problem-solving	I
	Helping the Noncompliant Child (McMahon and Forehand 2003)	3–8 years	Individual parent training	Positive discipline strategies	I
	Enhanced Family Treatment (Prinz and Miller 1994)	4–9 years	Individual parent training	Positive discipline strategies, parent-child relationship, family problems management skills	I
	Incredible Years Parenting Program (Spitzer et al. 1991; Webster-Stratton 1998)	2–8 years	Group parent training Self-administered	Positive discipline strategies, parent-child relationship, stress and conflict management skills	I + S
	Community-based program (Cunningham et al. 1995)	2–5 years	Group parent training	Parent problem-solving, positive discipline strategies	S
	DARE to be You (Miller-Heyle et al. 1998)	2–5 years	Group parent training	Positive discipline strategies, knowledge about developmental milestones, parent problem-solving skills	S

Multi-focused	First Step (CLASS) (Walker et al. 1998)	5 years	1. Classroom activities for children 2. Individual parent training	1. Regulatory skills (emotional and behavioral), task persistence 2. Positive discipline strategies	I
	Fast Track (CPPRG 1999a, b, 2002)	6–12 years	1. Classroom activities for children and teacher training 2. Individual parent training	1. Social skills, emotional regulation, learning abilities + classroom management strategies 2. HNC + Incredible Years Parent Training	U + I + S
	Incredible Years Training Series (Webster-Stratton et al. 2001; Webster-Stratton and Reid 2003)	4–8 years	1. Classroom activities for children and teacher training 2. Individual parent training	1. Compliance to rules, emotion understanding, emotion regulation, problem-solving, peer skills + teacher classroom management, parent-teacher partnership 2. Positive discipline strategies, parent-child interaction, parent problems management skills	U + I + S
	Al's Pals: Kids Making Healthy Choices (Lynch et al. 2004)	3–8 years	1. Classroom activities for children and teacher training 2. Individual parent training	1. Emotion recognition, peer skills, anger management, problem-solving + teacher classroom management 2. Positive discipline strategies	U + S

U universal, *I* indicated, *S* selective

employed in indicated/selective interventions (McMahon and Forehand 2003; Patterson et al. 1982; Prinz and Miller 1994), whereas individualized parental interventions are usually employed in early intervention programs (Cunningham et al. 1995; Spitzer et al. 1991).

However, this review of parent training is specifically focused on indicated interventions as summarized in Table 1.2. In terms of contents most parent trainings share a similar strategy, namely attempting to teach effective parent-child interactions (Valdez et al. 2005). This goal is achieved mainly through strategies aimed at enhancing the use of positive discipline strategies including limit setting (e.g., rules, commands, routines), appropriate use of reinforcement and managing misbehavior (e.g., ignoring, logical consequences, timeout) (Cunningham et al. 1995; Patterson et al. 1982; Miller-Heyle et al. 1998). However, some programs in addition to behavior management strategies, aim to expose parents to information about how to use play and communication as ways to teach children about emotions, emotion regulation and problem-solving (Spitzer et al. 1991; Webster-Stratton 1998).

Concerning parent training efficacy, a quantitative meta-analysis performed by Kazdin and Weisz (1998) concluded that these are effective in reducing children's risk of externalizing problems, as well as in decreasing levels of harsh and inconsistent discipline strategies employed by parents. However, some concerns have been raised by the lack of the interventions' specificity in terms of addressing parents' own difficulties (Sanders 2003). As suggested by the previous discussion on developmental pathways involved in children's risk of early onset conduct problems, it is apparent that contextual risk factors contribute to parental stress and enhance parents' difficulties in managing relationships with their children. Hence, some parent trainings began incorporating modules aimed at increasing parents' own stress management, conflict management, and problem-solving skills (Webster-Stratton 1990, 1998). The use of such strategies resulted not only in increased use of positive discipline, but it also triggered lower parental dropout rates, further supporting the notion that increasing the training's relevance for adults could act as a source of motivation for program completion especially for parents of high-risk children.

Multi-focused Interventions

Unlike, child or parent focused interventions, multi-focused prevention programs target not one type, but multiple risk factors that pertain to the child, parent, and the educational environment. The option of combining child, parent, and teacher interventions was driven by research suggesting that programs targeting a broader range of risk factors showed significantly higher improvements for both children and parents compared to single component interventions, and that these outcomes were maintained at follow-up (Webster-Stratton and Hammond 1997). Universal, classroom-based interventions have been criticized for their limited ability to support behavior generalization outside the original intervention setting, an outcome which has been attributed to lack of parental involvement (Webster-Stratton and Hammond 1997). Therefore, as mounting evidence suggested that multi-focused interventions were superior to interventions aimed at one source of risk, it has become obvious that multiple risk sources needed to be addressed especially in cases of indicated interventions aimed at reducing the levels of aggression and non-compliance in at risk children. Hence, some of the prevention programs mentioned in Table 1.2, which were initially either child focused (Walker et al. 1998) or parent focused (Patterson et al. 1982), were extended to include a multi-focused approach to preventing children's behavior problems.

While taking a closer look at intervention strategies employed in multi-focused interventions, it is apparent that at least some programs propose different intervention strategies depending on the target group of the intervention (Conduct Problems Prevention Research Group [CPPRG] 1999a, b; Lynch et al. 2004; Webster-Stratton et al. 2004). More precisely, some prevention programs support the use of different intervention methods for non-risk children vs. children who are at risk, proposing that the latter category might benefit from pullout small-group sessions as a complementary intervention strategy to classroom intervention (CPPRG 1999a, b). However, given children's propensity to interact with other children with similar behavior problems, some researchers argued that in fact such sessions do not result in lower levels of misbehavior (Lochman and Wells 2002).

Multi-focused interventions also include teacher training which was proven to positively affect children's classroom behavior (Kam et al. 2003; Webster-Stratton et al. 2001). Additionally, efficacy studies on multi-focused preventive interventions support the notion that at the indicated intervention level, teacher training is associated with decreased aggressive and non-compliant behavior 1–3 years after the intervention was implemented (CPPRG 1999a, b, 2002). Moreover, prevention programs such as *The Incredible Years* also aim to enhance the quality of the teacher-parent partnership, as one strategy to support parental involvement and children's reduced misbehavior (Webster-Stratton et al. 2001).

Parent training as part of community-based interventions represents a more recent development, which originates in interventions delivered to clinically referred children. However, interventions in school differ from those in clinical settings in terms of length, delivery format, and intervention content. Parent training in universal or indicated interventions varies from 12 to 24 hours, is delivered in groups and aims both to inform parents about children's skills, as well as to teach them positive discipline strategies (Webster-Stratton et al. 2001, 2004; Turner and Sanders 2006; Zubrick et al. 2005). Parent training in school based interventions was shown to promote the generalization of acquired skills from the classroom to parent-child interaction at home, and was associated with lower levels of reported externalizing problems especially in the case of children whose parents attended the interventions (Webster-Stratton and Hammond 1997; Webster-Stratton et al. 2001).

Considerations for Developing and Assessing Early Education Programs

Data on efficacy studies aimed at promoting children's mental health in school through social-emotional development suggest that this could be a relevant strategy for preventing behavior problems. Given these findings, several suggestions could be proposed in order to maximize intervention efficacy and possibly increasing the number of available evidence-based prevention practices for preschoolers.

Following, several guidelines are proposed for developing preventive programs.

- Prevention programs must be theory driven, meaning that proposed objectives and contents must be derived from fundamental research about children's development and best age-appropriate practices to ensure efficacy (Izard 2002; Webster-Stratton and Taylor 2001). Programs which are not informed by scientific evidence risk proposing erroneous practices with little or no impact for children, teachers and parents.
- Prevention programs should not only aim at developing knowledge, but also at providing contexts for skill development and practice (Nation et al. 2003; Nelson et al. 2003). For instance, the fact that a child is able to recognize emotions is relevant to the extent to which it allows her to better manage her own emotions and to establish proper

interactions with other children and adults. Conversely, teacher and parent training should be to a lesser extent lecture oriented, placing to a larger extent emphasis on practice during training and on homework assignments (McMahon 2006).

- Programs should ideally target a large spectrum of risk factors that are related to children's competencies, to adults' behaviors or to contextual variables. This recommendation is grounded in previous research suggesting that the most effective interventions are those that consider multiple risk factors, and as such their implementation results in lower dropout rates (Webster-Stratton 1990, 1998). This is especially important for parents of children at risk who are more likely to discontinue attending interventions, when these do not address issues parents consider relevant to them (Assemany and McIntosh 2002).
- The contents of preventive programs should be tailored to children who are at risk, as well as those who are not at risk. For instance, some programs propose different approaches for universal and indicated intervention levels (CPPRG 1999b), suggesting that children who are at risk should be trained in social skills development both in the classroom, and in small training groups outside the classroom. Furthermore, such programs aim to deliver parent training only to parents of at-risk children. Conversely, others suggest that children who are at risk would be better served by the inclusion of teacher training and consultations rather than pullout sessions (Lochman and Wells 2002). Additionally, some suggest that parent training is suitable for all parents, but different types of information and skills need to be considered: informing parents might be more relevant for parents of low-risk children, whereas parents of at-risk children might benefit from more skill development regarding parenting practices (Turner and Sanders 2006).
- Duration of prevention programs should be established considering symptom severity, meaning that interventions in community settings should take into account shorter timelines for implementation. Based on currently available data, effective programs include on average 4–5 months for classroom delivered activities, and fewer parent training sessions compared to training delivered in clinical settings. The latter strategy seems to be especially effective for increasing parent involvement (Rapee et al. 2005).
- Prevention programs should emphasize teacher-parent partnerships, because empirical evidence suggests that children whose parents are involved and communicate with teachers are less likely to exhibit

behavior problems than children of uninvolved parents, who do not communicate with teachers (Vickers and Minke 1995; Webster-Stratton 2006). Often, when parents are uninformed and uninvolved they elicit defensive responses when requested to support teachers' desire to address behavior problems (Knopf and Swick 2007). Hence, teacher-parent cooperation is key to helping children succeed, but also to their mental health (Webster-Stratton et al. 2001).

Following, a second set of guidelines are proposed considering the scientist-practitioner paradigm, which could contribute to more rigorous testing of intervention's efficacy in school settings (Chambless and Hollon 1998).

- Data concerning preventive program's efficacy should involve comparisons between an intervention and a control group (e.g., no intervention, wait list) (McMahon 2006; Nation et al. 2003). Also, data should be gathered on all outcome variables, both pre- and post-intervention measurements, to control for potential time related changes in children's behavior.
- Prevention programs must show both statistical and clinical relevance, meaning that differences between the intervention and control group should be reported together with effect sizes, as well as data on the intervention's practical relevance, interpreted in terms of the percentage of children from the intervention group compared to those from the control group whose at risk status was changed at post-intervention (Kazdin and Weisz 1998).
- Prevention programs must be associated with both post-intervention, as well as follow-up effects. Inclusion of follow-up assessments is important to determine the extent to which the program maintained its effects on the outcomes months or years after the intervention's completion. Furthermore, gathering follow-up data can provide a reliable perspective on whether skills taught within the program were maintained and transferred after the program ended (Webster-Stratton and Taylor 2001).
- Preventions program efficacy should be established based on selecting age-relevant outcomes. More precisely, preventive programs for children's behavioral problems aim to reduce juvenile delinquency, arrest rates, substance abuse, or school dropout in adolescence (Brotman et al. 2005; Kelly et al. 2005). While direct effects on such variables cannot be measured in preschoolers, relevant dependent variables

predictive of the targeted long-term outcomes could be selected (e.g., externalizing problems) (Webster-Stratton and Taylor 2001).
- Prevention programs must also provide a manual. This is important for 2 reasons: (1) it allows reliable implementation across different sites; and (2) it allows for independent replications of validity findings (Webster-Stratton and Taylor 2001).

The results reviewed in this chapter offer an integrative perspective on preschool children's social-emotional development, as well as the pathogenetic mechanisms involved in risk of developing early onset conduct disorders. Given the current knowledge about state of the art preventive programs, empirically supported interventions for preschoolers delivered in schools should aim: (1) to include all children and parents to avoid stigmatization of risk categories; (2) to include intervention strategies which respond to the different needs of children who are not at risk, as well as those who are at risk: (3) to design intervention strategies that consider maximizing parental involvement; and (4) to provide an in-depth analysis concerning the program's efficacy from classroom to individual level effects. These objectives were targeted through the development and efficacy assessment of the Social-Emotional Prevention Program (SEP). Consequently, the following chapters focus on describing the rationale and the contents of the proposed prevention program, as well as on presenting efficacy results of SEP at the classroom, risk group, and individual level.

References

Abe, J. A., & Izard, C. E. (1999). A longitudinal study of emotion expression and personality relations in early development. *Personality Processes and Individual Differences, 77*, 566–577. https://doi.org/10.1037/0022-3514.77.3.566.

Assemany, A., & McIntosh, D. (2002). Negative treatment outcomes of behavior parent training programs. *Psychology in the Schools, 39*, 209–219. https://doi.org/10.1002/pits.10032.

Babkie, A. M. (2006). Proactive in managing classroom behavior. *Intervention in School and Clinic, 41*, 183–191. https://doi.org/10.1177/10534512060410031001.

Bembenutty, H., & Karabenick, S. A. (2004). Inherent association between academic delay of gratification, future time perspective, and self-regulated learning. *Educational Psychology Review, 16*, 35–57. https://doi.org/10.1023/B:EDPR.0000012344.34008.5c.

Berlin, L. J., Cassidy, J., & Appleyard, K. (2008). The influence of early attachments on other relationships. In J. Cassidy & P. R. Shaver (Eds.), *Handbook of attachment: Theory, research, and clinical applications* (pp. 333–347). New York: Guilford Press.

Birch, S. H., & Ladd, G. W. (1997). The teacher-child relationship and children's early school adjustment. *Journal of School Psychology, 35*, 61–79. https://doi.org/10.1016/S0022-4405(96)00029-5.

Birch, S. H., & Ladd, G. W. (1998). Children's interpersonal behaviors and the teacher-child relationship. *Developmental Psychology, 34*, 934–946. https://doi.org/10.1037/0012-1649.34.5.934.

Blair, C. (2002). School readiness – Integrating cognition and emotion in a neurobiological conceptualization of children's functioning at school entry. *American Psychologist, 57*, 111–127. https://doi.org/10.1037/0003-066X.57.2.111.

Bor, W., & Sanders, M. R. (2004). Correlates of self-reported coercive parenting of preschool-aged children at risk for the development of conduct problems. *Australian and New Zealand Journal of Psychiatry, 38*, 738–745. https://doi.org/10.1080/j.1440-1614.2004.01452.x.

Bradley, R. H., & Corwyn, R. F. (2007). Externalizing problems in the fifth grade: Relations with productive activity, maternal sensitivity, and harsh parenting from infancy through middle childhood. *Developmental Psychology, 43*, 1390–1401. https://doi.org/10.1037/0012-1649.43.6.1390.

Brotman, L. M., Gouley, K. K., Chesir-Teran, D., Dennis, T., Klein, R. G., & Shrout, P. (2005). Prevention for preschoolers at high risk for conduct problems: Immediate outcomes on parenting practices and child social competence. *Journal of Clinical Child and Adolescent Psychology, 34*, 724–734. https://doi.org/10.1207/s15374424jccp3404_14.

Buckley, M., Storino, M., & Saarni, C. (2003). Promoting emotional competence in children and adolescents: Implications for school psychologists. *School Psychology Quarterly, 18*, 177–191. https://doi.org/10.1521/scpq.18.2.177.21855.

Burstein, M., Stanger, C., Kamon, J., & Dumeci, L. (2006). Parent psychpathology, parenting, and child internalizing problems in subtance abusing families. *Psychology of Addictive Behaviors, 20*, 97–106. https://doi.org/10.1037/0893-164X.20.2.97. 97.

Caldarella, P., & Merrell, K. W. (1997). Common dimensions of social skills of children and adolescents: A taxonomy of positive behaviors. *School Psychology Review, 26*, 264–278.

Calkins, S. D., & Dedmon, S. A. (2000). Physiological and behavioral regulation in two-year-old children with aggressive/destructive behavior problems. *Journal of Abnormal Child Psychology, 28*, 103–118. https://doi.org/10.1023/A:1005112912906.

Ceballo, R., Ramirez, C., Hearn, K. D., & Maltese, K. L. (2003). Community violence and children's psychological well-being: Does parental monitoring

matter? *Journal of Clinical Child and Adolescent Psychology, 32*, 586–592. https://doi.org/10.1207/S15374424JCCP3204_11.
Cemore, J. J., & Herwig, J. E. (2005). Delay of gratification and make-believe play of preschoolers. *Journal of Research in Childhood Education, 19*, 251–266. https://doi.org/10.1080/02568540509595069.
Chambless, D. L., & Hollon, S. D. (1998). Defining empirically supported psychotherapies. *Journal of Consulting and Clinical Psychology, 66*, 7–18. https://doi.org/10.1037/0022-006X.66.1.7.
Chang, L., Schwartz, D., Dodge, K. A., & McBride-Chang, C. (2003). Harsh parenting in relation to child emotion regulation and aggression. *Journal of Family Psychology, 17*, 598–606. https://doi.org/10.1037/0893-3200.17.4.598.
Chaplin, T. M., Cole, P. M., & Zahn-Waxler, C. (2005). Parental socialization of emotion expression: Gender differences and relations to child adjustment. *Emotion, 5*, 80–88. https://doi.org/10.1037/1528-3542.5.1.80.
Chronis, A. M., Lahey, B. B., Pelham, W. E., Jr., Hall Williams, S. H., Baumann, B. L., et al. (2007). Maternal depression and early positive parenting predict future conduct problems in young children with attention-deficit/hyperactivity disorder. *Developmental Psychology, 43*, 70–82. https://doi.org/10.1037/0012-1649.43.1.70.
Cole, P. M., Zahn-Waxler, C., Fox, N., Usher, B. A., & Welsh, J. D. (1996). Individual difference in emotion regulation and behavior problems in preschool children. *Journal of Abnormal Psychology, 105*, 518–529. https://doi.org/10.1037/0021-843X.105.4.518.
Cole, P. M., Teti, D. O., & Zahn-Waxler, C. (2003). Mutual emotion regulation and the stability of conduct problems between preschool and early school age. *Development and Psychopathology, 15*, 1–18. https://doi.org/10.1017/S0954579403000014.
Cole, P. M., Dennis, T. A., Smith-Simon, K. E., & Cohen, L. H. (2009). Preschoolers' emotion regulation strategy understanding: Relations with emotion socialization and child self-regulation. *Social Development, 18*, 324–252. https://doi.org/10.1111/j.1467-9507.2008.00503.x.
Colwell, M. J., & Lindsay, E. W. (2005). Preschool children's pretend and physical play and sex of play partner: Connections to peer competence. *Sex Roles, 52*, 497–509. https://doi.org/10.1007/s11199-005-3716-8.
Compas, B. E., Connor-Smith, J. K., Saltzman, H., Thomsen, A., & Wadsworth, M. E. (2001). Coping with stress during childhood and adolescence: Problems, progress, and potential in theory and research. *Psychological Bulletin, 127*, 87–127. https://doi.org/10.1037/0033-2909.127.1.87.
Conduct Problems Prevention Research Group. (1999a). Initial impact of the Fast Track prevention trial for conduct problems: I. The high risk sample. *Journal of Consulting and Clinical Psychology, 67*, 631–647. https://doi.org/10.1037/0022-006X.67.5.648.

Conduct Problems Prevention Research Group. (1999b). Initial impact of the Fast Track prevention trial for conduct problems: II. Classroom effects. *Journal of Consulting and Clinical Psychology, 67*, 648–657. https://doi.org/10.1037/0022-006X.67.5.648.

Conduct Problems Prevention Research Group. (2002). Evaluation of the first 3 years of the Fast Track prevention trial with children at high risk for adolescent conduct problems. *Journal of Abnormal Child Psychology, 30*, 19–35. https://doi.org/10.1023/A:1014274914287.

Crick, R. N., & Dodge, K. A. (1994). A review and reformulation of social-information-processing mechanisms in children's social adjustment. *Psychological Bulletin, 115*, 74–101. https://doi.org/10.1037/0033-2909.115.1.74.

Crick, N. R., Casas, J. F., & Mosher, M. (1997). Relational and overt aggression in preschool. *Developmental Psychology, 33*, 579–588. https://doi.org/10.1037/0012-1649.33.4.579.

Crick, R. N., Casas, H. F., & Ku, H.-C. (1999). Relational and physical forms of peer victimisation in preschool. *Developmental Psychology, 35*, 376–385. https://doi.org/10.1037/0012-1649.35.2.376.

Cummings, E. M., Kouros, C. D., & Papp, L. M. (2007). Marital aggression and children's responses to everyday interparental conflict. *European Psychologist, 12*, 17–28. https://doi.org/10.1027/1016-9040.12.1.17.

Cunningham, C. E., Bremner, R., & Boyle, M. (1995). Large group community-based parenting programs for families of preschoolers at risk for disruptive behavior disorders: Utilization, cost effectiveness, and outcome. *Journal of Child Psychology and Psychiatry, 36*, 1141–1159. https://doi.org/10.1111/j.1469-7610.1995.tb01362.x.

Curtner-Smith, M. E., Culp, A. M., Culp, R., Scheib, C., Owen, K., Tilley, A., et al. (2006). Mothers' parenting and young economically disadvantaged children's relational and overt bullying. *Journal of Child and Family Studies, 15*, 181–193. https://doi.org/10.1007/s10826-005-9016-7.

Cutting, A. L., & Dunn, J. (2006). Conversations with siblings and with friends: Links between relationship quality and social understanding. *British Journal of Developmental Psychology, 24*, 73–87. https://doi.org/10.1348/026151005X70337.

Denham, S. A. (2006). Social-emotional competence as support for school readiness: What is it and how do we assess it? *Early Education and Development, 17*, 57–89. https://doi.org/10.1207/s15566935eed1701_4.

Denham, S. A. (2007). Dealing with feelings: How children negotiate the worlds of emotions and social relationships. *Cognition, Brain, Behavior, 11*, 1–48.

Denham, S. A., Workman, E., Cole, P., Weissbrod, C., Kendziora, K., & Zahn-Waxler, C. (2000). Prevention of externalizing behavior problems from early to middle childhood: The role of parental socialization and emotion expression.

Development and Psychopathology, 12, 23–45. https://doi.org/10.1017/S0954579400001024.

Denham, S. A., Mason, T., Caverly, S., Schmidt, M., Hackney, R., Caswell, C., & DeMulder, E. (2001). Preschoolers at play: Co-socializers of emotional and social competence. *International Journal of Behavioral Development, 25*, 90–101. https://doi.org/10.1080/01650250143000067.

Denham, S. A., Blair, K. A., Schmidt, M. S., Blair, K., DeMulder, E., et al. (2002). Preschool understanding of emotions: Contributions to classroom anger and aggression. *Journal of Child Psychology and Psychiatry, 43*, 901–916. https://doi.org/10.1111/1469-7610.00139.

Denham, S. A., Blair, K. A., DeMulder, E., Levitas, J., Sawyer, K., Auerbach-Major, S., & Quinnan, P. (2003a). Preschool emotional competence: Pathway to social competence? *Child Development, 74*, 238–256. https://doi.org/10.1111/1467-8624.00533.

Denham, S. A., Blair, K. A., Schmidt, M. S., Blair, K., DeMulder, E., Caal, S., et al. (2003b). Preschool understanding of emotions: Contributions to classroom anger and aggression. *Journal of Child Psychology and Psychiatry, 43*, 901–916. https://doi.org/10.1111/1469-7610.00139.

Dennis, T. (2006). Emotional self-regulation in preschoolers: The interplay of child approach reactivity, parenting, and control capacities. *Developmental Psychology, 42*, 84–97. https://doi.org/10.1037/0012-1649.42.1.84.84.

Di Lalla, L. F., Marcus, J. L., & Wright-Phillips, M. V. (2004). Longitudinal effects of preschool behavioral styles on early adolescent school performance. *Journal of School Psychology, 42*, 385–401. https://doi.org/10.1016/j.jsp.2004.05.002.

Dishion, T. J., & McMahon, R. J. (1998). Parental monitoring and the prevention of child and adolescent problem behavior: A conceptual and empirical formulation. *Clinical Child and Family Psychology Review, 1*, 61–75. https://doi.org/10.1023/A:1021800432380.

Domitrovich, C. E., Cortes, R. C., & Greenberg, M. T. (2007). Improving young children's social and emotional competence: A randomized trial of the preschool "PATHS" curriculum. *The Journal of Primary Prevention, 28*, 67–91. https://doi.org/10.1007/s10935-007-0081-0.

Dunn, J., & Cutting, A. L. (1999). Understanding others, and individual differences in friendship interactions in young children. *Social Development, 8*, 201–219. https://doi.org/10.1111/1467-9507.00091.

Durlak, J. A., & Wells, A. M. (1998). Evaluation of indicated preventive intervention (secondary prevention) mental health programs for children and adolescents. *American Journal of Community Psychology, 26*, 775–802. https://doi.org/10.1023/A:1022162015815.

Eigisti, I. E., Zayas, M., Mischel, W., Shoda, Y., Ayduk, O., Dadlani, M. B., et al. (2006). Predicting cognitive control from preschool to late adolescence and young adulthood. *Psychological Science, 17*, 478–484. https://doi.org/10.1111/j.1467-9280.2006.01732.x.

Eisenberg, N., Spinrad, T. L., & Cumberland, A. (1998). Parental socialization of emotion. *Psychological Inquiry, 9*, 241–273.

Eisenberg, N., Guthrie, I. K., Murphy, B. C., Shepard, S. A., Cumberland, A., & Carlo, G. (1999). Consistency and development of prosocial dispositions: A longitudinal study. *Child Development, 70*, 1360–1372. https://doi.org/10.1111/1467-8624.00100.

Eisenberg, N., Fabes, R. A., Guthrie, I. K., & Reiser, M. (2000). Dispositional emotionality and regulation: Their role in predicting quality of social functioning. *Journal of Personality and Social Psychology, 78*, 136–157. https://doi.org/10.1037/0022-3514.78.1.136.

Eisenberg, N., Fabes, R. A., Guthrie, I. K., & Reiser, M. (2002). The role of emotionality and regulation in children's social competence and adjustment. In L. Pulkinnen & A. Caspi (Eds.), *Paths to successful development: Personality in the life course* (pp. 46–70). Cambridge: Cambridge University Press.

Eisenberg, N., Valiente, C., Morris, A. S., Fabes, R. A., Cumberland, A., & Reiser, M. (2003). Longitudinal relations among parental emotional expressivity, children's regulation, and quality of socioemotional function. *Developmental Psychology, 39*, 3–19. https://doi.org/10.1037/0012-1649.39.1.3.

Eisenberg, N., Liew, J., & Pidada, S. U. (2004). The longitudinal relations of regulation and emotionality of Indonesian children's socioemotional functioning. *Developmental Psychology, 40*, 790–804. https://doi.org/10.1037/0012-1649.40.5.790.

Eisenberg, N., Sadovsky, A., & Spinrad, T. L. (2005a). Associations of emotion-related regulation with language skills, emotion knowledge, and academic outcomes. *New Directions for Child and Adolescent Development, 109*, 109–118. https://doi.org/10.1002/cd.143.

Eisenberg, N., Sadovsky, A., Spinrad, T. L., Fabes, R. A., Losoya, S. H., Valiente, C., et al. (2005b). The relations of problem behavior status to children's negative emotionality, effortful control, and impulsivity: Concurrent relations and prediction of change. *Developmental Psychology, 42*, 193–211. https://doi.org/10.1037/0012-1649.41.1.193.

Elgar, F. J., McGrath, P. J., & Washbusch, D. A. (2004). Mutual influences on maternal depression and child adjustment problems. *Clinical Psychology Review, 24*, 441–459. https://doi.org/10.1016/j.cpr.2004.02.002.

Erdena, F., & Wolfgang, C. H. (2004). An exploration of the differences in pre-kindergarten, kindergarten, and first grade teachers' beliefs related to discipline when dealing with male and female students. *Early Childhood Development and Care, 174*, 3–11. https://doi.org/10.1080/0300443032000103098.

Fabes, R. A., Martin, C. L., & Hanish, L. D. (2003). Young children's play qualities in same-, other-, and mixed-sex peer groups. *Child Development, 74*, 921–932. https://doi.org/10.1111/1467-8624.00576.

Fabes, R. A., Gaertner, M. B., & Popp, T. K. (2006). Getting along with others: Social competence in early childhood. In K. M. D. Phillips (Ed.), *Handbook of early childhood development* (pp. 297–315). Malden: Blackwell Publishing.

Fantuzzo, J., & McWayne, C. (2002). The relationship between peer-play interactions in the family context and dimensions of school readiness for low-income preschool children. *Journal of Educational Psychology, 92*, 79–87. https://doi.org/10.1037/0022-0663.94.1.79.

Filcheck, H. A., McNeil, C. B., Greco, L. A., & Bernard, R. S. (2004). Using a whole-class token economy and coaching of teacher skills in a preschool classroom to manage disruptive behavior. *Psychology in the Schools, 4*, 351–361. https://doi.org/10.1002/pits.10168.

Gilliom, M., Shaw, D. S., Beck, J. E., Schonberg, M. A., & Lukon, J. L. (2002). Anger regulation in disadvantaged preschool boys: Strategies, antecedents, and the development of self-control. *Developmental Psychology, 38*, 222–235. https://doi.org/10.1037/0012-1649.38.2.222.

Gutermuth-Anthony, L., Anthony, B. J., Glanville, D. N., Naiman, D. Q., Waandres, C., & Shaffer, S. (2005). The relationship between parenting stress, parenting behavior and preschoolers' social competence and behavior problems in the classroom. *Infant and Child Development, 14*, 133–154. https://doi.org/10.1002/icd.385.

Haight, W. L., Wang, X., Fung, H. H., Williams, K., & Mintz, J. (1999). Universal, developmental, and variable aspects of young children's play: A cross-cultural comparison of pretending at home. *Child Development, 70*, 1477–1488. https://doi.org/10.1111/1467-8624.00107.

Halberstadt, A. G., Denham, S. A., & Dunsmore, J. C. (2001). Affective social competence. *Social Development, 10*, 10–20. https://doi.org/10.1111/1467-9507.00150.

Hastings, P. D., Zahn-Waxler, C., Robinson, J., Usher, B., & Bridges, D. (2000). The development of concern for others in children with behavior problems. *Developmental Psychology, 36*, 531–546. https://doi.org/10.1037//0O12-1649.36.5.531.

Hay, D. F., Payne, A., & Chadwick, A. (2004). Peer relations in childhood. *Journal of Child Psychology and Psychiatry, 45*, 84–108. https://doi.org/10.1046/j.0021-9630.2003.00308.x.

Hess, C. R., Teti, D. M., & Hussey-Gardner, B. (2004). Self-efficacy and parenting of high-risk infants: The moderating role of parent knowledge of infant development. *Journal of Applied Developmental Psychology, 25*, 423–437. https://doi.org/10.1016/j.appdev.2004.06.002.

Hill, A. L., Degnan, K. A., Calkins, S. A., & Keane, S. P. (2006). Profiles of externalizing behavior problems for boys and girls across preschool: The roles of emotion regulation and inattention. *Developmental Psychology, 42*, 913–928. https://doi.org/10.1037/0012-1649.42.5.913.

Hinshaw, S. P., Owens, E. B., Wells, K. C., Kraemer, H. C., Abikoff, H. B., Arnold, E., et al. (2000). Family processes and treatment outcome in the MTA: Negative/ineffective parenting practices in relation to multimodal treatment. *Journal of Abnormal Child Psychology, 28*, 555–568. https://doi.org/10.1023/A:1005183115230.

Howe, N., Rinaldi, C. M., Jennings, M., & Petrakos, H. (2002). "No! The lambs can stay out because they got cozies": Constructive and destructive sibling conflict, pretend play, and social understanding. *Child Development, 75*, 1460–1473. https://doi.org/10.1111/1467-8624.00483.

Howe, N., Petrakos, H., Rinaldi, C. M., & LeFebre, R. (2005). 'This is a bad dog, you know...': Constructing shared meanings during sibling pretend play. *Child Development, 76*, 783–794. https://doi.org/10.1111/j.1467-8624.2005.00877.x.

Howes, C., Hamilton, C. E., & Matheson, C. C. (1994). Children's relationships with peers: Differential associations with aspects of the teacher-child relationship. *Child Development, 65*, 253–263. https://doi.org/10.2307/1131380.

Izard, C. E. (2002). Translating emotion theory and research into preventive interventions. *Psychological Bulletin, 128*, 796–824. https://doi.org/10.1037//0033-2909.128.5.796.

Izard, C. E., Fine, S., Schultz, D., Mostow, A., Ackerman, B., & Youngstrom, E. (2001). Emotion knowledge as a predictor of social behaviour and academic competence in children at risk. *Psychological Science, 12*, 18–23. https://doi.org/10.1111/1467-9280.00304.

Kam, C.-M., Greenberg, M. T., & Walls, C. T. (2003). Examining the role of implementation quality in school-based prevention using the PATHS curriculum. *Prevention Science, 4*, 55–63. https://doi.org/10.1023/A:1021786811186.

Kam, C.-M., Greenberg, M. T., & Kusche, C. A. (2004). Sustained effects of the PATHS curriculum on the social and psychological adjustment of children in special education. *Journal of Emotional and Behavioral Disorders, 12*, 66–78. https://doi.org/10.1177/10634266040120020101.

Kazdin, A. E., & Weisz, J. R. (1998). Identifying and developing empirically supported child and adolescent treatments. *Journal of Consulting and Clinical Psychology, 66*, 19–36. https://doi.org/10.1037/0022-006X.66.1.19.

Kellam, S. G., Ling, X., Merisca, R., Brown, C. H., & Ialongo, N. (1998). The effect of the level of aggression in the first grade classroom on the course and malleability of aggressive behavior in middle school. *Development and Psychopathology, 10*, 165–186. https://doi.org/10.1017/S0954579498001564.

Kelly, B., Longbottom, J., Potts, F., & Williamson, J. (2005). Applying emotional intelligence: Exploring the Promoting Alternative Thinking Strategies curriculum. *Educational Psychology in Practice, 20*, 221–241. https://doi.org/10.1080/0266736042000251808.

Kilgore, K., Snyder, J., & Lentz, C. (2000). The contribution of parental discipline, parental monitoring, and school risk to early-onset conduct problems in

African American boys and girls. *Developmental Psychology, 36*, 835–845. https://doi.org/10.1037/0012-1649.36.6.835.

Kitzman, K. M. (2000). Effects of marital conflict on subsequent triadic family interactions and parenting. *Developmental Psychology, 36*, 3–13. https://doi.org/10.1037/0012-1649.36.1.3.

Knopf, H. T., & Swick, K. J. (2007). How parents feel about their child's teacher/school: Implications for early childhood professionals. *Early Childhood Education Journal, 34*, 291–296. https://doi.org/10.1007/s10643-006-0119-6.

Kochanska, G. (2002). Committed compliance, moral self, and internalization: A meditational model. *Developmental Psychology, 38*, 339–351. https://doi.org/10.1037/0012-1649.38.3.339.

Kochanska, G., Murray, K. T., & Harlan, E. T. (2000). Effortful control in early childhood: Continuity and change, antecedents, and implications for social development. *Developmental Psychology, 36*, 220–232. https://doi.org/10.1037/0012-1649.36.2.220.

Krueger, R. F., Hicks, B. M., & McGue, M. (2001). Altruism and antisocial behavior: Independent tendencies, unique personality correlates, distinct etiologies. *Psychological Science, 12*, 397–402. https://doi.org/10.1111/1467-9280.00373.

Lee, D. L., Belfiore, P. J., Scheeler, M. C., Hua, Y., & Smith, R. (2004). Behavioral momentum in academics: Using embedded high-p sequence to increase academic productivity. *Psychology in the Schools, 41*, 789–801. https://doi.org/10.1002/pits.20014.

Lee, D. L., Belfiore, P. J., & Gormley, S. (2008). Riding the wave: Creating a momentum of school success. *Teaching Exceptional Children, 40*, 65–70.

Lemerise, A. E., & Arsenio, C. R. (2000). An integrated model of emotion processes and cognition in social information processing. *Child Development, 71*, 107–118. https://doi.org/10.1111/1467-8624.00124.

Lewis, R. (1999). Teachers coping with the stress of classroom discipline. *Social Psychology in Education, 3*, 155–171. https://doi.org/10.1023/A:1009627827937. 36.

Lochman, J. E., & Wells, K. C. (2002). The Coping Power program at the middle-school transition: Universal and indicated prevention effects. *Psychology of Addictive Behaviors, 16*, S40–S54. https://doi.org/10.1037/0893-164X.16.4S.S40.

Lynch, K. B., Geller, S. R., & Schmidt, M. G. (2004). Multi-year evaluation of the effectiveness of a resilience-based prevention program for young children. *Journal of Primary Prevention, 24*, 335–353. https://doi.org/10.1023/B:JOPP.0000018052.12488.d1.

Maguire, M. C., & Dunn, J. (1997). Friendships in early childhood, and social understanding. *International Journal of Behavioral Development, 21*, 669–686. https://doi.org/10.1080/016502597384613.

Martin, R. M., & Green, J. A. (2005). The use of emotion explanations by mothers: Relation to preschoolers' gender and understanding of emotions. *Social*

Development, 14, 229–249. https://doi.org/10.1111/j.1467-9507.2005.00300.x.
Masten, A., & Coatesworth, J. (1998). The development of competence in favorable and unfavorable environments: Lessons on research on successful children. *American Psychologist, 53*, 205–220. https://doi.org/10.1037/0003-066X.53.2.205.
Mayer, J. D., & Salovey, P. (1997). What is emotional intelligence? In P. Salovey & D. J. Sluyter (Eds.), *Emotional development and emotional intelligence: Educational implications* (pp. 3–31). New York: Basic Books.
McMahon, R. J. (2006). Parent training interventions for preschool-age children. In R. E. Tremblay, R. G. Barr, & R. V. De Peters (Eds.), *Encyclopedia on early childhood development*. Retrieved March 13, 2008, from www.excellence-earlychildhood.ca
McMahon, R. J., & Forehand, R. J. (2003). *Helping the noncompliant child: Family-based treatment for oppositional behaviour* (2nd ed.). New York: The Guilford Press.
Mendez, J. L., Fantuzzo, J., & Cicchetti, D. (2002a). Profiles of social competence among low income African American preschool children. *Child Development, 73*, 1085–1100. https://doi.org/10.1111/1467-8624.00459.
Mendez, J. L., McDermott, P., & Fantuzzo, J. (2002b). Identifying and promoting social competence with African American preschool children: Developmental and contextual considerations. *Psychology in the Schools, 39*, 111–123. https://doi.org/10.1002/pits.10039.
Merikangas, K. R., Dierker, L. C., & Szatmari, P. (1998). Psychopathology among offspring of parents with substance abuse and/or anxiety disorders: A high-risk study. *Journal of Child Psychology and Psychiatry, 39*, 711–720. https://doi.org/10.1111/1469-7610.00370.
Merrell, K. W., & Gimpel, G. A. (1998). On the nature and value of social skills. In K. W. Merrell & G. A. Gimpel (Eds.), *Social skills of children and adolescents: Conceptualization, assessment, treatment* (pp. 1–28). Mahwah: Lawrence Erlbaum.
Miller-Heyle, J., MacPhee, D., & Fritz, J. J. (1998). DARE to be You: A family support, early prevention program. *Journal of Primary Prevention, 18*, 257–285. https://doi.org/10.1023/A:1024602927381.
Mischel, W. (1974). Processes in delay of gratification. In L. Berkowitz (Ed.), *Advances in experimental social psychology* (Vol. 7, pp. 249–292). New York: Academic Press.
Moffitt, T. E., & Caspi, A. (2001). Childhood predictors differentiate life-course persistent and adolescence limited antisocial pathways among males and females. *Development and Psychopathology, 13*, 355–375. https://doi.org/10.1017/S0954579401002097.
Nation, M., Crusto, C., Wandersman, A., Kumpfer, A., Seybolt, D., Morrissey-Kane, E., & Davino, K. (2003). What works in prevention – Principles of effective prevention programs. *American Psychologist, 58*, 449–456. https://doi.org/10.1037/0003-066X.58.6-7.449.

Nelson, G., Westhues, A., & MacLeod, J. (2003). A meta-analysis of longitudinal research on preschool prevention programs for children. *Prevention and Treatment, 6*, 1–25.

Nelson, J. R., Stage, S., Duppong-Hurley, K., Synhorst, L., & Epstein, M. H. (2007). Risk factors predictive of problem behavior of children at risk for emotional and behavioral disorders. *Exceptional Children, 73*, 367–379. https://doi.org/10.1177/001440290707300306.

Nicholson, B. C., Fox, R. A., & Johnson, S. D. (2005). Parenting young children with challenging behaviour. *Infant and Child Development, 14*, 425–428. https://doi.org/10.1002/icd.403.

Patterson, G. R., Chamberlain, P., & Reid, J. B. (1982). A comparative evaluation of a parent training program. *Behavior Therapy, 13*, 638–650. https://doi.org/10.1016/S0005-7894(82)80021-X.

Prinz, R. J., & Miller, G. E. (1994). Family-based treatment for childhood antisocial behavior: Experimental influences on dropout and engagement. *Journal of Consulting and Clinical Psychology, 62*, 645–650. https://doi.org/10.1037/0022-006X.62.3.645.

Prinz, R. J., & Sanders, M. R. (2007). Adopting a population-level approach to parenting and family support interventions. *Clinical Psychology Review, 27*, 739–749. https://doi.org/10.1016/j.cpr.2007.01.005.

Rapee, R. M., Kennedy, S., Ingram, M., Edwards, S., & Sweeney, L. (2005). Prevention and early intervention of anxiety disorders in inhibited preschool children. *Journal of Consulting Clinical Psychology, 73*, 488–497. https://doi.org/10.1037/0022-006X.73.3.488.

Ricaud-Droisy, H., & Zaouche-Gaudron, C. (2003). Interpersonal conflict resolution strategies in children: A father-child co-construction. *European Journal of Psychology of Education, 18*, 157–169. https://doi.org/10.1007/BF03173482.

Roberts, W. (1999). The socialization of emotion expression: Relations with prosocial behavior and competence in five samples. *Canadian Journal of Behavioural Science, 31*, 72–85. https://doi.org/10.1037/h0087075.

Roberts, W., & Strayer, J. (1996). Empathy, emotional expressiveness, and prosocial behavior. *Child Development, 67*, 449–470. https://doi.org/10.1111/j.1467-8624.1996.tb01745.x.

Romano, E., Tremblay, R. E., Boulerice, B., & Swisher, R. (2005). Multilevel correlates of childhood physical aggression and prosocial behavior. *Journal of Abnormal Child Psychology, 33*, 565–578. https://doi.org/10.1007/s10802-005-6738-3.

Rothbart, M. K., & Bates, J. E. (1998). Temperament. In W. Damon & N. Eisenberg (Eds.), *Handbook of child psychology: Vol. 3. Social, emotional, and personality development* (5th ed., pp. 105–176). New York: Wiley.

Ryan, R. M., & Stiller, J. D. (1994). Representations of relationships to teachers, parents, and friends as predictors of academic success. *Journal of Early Adolescence, 14*, 226–250. https://doi.org/10.1177/027243169401400207.

Rydell, A.-M., Berlin, L., & Bohlin, G. (2003). Emotionality, emotion regulation, and adaptation among five-to-eight-year old children. *Emotion, 31*, 30–47. https://doi.org/10.1037/1528-3542.3.1.30.

Saarni, C. (2001). The continuity dilemma in emotional competence. *Psychological Inquiry, 12*, 94–96.

Sanders, M. R. (2003). Triple P – Positive Parenting Program: A population approach to promoting competent parenting. *Australian e-Journal for the Advancement of Mental Health, 2*(3). Retrieved March 23, 2008, from www.ausienet.com/journal/vol2iss3/sanders.pdf

Sanders, M. R., & Morawska, A. (2005). Can changing parental knowledge, dysfunctional expectations and attributions, and emotion regulation improve outcomes for children? In R. E. Tremblay, R. G. Barr, & R. V. De Peters (Eds.), *Encyclopedia on early childhood development.* Retrieved March 13, 2010, from www.excellence-earlychildhood.ca

Schultz, D., Izard, C. E., Ackerman, B. P., & Youngstrom, E. A. (2001). Emotion knowledge in economically disadvantaged children: Self-regulatory antecedents and relations to social difficulties and withdrawal. *Development and Psychopathology, 13*, 53–68. https://doi.org/10.1017/S0954579401001043.

Sebanc, A. M. (2003). The friendship features of preschool children: Links with prosocial behavior and aggression. *Social Development, 12*, 249–268. https://doi.org/10.1111/1467-9507.00232.

Sheffield, J. K., Spence, S. H., Rapee, R. M., Kowalenko, N., Wignall, A., Davis, A., & McLoone, J. (2006). Evaluation of universal, indicated, and combined cognitive-behavioral approaches to the prevention of depression among adolescents. *Journal of Consulting and Clinical Psychology, 74*, 66–79. https://doi.org/10.1037/0022-006X.74.1.66.

Shure, M. B., & Spivak, G. (1982). Interpersonal problem-solving in young children: A cognitive approach to prevention. *American Journal of Community Psychology, 10*, 341–356. https://doi.org/10.1007/BF00896500.

Snyder, H. (2001). Epidemiology of official offending. In R. Loeber & D. P. Farmington (Eds.), *Child delinquents: Development, intervention and service needs* (pp. 25–46). Thousand Oaks: Sage.

Snyder, J., Cramer, A., Afrank, J., & Patterson, G. R. (2005a). The contributions of ineffective discipline and parental hostile attributions of child misbehavior to the development of conduct problems at home and school. *Developmental Psychology, 41*, 30–41. https://doi.org/10.1037/0012-1649.41.1.30.

Snyder, J., Schrepferman, L., Oeser, J., Patterson, G., Stoolmiller, M., Johnson, K., & Snyder, A. (2005b). Deviancy training and association with deviant peers in young children: Occurrence and contribution to early-onset conduct problems. *Development and Psychopathology, 17*, 397–413. https://doi.org/10.1017/S0954579405050194.

Spinrad, T. L., Eisenberg, N., Cumberland, A., Fabes, R. A., Valiente, C., Shepard, S. A., et al. (2006). Relation of emotion-related regulation to children's social competence: A longitudinal study. *Emotion, 6*, 498–510. https://doi.org/10.1037/1528-3542.6.3.498.

Spitzer, A., Webster-Stratton, C., & Hollinsworth, T. (1991). Coping with conduct-problem children: Parents gaining knowledge and control. *Journal of Clinical Child Psychology, 20*, 413–427. https://doi.org/10.1207/s15374424jccp2004_10.

Stanger, C., Dumenci, L., Kamon, J., & Burstein, M. (2004). Parenting and children's externalizing problems in substance abusing families. *Journal of Clinical Child and Adolescent Psychology, 33*, 590–600. https://doi.org/10.1207/s15374424jccp3303_16.

Stansbury, K., & Sigman, M. (2000). Responses of preschoolers in two frustrating episodes: Emergence of complex strategies for emotion regulation. *Journal of Genetic Psychology, 161*, 182–202. https://doi.org/10.1080/00221320009596705.

Stoiber, K. C. (1992). Parents' beliefs about their children's cognitive, social, and motor functioning. *Early Education and Development, 3*, 244–257. https://doi.org/10.1207/s15566935eed0303_4.

Stoolmiller, M., Eddy, M., & Reid, J. B. (2000). Detecting and describing preventive intervention effects in a universal school-based randomized trial targeting delinquent and violent behavior. *Journal of Consulting and Clinical Psychology, 68*, 296–306. https://doi.org/10.1037//0022-006X.68.2.296.

Strayer, J., & Roberts, W. (2004). Empathy and observed anger and aggression in 5-year-olds. *Social Development, 13*, 1–13. https://doi.org/10.1111/j.1467-9507.2004.00254.x.

Sturge-Apple, M. L., Davies, P. T., & Cummings, E. M. (2006). Hostility and withdrawal in marital conflict: Effects on parental emotional unavailability and inconsistent discipline. *Journal of Family Psychology, 20*, 227–238. https://doi.org/10.1037/0893-3200.20.2.227.

Swick, K. (2004). What parents seek in relations with early childhood family helpers. *Early Childhood Education Journal, 31*, 217–220. https://doi.org/10.1023/B:ECEJ.0000012316.93327.6b.

Swick, K., & Hooks, L. (2005). Parental experiences and beliefs regarding inclusive placements of their special needs children. *Early Childhood Education Journal, 32*, 1–6. https://doi.org/10.1007/s10643-005-0011-9.

Thompson, R. A. (1994). Emotion regulation: A theme in search of definition. *Monographs of the Society for Research in Child Development, 59*., (Serial No. 240), 25–52. https://doi.org/10.1111/j.1540-5834.1994.tb01276.x.

Trapolini, T., Ungerer, J. A., & McMahon, C. A. (2007). Maternal depression and children's attachment representations during the preschool years. *British Journal of Developmental Psychology, 25*, 247–261. https://doi.org/10.1348/026151006X118739.

Turner, K. M. T., & Sanders, M. R. (2006). Dissemination of evidence-based parenting and family support strategies: Learning from the Triple P – Positive

Parenting Program system approach. *Aggression and Violent Behavior, 11*, 176–193. https://doi.org/10.1016/j.avb.2005.07.005.
Valdez, C. R., Carlson, C., & Zanger, D. (2005). Evidence-based parent training and family interventions for school behavior change. *School Psychology Quarterly, 20*, 403–433. https://doi.org/10.1521/scpq.2005.20.4.403.
van Lier, P. A. C., Vuijk, P., & Crijnen, A. A. M. (2005). Understanding mechanisms of change and development of antisocial behavior: The impact of a universal intervention. *Journal of Abnormal Child Psychology, 33*, 521–535. https://doi.org/10.1007/s10802-005-6735-7.
Vaughan Van Hecke, A., Mundy, P. C., Acra, C. F., Block, J. J., Delgado, C. E. F., et al. (2007). Infant joint attention, temperament, and social competence in preschool children. *Child Development, 78*, 53–69. https://doi.org/10.1111/j.1467-8624.2007.00985.x.
Vickers, H. S., & Minke, K. M. (1995). Exploring parent-teacher relationship: Joining and communication to others. *School Psychology Quarterly, 10*, 133–150. https://doi.org/10.1037/h0088300.
Vitaro, F., Brendgen, M., Larose, S., & Tremblay, R. E. (2005). Kindergarten disruptive behaviors, protective factors, and educational achievement by early adulthood. *Journal of Educational Psychology, 97*, 617–629. https://doi.org/10.1037/0022-0663.97.4.617.
Wahler, R. G. (1997). On the origins of children's compliance and opposition: Family context, reinforcement, and rules. *Journal of Child and Family Studies, 6*, 191–208. https://doi.org/10.1023/A:1025050724559.
Walker, H. M., Kavanagh, K., Stiller, B., Golly, A., Severson, H. H., & Feil, E. G. (1998). First step to success: An early intervention approach for preventing school antisocial behavior. *Journal of Emotional and Behavioral Disorders, 6*, 66–80. https://doi.org/10.1177/106342669800600201.
Warnes, E. D., Sheridan, S. M., Geske, J., & Warnes, W. A. (2005). A contextual approach to the assessment of social skills: Identifying meaningful behaviors for social competence. *Psychology in the Schools, 42*, 173–187. https://doi.org/10.1002/pits.20052.
Webster-Stratton, C. (1990). Long-term follow-up of families with young conduct-problem children: From preschool to grade school. *Journal of Clinical Child Psychology, 19*, 1344–1349.
Webster-Stratton, C. (1996). Early-onset conduct problems: Does gender make a difference? *Journal of Consulting and Clinical Psychology, 64*, 540–551. https://doi.org/10.1037/0022-006X.64.3.540.
Webster-Stratton, C. (1998). Preventing conduct problems in Head Start children: Strengthening parenting competencies. *Journal of Consulting and Clinical Psychology, 66*, 715–730. https://doi.org/10.1037/0022-006X.66.5.715.

Webster-Stratton, C. (2006). *The incredible years: A trouble-shooting guide for parents of children ages 3–8 years*. Seattle: Incredible Years Press.

Webster-Stratton, C., & Hammond, M. (1997). Treating children with early-onset conduct problems: A comparison of child and parent training interventions. *Journal of Consulting and Clinical Psychology, 65*, 93–109. https://doi.org/10.1037/0022-006X.65.1.93.

Webster-Stratton, C., & Reid, J. M. (2003). Treating conduct problems and strengthening social and emotional competence in young children: The Dina Dinosaur Program. *Journal of Emotional and Behavioral Disorders, 2*, 130–143. https://doi.org/10.1177/10634266030110030101.

Webster-Stratton, C., & Taylor, T. (2001). Nipping early risk factors in the bud: Preventing substance abuse, delinquency, and violence in adolescence through interventions targeted at young children (0–8 years). *Prevention Science, 2*, 165–192. https://doi.org/10.1023/A:1011510923900.

Webster-Stratton, C., Reid, J. M., & Hammond, M. (2001). Preventing conduct problems, promoting social competence: A parent-teacher training partnership in Head Start. *Journal of Clinical Child Psychology, 30*, 283–302.

Webster-Stratton, C., Reid, J. M., & Hammond, M. (2004). Treating children with early-onset conduct problems: Intervention outcomes for parent, child, and teacher training. *Journal of Clinical Child and Adolescent Psychology, 33*, 105–124. https://doi.org/10.1207/S15374424JCCP3301_11.

Wilburn, R. E. (2000). *Understanding the preschooler*. New York: Peter Lang Publishing.

Witherington, D. C., & Crichton, J. A. (2007). Frameworks for understanding emotions and their development: Functionalist and dynamic systems approaches. *Emotion, 7*, 628–637. https://doi.org/10.1037/1528-3542.7.3.628.

Wulfert, E., Block, J. A., Santa Ana, E., Rodriguez, M. L., & Colsman, M. (2002). Delay of gratification: Impulsive choices and problem behaviors in early and late adolescence. *Journal of Personality, 70*, 533–552. https://doi.org/10.1111/1467-6494.05013.

Zanolli, K. M., Paden, P., & Cox, K. (1997). Teaching prosocial behavior to typically developing toddlers. *Journal of Behavioral Education, 7*, 373–391. https://doi.org/10.1023/A:1022883807927.

Zubrick, S. R., Ward, K. A., Silburn, S. R., Lawrence, D., Williams, A. A., Blair, E., et al. (2005). Prevention of child behavior problems through universal implementation of a group behavioral family intervention. *Prevention Science, 6*, 176–193. https://doi.org/10.1007/s11121-005-0013-2.

CHAPTER 2

The Conceptual Framework of the Social-Emotional Prevention Program

As suggested by the review of the literature presented in the previous chapter, several informative conclusions can be drawn from current research on preschool children's social-emotional competencies. First, children's social-emotional development seems to be a key element supporting long-term social and academic adjustment, and hence, it could be conceptualized as an important focus of early education programs aiming to enhance preschoolers' ability to adapt to social relationships and to later academic requirements (Linares et al. 2005; Mantzicopoulos and Neurath-Pritchett 1998; Trentacosta et al. 2006). In addition to these positive outcomes, social-emotional competencies have been found to increase resilience to mental health problems, particularly externalizing problems (Eisenberg et al. 2005; Hastings et al. 2000). Moreover, longitudinal studies have shown that these competencies are relatively stable over time from preschool to adolescence (Abe and Izard 1999; Eisenberg et al. 1999, 2003), meaning that maladaptive interaction patterns acquired by preschoolers become more resistant to change once they are reinforced over time (Moffitt and Caspi 2001; Snyder 2001). Therefore, early intervention is an essential step in ensuring that children's developmental trajectories are deflected from negative outcomes such as juvenile delinquency or conduct disorders.

Second, there is compelling empirical evidence supporting the notion that early education programs targeting social-emotional development in preschool children may be relevant in preventing the escalation of

C. A. Ştefan, *Social-Emotional Prevention Programs for Preschool Children's Behavior Problems*,
https://doi.org/10.1007/978-3-319-74751-4_2

maladaptive behaviors (Nation et al. 2003; Nelson et al. 2003). Moreover, data on the efficacy of prevention programs focusing on social-emotional learning have largely supported the notion that the most promising types of interventions for children are multi-focused, meaning that they not only target the child, but also parents' and teachers' behaviors (Webster-Stratton and Taylor 2001). Consequently, the Social-Emotional Prevention Program (SEP) was developed as a multi-component intervention with the aim of enhancing children's social-emotional development and reducing their risk of externalizing problems.

Underlying Assumptions of SEP Development

The SEP was developed considering the following: (1) reviewing currently available evidence-based practices considered effective in developing preschoolers' social-emotional competencies (see Chap. 1); (2) identifying an intervention framework which would allow SEP to address the intervention needs of all children, irrespective of their risk status; (3) linking the intervention to a screening system; and (4) adapting SEP contents to the Romanian preschool education system.

Based on the literature review, it is obvious that the most often employed approaches to delivering social-emotional learning programs in community-based settings are the universal and the indicated interventions (Denham and Burton 2003; Ştefan and Miclea 2010; Webster-Stratton and Taylor 2001). The former are aimed at developing social-emotional skills in all children, while the latter are aimed at developing such skills in children who are at risk of maladjustment. Given the call for preventive interventions to address the needs of all children, not only those who are at risk, SEP development was inspired by the hybrid approach of the Fast Track program (Conduct Prevention Program Research Group [CPPRG] 1999a, b). The Fast Track represents a multi-focused preventive approach designed for school-aged children, which allows for the concomitant implementation of a universal and an indicated prevention program. Hence, the SEP employs the same intervention rationale, but with some changes to the original framework which are mainly related to the indicated intervention level.

First, the Fast Track program's indicated intervention included *pullout* sessions for children at risk of externalizing problems (CPPRG 1999b). However, some researchers have raised doubts about the efficacy of small-group training, given that children exhibiting high levels of aggression and non-compliance do not benefit from such approaches, because negative behaviors are generally reinforced by interactions with peers manifesting similar difficulties (Lochman and Wells 2002; van Lier et al. 2005). Consequently, SEP relies on the assumption that at risk children are better served by an intervention which emphasizes their opportunities to interact with peers who have better developed social skills. In turn, it could be assumed that such peers could provide a positive model for their less skilled counterparts.

A second way in which SEP departs from the Fast Track framework is related to the contents of the parent training. In its original format, parent training was only offered to parents of high-risk children (CPPRG 1999a). This could have potentially damaging effects on parental involvement in the intervention, because parents of high-risk children could feel ashamed of being singled out. Conversely, parents of children who are not at risk would be denied access to training, when in fact participation could positively affect their children's skills, as well as their own ability to support children's healthy development. Such an assumption is supported by findings on the efficacy of the Triple P – Positive Parenting Program, a community-based prevention program which elicited increased parental attendance when both parents of non-risk and at-risk children were involved in the training (Turner and Sanders 2006; Zubrick et al. 2005). The Triple P is grounded in the assumption that parental involvement could be enhanced by providing different types of learning opportunities depending on parents' needs: parents of non-risk children might benefit from an approach which emphasizes exposure to information on children's social-emotional skills development, whereas parents of high-risk children might benefit from a more consistent training in managing parent-child interactions (Sanders and Morawska 2005). This rationale was employed in designing the SEP parent training, and its content was organized to reflect the needs of both categories of parents.

In conclusion, the SEP was designed considering the hybrid framework of the Fast Track program, but its contents were adjusted to maximize the program's efficacy. Including such an approach, which targets children irrespective of their risk status, raises the question of how to adequately establish whether children are the focus of the universal or the indicated intervention. Most of the current approaches rely on: (1) identifying children who exhibit high levels of externalizing problems, usually signaled by below cutoff scores on measures of behavior problems (Webster-Stratton et al. 2008); and (2) indicators related to children's socio-economic status or juvenile delinquency rates in a given area (CPPRG 1999a; Raver et al. 2009). However, these approaches do not take into account the fact that recent developments in universal screening practices began emphasizing the assessment of children's social-emotional development as a primary strategy in defining and establishing risk of emotional and behavior problems (Severson and Walker 2002). Second, some researchers even called for screening procedures to be associated with specific intervention practices, thus proactively rather than reactively addressing children's mental health needs (Essex et al. 2009; Severson et al. 2007). Consequently, the SEP relies on a multiple gate screening procedure similar to that proposed by Durlak and Wells (1998): (1) in the first step a universal screener of children's social-emotional competencies is employed; and (2) in the second step, an additional measure of children's behavior problems is used to establish further need for assessment. Hence, children who exhibit insufficiently developed social-emotional skills become the target group for the indicated intervention, whereas the measure for externalizing problems becomes a second marker of risk status. In line with these assumptions, the SEP was associated with a universal screener developed to assess children's risk status. The Emotional Competence Screening and the Social Competence Screening were developed as measures of children's skills, which showed appropriate psychometric properties (Ştefan et al. 2009), and were consequently incorporated as a universal screening system associated with SEP implementation.

Finally, the SEP was developed considering the specific context of the Romanian preschool education system. Post-communist reforms of the education system undertaken by the Romanian Ministry of Education included the development of a national curriculum for preschool children specifically addressing social-emotional development in addition to the previous focus on cognitive development and school readiness prerequisites for reading/writing and mathematics. This update was intended to reflect recent conceptualizations of school readiness, suggesting that not only cognitive abilities, but also children's social-emotional competencies could play a key role in their adjustment to school requirements (Denham 2006; Ramey and Ramey 2004; Snow 2006). Although the curriculum states age-appropriate objectives for social-emotional learning, the suggested educational strategies which are supposed to facilitate the attainment of such goals cover activities which are embedded within other teaching activities and do not have a specific focus on social-emotional competence development. Therefore, the SEP was intended to provide teachers with clear guidelines for social-emotional learning in the classroom. In order to achieve this goal, SEP incorporates a stand-alone approach, encompassing a structured curriculum of classroom activities designed to develop social-emotional competencies, but it also emphasizes training teachers to support children's skill development by transferring learning during structured activities to daily interactions/activities in the classroom, meaning that the SEP can also be construed as an embedded intervention. The combination between the stand-alone and embedded intervention is a result of research emphasizing that children's skill development is facilitated mainly when adults provide them with contexts for practicing newly learned emotion regulation, problem-solving or friendship skills (Nation et al. 2003; Nelson et al. 2003).

The SEP Framework in the Context of Evidence-Based Preventive Programs from the Field of Early Education

During SEP development, recent advances in research concerning preventive program's efficacy were considered in order to design intervention contents which reflected updated approaches for each intervention component. The first component, the *classroom curriculum*, included activities for developing children's social-emotional competencies. In keeping with research suggesting that emotional and social competencies are highly related constructs encompassing rather distinct skills and behaviors, as more extensively argued in Chap. 1, SEP proposed a separate conceptualization of emotional and social competencies (Denham et al. 2001, 2003). Similar approaches to children's skill development were previously proposed in 2 empirically supported preventive interventions (CPPRG 1999b; Webster-Stratton 2000). Consequently, drawing from the structure of the Fast Track and the Incredible Years prevention programs, SEP includes 2 modules targeting the development of emotional competencies (i.e., emotion knowledge, emotion regulation) and 3 modules targeting the development of social competencies (i.e. rule compliance, peer play, problem-solving).

As suggested by the literature on evidence-based interventions in community settings, simply addressing social-emotional competence development through a curriculum of structured activities might be insufficient, especially for children who already exhibit signs of behavior problems (Domitrovich et al. 2007; CPPRG 1999b). Thus, prevention programs that specifically address behavior problems include more complex intervention strategies. For instance, coupling the classroom curriculum with teacher training was proposed as an effective strategy for improving adults' ability to effectively address children's behavior problems (CPPRG 1999b; Webster-Stratton et al. 2008). Given that these combined strategies resulted in significantly lower levels of externalizing problems in children who were at risk, these results further supported the decision to develop a teacher training as part of SEP (CPPRG 1999b; Filcheck et al. 2004; Raver et al. 2009).

A significant amount of empirical evidence suggests that in fact preventing and mainly managing misbehavior is effectively achieved through increasing teachers' use of positive discipline strategies (e.g., establishing rules, praising positive behaviors, establishing logical consequences for misbehaviors) (CPPRG 1999a; Webster-Stratton 2000). Also, establishing parent-teacher partnerships seems to enhance teachers' ability to manage behavior problems by creating more opportunities for parents to be involved in their children's activities both at home and in the classroom (Webster-Stratton et al. 2001, 2004). Hence, these 2 strategies were considered as part of the SEP teacher training.

However, research also suggests that simply managing children's behavior is a required, but insufficient skill when it comes to replacing maladaptive behavior patterns with more adaptive ones. More precisely, behavior management strategies focus on preventing or managing misbehavior, but not on actually building children's skills. Therefore, considering evidence supporting the fact that teacher consultations could complement behavior management training in order to facilitate teachers' ability to implement the classroom curriculum, and therefore to effectively support children's skill development (Domitrovich et al. 2007; Kam et al. 2003), SEP was designed to include consulations as part of the teacher training. These consultations were employed with 2 aims: (1) facilitating the implementation of the classroom curriculum; and (2) providing teachers with support for better managing difficult behavior mainly in at risk children, as well as with the opportunity to learn specific coaching strategies for supporting children's emotion regulation, problem-solving, or cooperative play skills development. The consultation component was deemed as especially important, because the child-focused intervention, as previously discussed, required teachers besides implementing the classroom activities to embed children's learning about social-emotional skills within daily classroom interactions. Hence, including teacher consultations created the context for practicing and discussing how to approach social-emotional learning by modeling and reinforcing appropriate behaviors when children are expected to manage and implement skills taught through the activities for the classroom curriculum in ecological situations.

A more recent trend in community-based settings is represented by the inclusion of *parent training*. The reason for including parent training as a part of a community-based intervention was twofold: (1) parent training supports the transfer and generalization of classroom acquired skills to parent-child interactions at home (Hughes et al. 2005); and (2) parental involvement in the intervention is consistently associated with lower levels of aggression and non-compliance in at risk children (Webster-Stratton et al. 2001, 2004). Initially, this intervention strategy was mostly employed in early intervention programs targeting children with clinical symptoms of conduct disorders (Webster-Stratton and Hammond 1997). In such instances, parent training usually included sessions ranging from 12 to 24 hours, which is less feasible in community-based settings, and thus raising sustainability issues in non-clinical settings (Dadds and Roth 2008). Previous research on the efficacy of multi-focused interventions for preschoolers' internalizing problems, comprising no more than 10 hours of parent training found that this type of approach supported changes in children's behavior and attracted relatively consistent attendance rates, with approximately 60% of parents participating in more than half of the intervention's training sessions (Dadds and Roth 2008; Izard et al. 2008). Also, as suggested by Kazdin and Wassell (1999), parental engagement in the intervention could be related to the perceived relevance of the intervention. Data on the sustainability of parent trainings in community-based settings point to a self-selective process, in which parents who perceive their children as more difficult are more interested in attending (Prinz and Sanders 2007), as opposed to parents of low-risk children who are more likely to drop-out (Andrews and Erskine 2001). Therefore, SEP comprised a brief, 4-session group training, as well as brief individual training sessions which could be held at parents' request. Hence, it was expected that the flexibility of the intervention format would prompt more interest from parents of at risk children to participate in the group sessions, as well as to potentially seek further support and assistance through individual training sessions, while also maintaining the interest of parents of low-risk children in participating in the group training.

In addition to the training session type, another strategy for increasing parental attendance was by adapting the intervention principles of the Triple P, as indicated in the previous section of this chapter. Considering the "minimally sufficient" framework of the Triple P, the SEP included different strategies depending on children's risk status: (1) informing and educating about social-emotional development for parents of low-risk children; and (2) supporting the development of behavior management and coaching skills of parents whose children were at risk of behavior problems (Turner and Sanders 2006; Zubrick et al. 2005). Moreover, in a similar vein to the teacher training, the SEP parent training was developed to include both strategies for behavior management and for social-emotional competence development. The behavior training component of SEP was largely similar to that proposed by the Fast Track or the Incredible Years (CPPRG 1999a; Webster-Stratton 2000) and it was intended to teach parents the skills needed to counteract the negative effects of harsh and/or inconsistent discipline on children's social-emotional development (Chang et al. 2003; Dennis 2006), and how to effectively support their children's skill development.

Objectives, Structure, and Contents of the SEP Program

Drawing on the theoretical assumptions of evidence-based preventive programs reviewed in the previous sections of this chapter, the SEP was developed as a multi-focused approach consisting of child, parent, and teacher focused activities. The SEP objectives were twofold: (1) to enhance children's social-emotional competencies; and (2) to reduce the frequency of externalizing type behaviors. Below, the main components of the SEP are described, namely the classroom curriculum, teacher training, and parent training.

The Classroom Curriculum

The classroom curriculum[1] targeting children's social and emotional development was designed to include 37 teacher implemented activities. These lessons were intended to be implemented with all the children irrespective of their risk status during 15 weeks with a frequency of 2–3 activities/week. The activities covered 5 modules focusing on: (1) emotional competencies (i.e., emotion recognition and emotion regulation); and (2) social competencies (i.e., compliance with rules, problem-solving, and prosocial behaviors). The order of implementing the modules was determined based on the following rationale: (1) compliance with rules was implemented first because setting expectations and establishing a proactive approach to discipline was regarded as fundamental for preparing the setting for social-emotional learning; setting expectations and consistent attitudes from teachers were found to predict children's ability to learn in the classroom (Stifter et al. 1999); (2) the emotion recognition and emotion regulation modules preceded the other modules targeting social skills, because previous research supported the notion that emotion awareness and children's ability to manage anger are prerequisites for adaptive social functioning (Denham et al. 2001, 2003); and (3) the problem-solving module, which emphasized children's ability to manage conflict was considered a prerequisite for supporting their ability to elicit prosocial behaviors and establish friendships with same-age peers, as suggested by previous research (Marion 2003; Sheridan et al. 1999). The contents of the 5 modules is described below. It is noteworthy that each module description provides insights concerning the standard activities from the classroom curriculum, while also highlighting strategies for embedding social-emotional learning during daily activities in the classroom.

Compliance with Rules The main objective of this module was to increase children's compliance with classroom rules. Compliance with rules from the SEP perspective includes a focus on guiding children to become responsible for their own behavior and to promote self-control, rather than training children to become obedient to adults' requests (Bear 2005; Brophy 1999). Lessons from this module were implemented as classroom activities for 2 weeks, whereas the supporting reward system was implemented for an additional 2 weeks after the start of the second module targeting emotion knowledge. Teachers were asked to select a maximum of 3–4 classroom rules (e.g., listening to others, asking permission before speaking, gathering toys, speaking with an "indoor" voice), which they considered important for their classroom management. Depending on the selected rules, teachers were asked to read them out in order to familiarize children with the rules, as well as to employ role-play scenarios for children to exercise rule appropriate behaviors. Also, classroom materials such as posters depicting the rules were used as visual cues, intended as reminders of expected behavior. Additionally, teachers were instructed to consistently implement a reward system for behaviors consistent with the rules (e.g., receiving a stamp with Ami the main character of the module), as well as establishing logical consequences for misbehaviors (e.g., not being allowed to play with a favorite toy, if the child did not participate in gathering the toys). Hence, circle time was selected as an appropriate context for teachers to discuss each child's behavior during the day. Due to the fact that the median classroom size consisted of approximately 25 children, the teachers were instructed to use a reward system for 1 or 2 rules. The criterion for choosing among the rules was the teachers' judgement regarding the difficulty with which a rule consistent behavior could be learned by most of the children in the classroom.

Emotion Recognition The main aim of this module was to develop children's expressive (i.e., naming emotions) and receptive (i.e., recognizing emotions based on facial features) emotion recognition abilities. As research with preschoolers suggests, 3- to 5-year-olds are more consistely able to recognize happiness, anger, sadness, and fear, which supported the option of focusing the contents of the lessons on these emotions (Widen and Russell 2002, 2003). The activities from this module were implemented for 3 weeks. Stories, mime games, and drawing activities were used to teach children about the way emotions can be recognized based on facial features. Also, children were presented with vignettes in which they were asked to label the characters' emotions and to think about the behavioral consequences of those emotion-eliciting situations. Additionally, the module was designed to enhance children's empathy by teaching them about perspective-taking, with the emphasis on emotional perspective-taking (i.e., *how* does the character feel in a particular situation?), and cognitive perspective-taking (i.e., *why* does the character feel in a certain way?). Such activities contained puppet-play scenarios depicting conflict situations, in which children were provided with the opportunity to identify emotions of all the story's characters. Such skills were considered particularly important, because perspective-taking skills prepare children for learning about problem-solving. In fact, as research has pointed out, children who exhibit more empathy are more socially competent, because they are able to understand different perspectives and hence are more likely to problem-solve in conflict situaions (Spinrad et al. 2006; Strayer and Roberts 2004).

During the implementation of this module, teachers continued implementing the reward system for encouraging compliance with classroom rules. However, in order to maintain children's motivation and to ensure that their behavior did not become dependent on rewards, circle times for discussing rule consistent or inconsistent behavior were scheduled at increased time intervals. Furthermore, teachers were encouraged to coach children's abilities to recognize emotions during other classroom activities such as discussing the emotions of story book or cartoon characters, or just by reflecting on children's emotions and discussing them (e.g., "I see you are sad because of your drawing. Maybe we can draw another one together?").

Emotion Regulation The third intervention module consisted of activities implemented over a 2-week period, which were aimed at increasing children's ability to regulate emotions. The focus of this module's activities on anger regulation was supported by evidence suggesting that difficulties in regulating this emotion might place children at increased risk of externalizing problems (Hill et al. 2006; Spinrad et al. 2006). Consequently, this module was intended to teach children about the steps of the "turtle technique" (Robin et al. 1976), an anger management strategy which allows children to regulate anger by reducing physiological reactivity through deep breathing, and afterwards, by teaching children to focus on finding a solution to the anger-eliciting situation. The technique was introduced to children through a story as a strategy to familiarize children with the actions of the turtle in an anger provoking context. Children were also shown puppet plays, in which the characters became angry and misbehaved. Consequently, they were asked to role-play how the turtle would handle the situation, while also providing a solution to the conflict. Solutions included developmentally appropriate strategies, which were shown to be consistently employed by preschoolers such as: redirecting attention (i.e., thinking about something nice), redirecting behavior (i.e., doing something else, finding another friend/toy to play with), seeking support (i.e. telling an adult), or problem-solving (i.e., finding a solution to the problem) (Cole et al. 2009; Dennis and Kelemen 2009). Again, skills developed during classroom activities were further reinforced by teachers, who were trained to remind children about the steps of the technique employing visual cues (i.e., a drawing containing the steps taken by the turtle to manage anger), and by reminding children to use this strategy when they felt angry.

Problem-Solving The fourth module was aimed at teaching children about problem-solving, and the corresponding lessons covered 4 weeks from the classroom curriculum implementation schedule. Problem-solving for preschoolers included teaching them to identify a problem, to discover multiple possible solutions to a problem, to evaluate the alternatives for solving a problem, and to implement the solution which seems like the best choice (Ashley and Tomasello 1998). The choice of focusing this module on problem-solving was supported by research suggesting that the development of such skills is positively associated with children's ability to manage conflicts in non-aggressive ways (Rubin and Rose-Krasnor 1992; Youngstrom et al. 2000). To develop these abilities, stories and short vignettes were employed with the purpose of teaching children to generate as many solutions as possible for each situation. Next, puppet-play scenarios depicting conflicts between children (e.g., refusing to share a toy, being excluded from group play, being hit), or between children and adults (e.g., refusing to do something that the teacher/parent asked, lying, not following rules, having to wait for something they want) were used to help children learn about assessing alternatives: either by evaluating the solutions provided by the characters in the story/vignette, or by finding solutions themselves. In all activities role-play was used as a strategy for modeling and exercising appropriate solutions to conflicts. Similar to previous modules, classroom lessons were associated with practicing problem-solving during conflict situations arising during daily activities in the classroom.

Play Cooperation The final module's objective was to teach children about skills needed to establish and to maintain friendships. This module was implemented over 4 weeks and it was designed to enhance children's use of prosocial behaviors (e.g., turn-taking, sharing, providing help, cooperating during play). The rationale for targeting these behaviors was related to the fact that previous research had established that prosocial behaviors could act as protective factors against developing aggression, a hallmark of externalizing problems (Crick et al. 1997; Sebanc 2003). In order to achieve the objective of this module, stories were developed to ensure that children would be able to distinguish friendly from unfriendly behaviors. Also, play activities were devised that encouraged children to cooperate to solve group tasks. Activities were designed so that the number of children from a group was gradually increased from 2 or 3 to 4 or 5 as the tasks became more complex. In addition to these scheduled activities, teachers were provided with suggestions for using cooperative activities mainly during children's daily learning tasks or structured play sessions, as a strategy for exercising prosocial behaviors.

Teacher Training[2]

Teacher training was aimed at: (1) developing teachers' classroom management abilities; and (2) enhancing teachers' ability to implement the classroom curriculum, as well as their ability to coach social-emotional learning in the classroom. Hence, teacher training included 2 components: (1) *group workshops* conducted prior to implementing the classroom curriculum; and (2) *consultations* conducted before the beginning of each intervention module of the classroom curriculum. Teacher training lasted 12 hours and included training in classroom management strategies (2 sessions x 2.5 hours), communication and teacher-parent partnership (1 session of 2 hours), and consultations (5 sessions of 1 hour). During the training, teachers were provided with handouts containing PowerPoint presentations, and a summary of the strategies taught and exercised during a particular session. Also, after each consultation, teachers received the training materials needed for the child-focused activities. These included each activity's objective, a short description of the steps involved in implementing the activity, together with corresponding supporting materials (i.e., story, vignette, drawings, posters, etc.). Descriptions are provided below for 2 components of the teacher training, namely group workshops and consultations.

Group Workshops Group workshops included 4 teacher training modules. The first module was focused on *classroom management strategies*. This part of the training was aimed at developing teacher's knowledge about behavior management strategies with the emphasis on both prevention and intervention type strategies for managing children's behavior. Training teachers in proactive strategies for maintaining discipline is rooted in research suggesting that reactive, punitive, and exclusionary strategies represent the means of unwittingly reinforcing negative behaviors (Horner and Sugai 2000; Taylor-Greene et al. 1997). Therefore, an improved classroom climate is more likely to ensure children's involvement in learning activities, and to provide an environment supportive of their social-emotional skills development (Luiselli et al. 2005; Sutherland et al. 2000).

The first part of the training was intended to describe the importance of preventing negative behavior through rule-setting, establishing limits (i.e., explaining children why a given behavior is appropriate, whereas another is not), and communicating positive expectations about children's behavior even in circumstances which could potentially lead to misbehavior, such as transitions from one activity to another (Chaplain 2003; McGinnis et al. 1995). The second component of the workshop on discipline was aimed at increasing teachers' knowledge about motivating children. Reinforcement of positive behaviors was introduced as a strategy for increasing children's self-esteem, confidence and sense of self-efficacy. The main topics approached during this session were social reinforcement and strategies for implementing reward systems. The next part of the training highlighted the importance of positive discipline strategies for managing children's recurrent negative behaviors with emphasis on behavioral analysis as a strategy for determining the function of a given behavior, as well as for establishing an appropriate strategy to reduce the frequency of misbehaviors (i.e., ignoring, logical consequences, timeout) (Azoulay 1999; Babkie 2006). The choice for training teachers in these particular behavior management strategies is supported by empirical research indicating that token economies and response cost procedures were associated with a reduction of behavior problems in at risk children (McGoey and DuPaul 2000).

Each theme approached during the training on classroom management included, besides sharing theoretical knowledge, activities which relied on practicing the skills teachers required to implement these strategies. Handouts, work sheets, and case studies were employed for exercising newly developed skills, as well as for identifying possible difficulties or errors in effectively employing these strategies.

The second component of the teacher workshops was aimed at enhancing *communication and parent-teacher partnerships*. This part of the training included discussing strategies that increase teachers' ability to effectively communicate disapproval, but also strategies for increasing communication about emotions or during children's play. Again, the discussion of the underlying theoretical assumptions was complemented by exercises and role-playing "I" statements, reflecting on children's emotions and validating them, or using descriptive rather than directive language during children's play. The rationale for targeting these strategies was related to previous research supporting the notion that appropriate teacher-child communication increases children's trust and attachment to teachers, both of which are essential for maintaining a positive classroom environment and for supporting children's social adjustment (Howes 2000; Howes et al. 1994, 2000).

Conversely, training was also developed to target improved teacher-parent communication as a strategy of supporting a partnership between the adults involved in children's education. The need to create a collaborative teacher-parent relationship is supported by empirical evidence suggesting that increased communication between adults provides the optimal context for ensuring children's skills development and transfer from classroom to home (Christenson and Sheridan 2001; Swick 2003). The training included discussions about strategies that could increase parental participation (e.g., parties, visits to the movies/zoo, school trips, and school "*open doors days*", in which parents are invited to participate in an activity), and ensure parents' access to more frequent communication with the teacher (e.g., email, teacher-parent conferences/consultations, parental access to information about children's educational progress). Also, role-plays were devised for exercising how to prevent defensive parental communication and increase parents' support for teachers through: (1) striving for a positive approach rather than a crisis orientation; (2) focusing on how to communicate (e.g., tone of voice) and how to achieve a "win-win" solution rather than placing blame; and (3) ensuring that parents can easily access information needed to support their children's progress.

Teacher Consultations All teacher consultations were designed to include a similar approach: (1) discussing developmental milestones for the competence targeted by each classroom curriculum module; (2) presenting methods for supporting the development of each competence during daily classroom interactions; and (3) discussing the content of the child-focused activities of each intervention module. As previously suggested, these consultations were employed to provide teachers with the opportunity to understand the rationale and the content of each intervention module, but also to increase their awareness and ability to effectively coach and support the development of children's social-emotional competencies during daily routines, such as: (1) discussing and validating children's emotions; (2) supporting their attempts to manage anger, helping them to engage in problem-solving as a strategy for solving conflicts; and (3) and getting involved in children's play to model prosocial behaviors through non-directive, cooperative play attitudes.

Parent Training[3]

The main aims of the parent training were similar to those proposed for the teacher training: (1) informing parents about the developmental milestones of preschoolers' social-emotional competencies; (2) developing parents' ability to employ positive discipline strategies to either prevent or manage negative behavior; and (3) enhancing parents' ability to coach their children's social-emotional skills. The training consisted of 2 approaches: (1) group training including 4 sessions lasting between 90 and 120 minutes each; and (2) individual training sessions, which were held at parents' request, which lasted approximately 20–30 minutes.

Group Training Each group session was developed following a similar rationale, encompassing 4 major training topics: discipline strategies, developmental milestones concerning preschoolers' social-emotional competencies, coaching strategies for children's social-emotional skills, and management of children's difficult behavior (e.g., going to sleep, food rejection, excessive TV watching, bed-wetting, fighting with siblings). Group training sessions were followed by a homework assignment, which served 2 purposes: (1) it provided parents with the opportunity to implement newly developed skills; and (2) it supported children's transfer of social-emotional competencies from the classroom to parent-child interactions at home. During each training session parents received handouts summarizing the main ideas and strategies presented throughout the session, as well as instructions for the homework assignments.

The first module targeted *compliance with rules*. The module included familiarizing parents with different types of compliant vs. non-compliant behavior, with an emphasis on understanding those types of non-compliance which might be harmful to the parent-child relationship, and might increase risk of maladjustment. This was considered especially important because parents need to recognize that children will sometime try to assert their autonomy and to test imposed limitations on their behavior (Webster-Stratton 1999). Consequently, the training addressed the strategies which parents could employ to gently, but effectively, encourage children to assume responsibility for their behavior (Matheson and Shriver 2005; Walker and Walker 1991). The training focused on strategies for establishing rules, and properly communicating requests to children so that parents could reduce the frequency of non-compliant behaviors. A particularly strong emphasis was placed on teaching parents the importance of being consistent in implementing rules, and of age-appropriate expectations regarding their children's behavior. Exercises and role-play were used to teach about proper ways to give instructions, reward rule compliant behavior, and establish logical consequences for rule breaking behavior. Parents received 2 homework assignments: the first involved establishing rules at home and exercising proper ways to communicate requests to children, whereas the second required parents to self-monitor their own behaviors in response to children's appropriate or inappropriate behaviors.

The second module was focused on *praise and emotional development*. First, the module was intended to explain parents the differences between reinforcers (i.e., social, activity, symbolic, material), as well as how each type of reward influences children's motivation for eliciting expected behaviors (Filcheck and McNeil 2004; McGoey and DuPaul 2000). The next component of the module was focused on familiarizing parents with emotion recognition and emotion regulation developmental milestones. In a similar vein to the teacher training, the parent training included providing adults with strategies to promote the development of their children's emotion knowledge (i.e., discussions about emotions, modeling empathy, validating children's emotions), and anger regulation strategies (i.e., exercising the "turtle technique", helping the child to calm down by reframing the situation or by helping him to redirect attention). This option was grounded in research suggesting that parental positive attitudes about emotions, and scaffolding children's attempt to regulate emotional arousal, lead to positive outcomes for their children (Morris et al. 2007; Zeman et al. 2006). The module's homework assignment required parents to implement strategies for supporting children's emotional development and to continue the self-monitoring exercise.

The third intervention module covered *positive discipline strategies and problem-solving*. First, this session was intended to raise parents' awareness about how harsh and/or inconsistent parenting actually increases the frequency with which children engage in misbehavior (Chang et al. 2003; Dennis 2006). Second, the module was intended to emphasize the benefits of positive discipline strategies and to teach parents how and when to implement them. Role-play, case studies, and other exercises were developed to provide parents with opportunities to understand the benefits, but also the potential pitfalls, of incorrectly or inconsistently employing these strategies. The social-emotional skill targeted during this module was problem-solving. Problem-solving steps together with problem-solving strategies were discussed and role-played, because this provided parents with a skill-building approach to preventing their children's aggressive behavior (Rubin and Rose-Krasnor 1992; Youngstrom et al. 2000). The homework assignment included implementing problem-solving strategies at home and continuing the self-monitoring exercise.

The last component of the group parent training was the module on *play cooperation and adult-child communication*. This module was aimed at familiarizing parents with the developmental milestones of pretend play, and pretend play's relevance to children's learning and to their ability to develop positive relationships, as this type of play offers valuable opportunities for children to exercise perspective-taking, a skill which is of significant importance to building and maintaining friendships (Dunn and Cutting 1999; Elkind 2007; Hughes and Dunn 1997). Also, special emphasis was placed on the need to encourage non-aggressive pretend play, which was found to predict children's improved ability to establish friendships (Dunn and Cutting 1999; Dunn and Hughes 2001). The practical skills learned by parents during this module were focused on how they can help children develop prosocial behaviors (i.e., sharing, turn-taking, helping, cooperating) by being involved in their play activities. Role-play scenarios were used to help parents identify directive adult behaviors during play (e.g., telling the child what to do next, trying to impose grown-up expectations on the child's behaviors during play), as opposed to supportive strategies (e.g., describing the child's actions, conversing with the child about the activity, establishing a common goal). Exercising strategies for effective communication during play were followed by exercising communication strategies during daily parent-child interactions such as criticizing behaviors instead of criticizing the child, using "I" statements, and properly saying "no" to the child's requests. Homework assignments required parents to employ principles of effective communication at home and to continue the self-monitoring exercise.

Individual Training As previously discussed, individual parent training sessions were held only at parents' request. Two reasons prompted offering parents this option. First, it was expected that some parents might feel discomfort when discussing their children's problem behavior in a group setting. Second, while group discussions and practice might constitute enough support for most parents, other parents, especially those of high-risk children, could feel the need for more guidance in managing particular behaviors or parent-child interactions. The format of these sessions included a first meeting, in which the problem was identified and an intervention strategy was devised, whereas the second session was a follow-up meeting in which outcomes would be evaluated, and further actions might be suggested if needed. The format of this intervention component was flexible and, depending on the severity or the number of problems raised by the parent, extra sessions could be scheduled.

Notes

1. A detailed description of the classroom curriculum is provided in Appendix 1.
2. A detailed description of the teacher training is provided in Appendix 2.
3. A detailed description of the parent training is provided in Appendix 3.

References

Abe, J. A., & Izard, C. E. (1999). A longitudinal study of emotion expression and personality relations in early development. *Personality Processes and Individual Differences, 77*, 566–577. https://doi.org/10.1037/0022-3514.77.3.566.

Andrews, G., & Erskine, A. (2001). Within our reach: The economics of prevention. *Current Opinion in Psychiatry, 14*, 103–105. https://doi.org/10.1097/00001504-200103000-00001.

Ashley, J., & Tomasello, M. (1998). Cooperative problem-solving and teaching in preschoolers. *Social Development, 7*, 143–163. https://doi.org/10.1111/1467-9507.00059.

Azoulay, D. (1999). Encouragement and logical consequences versus rewards and punishment: A reexamination. *Journal of Individual Psychology, 55*, 92–99.

Babkie, A. M. (2006). Proactive in managing classroom behavior. *Intervention in School and Clinic, 41*, 183–191. https://doi.org/10.1177/10534512060410031001.

Bear, G. G. (2005). *School discipline and self-discipline: A practical guide to promoting prosocial student behavior*. New York: The Guilford Press.

Brophy, J. (1999). Perspectives of classroom management: Yesterday, today, and tomorrow. In H. J. Freiberg (Ed.), *Beyond behaviorism: Changing the classroom management paradigm* (pp. 43–56). Boston: Allyn & Bacon.

Chang, L., Schwartz, D., Dodge, K. A., & McBride-Chang, C. (2003). Harsh parenting in relation to child emotion regulation and aggression. *Journal of Family Psychology, 17*, 598–606. https://doi.org/10.1037/0893-3200.17.4.598.

Chaplain, R. (2003). *Teaching without disruption in the primary school: A model for managing behaviour*. London: Routledge Falmer.

Christenson, S. L., & Sheridan, S. M. (2001). *School and families: Creating essential connections for learning*. New York: The Guilford Press.

Cole, P. M., Dennis, T. A., Smith-Simon, K. E., & Cohen, L. H. (2009). Preschoolers' emotion regulation strategy understanding: Relations with emotion socialization and child self-regulation. *Social Development, 18*, 324–252. https://doi.org/10.1111/j.1467-9507.2008.00503.x.

Conduct Problems Prevention Research Group. (1999a). Initial impact of the Fast Track prevention trial for conduct problems: I. The high risk sample. *Journal of Consulting and Clinical Psychology, 67*, 631–647. https://doi.org/10.1037/0022-006X.67.5.648.

Conduct Problems Prevention Research Group. (1999b). Initial impact of the Fast Track prevention trial for conduct problems: II. Classroom effects. *Journal of Consulting and Clinical Psychology, 67*, 648–657. https://doi.org/10.1037/0022-006X.67.5.648.

Crick, N. R., Casas, J. F., & Mosher, M. (1997). Relational and overt aggression in preschool. *Developmental Psychology, 33*, 579–588. https://doi.org/10.1037/0012-1649.33.4.579.

Dadds, M. R., & Roth, J. H. (2008). Prevention of anxiety disorders: Results of a universal trial with young children. *Journal of Child and Family Studies, 17*, 320–335. https://doi.org/10.1007/s10826-007-9144-3.

Denham, S. A. (2006). Social-emotional competence as support for school readiness: What is it and how do we assess it? *Early Education and Development, 17*, 57–89. https://doi.org/10.1207/s15566935eed1701_4.

Denham, S. A., & Burton, R. (2003). *Social and emotional prevention and intervention programming for preschoolers.* New York: Kluwer Academic/Plenum Press.

Denham, S. A., Mason, T., Caverly, S., Schmidt, M., Hackney, R., Caswell, C., & DeMulder, E. (2001). Preschoolers at play: Co-socializers of emotional and social competence. *International Journal of Behavioral Development, 25*, 90–101. https://doi.org/10.1080/016502501143000067.

Denham, S. A., Blair, K. A., Schmidt, M. S., Blair, K., DeMulder, E., Caal, S., et al. (2003). Preschool understanding of emotions: Contributions to classroom anger and aggression. *Journal of Child Psychology and Psychiatry, 43*, 901–916. https://doi.org/10.1111/1469-7610.00139.

Dennis, T. (2006). Emotional self-regulation in preschoolers: The interplay of child approach reactivity, parenting, and control capacities. *Developmental Psychology, 42*, 84–97. https://doi.org/10.1037/0012-1649.42.1.84.84.

Dennis, T. A., & Kelemen, D. (2009). Children's views on emotion regulation: Functional links and implications for socio-emotional adjustment. *International Journal of Behavioral Development, 33*, 243–252. https://doi.org/10.1177/0165025408098024.

Domitrovich, C. E., Cortes, R. C., & Greenberg, M. T. (2007). Improving young children's social and emotional competence: A randomized trial of the preschool "PATHS" curriculum. *The Journal of Primary Prevention, 28*, 67–91. https://doi.org/10.1007/s10935-007-0081-0.

Dunn, J., & Cutting, A. L. (1999). Understanding others, and individual differences in friendship interactions in young children. *Social Development, 8*, 201–219. https://doi.org/10.1111/1467-9507.00091.

Dunn, J., & Hughes, C. (2001). "I got some swords and you're dead!": Violent fantasy, antisocial behavior, friendship, and moral sensibility in young children. *Child Development, 72*, 491–505.

Durlak, J. A., & Wells, A. M. (1998). Evaluation of indicated preventive intervention (secondary prevention) mental health programs for children and adoles-

cents. *American Journal of Community Psychology, 26*, 775–802. https://doi.org/10.1023/A:1022162015815.
Eisenberg, N., Guthrie, I. K., Murphy, B. C., Shepard, S. A., Cumberland, A., & Carlo, G. (1999). Consistency and development of prosocial dispositions: A longitudinal study. *Child Development, 70*, 1360–1372. https://doi.org/10.1111/1467-8624.00100.
Eisenberg, N., Valiente, C., Morris, A. S., Fabes, R. A., Cumberland, A., & Reiser, M. (2003). Longitudinal relations among parental emotional expressivity, children's regulation, and quality of socioemotional function. *Developmental Psychology, 39*, 3–19. https://doi.org/10.1037/0012-1649.39.1.3.
Eisenberg, N., Sadovsky, A., Spinrad, T. L., Fabes, R. A., Losoya, S. H., Valiente, C., et al. (2005). The relations of problem behavior status to children's negative emotionality, effortful control, and impulsivity: Concurrent relations and prediction of change. *Developmental Psychology, 42*, 193–211. https://doi.org/10.1037/0012-1649.41.1.193.
Elkind, D. (2007). *The power of play*. Cambridge, MA: Da Capo Lifelong Books.
Essex, M. J., Kraemer, H. C., Slattery, M. J., Burk, L. R., Boyce, W. T., Woodward, H. R., & Kupfer, D. J. (2009). Screening for childhood mental health problems: Outcomes and early identification. *Journal of Child Psychology and Psychiatry, 50*, 562–570. https://doi.org/10.1111/j.1469-7610.2008.02015.x.
Filcheck, H. A., & McNeil, C. B. (2004). The use of token economies in preschool classrooms: Practical and philosophical concerns. *Journal of Early and Intensive Behavior Intervention, 1*, 94–104. https://doi.org/10.1037/h0100281.
Filcheck, H. A., McNeil, C. B., Greco, L. A., & Bernard, R. S. (2004). Using a whole-class token economy and coaching of teacher skills in a preschool classroom to manage disruptive behavior. *Psychology in the Schools, 4*, 351–361. https://doi.org/10.1002/pits.10168.
Hastings, P. D., Zahn-Waxler, C., Robinson, J., Usher, B., & Bridges, D. (2000). The development of concern for others in children with behavior problems. *Developmental Psychology, 36*, 531–546. https://doi.org/10.1037/0012-1649.36.5.531.
Hill, A. L., Degnan, K. A., Calkins, S. A., & Keane, S. P. (2006). Profiles of externalizing behavior problems for boys and girls across preschool: The roles of emotion regulation and inattention. *Developmental Psychology, 42*, 913–928. https://doi.org/10.1037/0012-1649.42.5.913.
Horner, R. H., & Sugai, G. (2000). School-wide behavior support: An emerging initiative. *Journal of Positive Behavioral Interventions, 2*, 231–232. https://doi.org/10.1177/109830070000200407.
Howes, C. (2000). Social-emotional classroom climate in child care, child-teacher relationships and children's second grade peer relations. *Social Development, 9*, 191–204. https://doi.org/10.1111/1467-9507.00119.

Howes, C., Hamilton, C. E., & Matheson, C. C. (1994). Children's relationships with peers: Differential associations with aspects of the teacher-child relationship. *Child Development, 65*, 253–263. https://doi.org/10.2307/1131380.

Howes, C., Phillipsen, L. C., & Peisner-Feinberg, E. (2000). The consistency of perceived teacher-child relationships between preschool and kindergarten. *Journal of School Psychology, 38*, 113–132. https://doi.org/10.1016/S0022-4405(99)00044-8.

Hughes, C., & Dunn, J. (1997). "Pretend you didn't know": Preschoolers' talk about mental states in pretend play. *Cognitive Development, 12*, 477–497. https://doi.org/10.1016/S0885-2014(97)90019-8.

Hughes, J. N., Cavell, T. M., Meehan, B. T., Zhang, D., & Collie, C. (2005). Adverse school context moderates the outcomes of selective interventions for aggressive children. *Journal of Consulting and Clinical Psychology, 73*, 731–736. https://doi.org/10.1037/0022-006X.73.4.731.

Izard, C. E., King, K. A., Trentacosta, C. J., Morgan, J. K., Laurenceau, J. P., Krauthamer-Ewing, E. S., & Finlon, K. J. (2008). Accelerating the development of emotion competence on Head Start children: Effects on adaptive and maladaptive behavior. *Development and Psychopathology, 20*, 369–397. https://doi.org/10.1017/S0954579408000175.

Kam, C.-M., Greenberg, M. T., & Walls, C. T. (2003). Examining the role of implementation quality in school-based prevention using the PATHS curriculum. *Prevention Science, 4*, 55–63. https://doi.org/10.1023/A:1021786811186.

Kazdin, A. E., & Wassell, G. (1999). Barriers to treatment participation and therapeutic change among children referred for conduct disorder. *Journal of Clinical Child Psychology, 28*, 160–172. https://doi.org/10.1037/0022-006X.69.2.262.

Linares, L. O., Rosbruch, N., Stern, M. B., Edwards, M. E., Walker, G., Abikoff, H. B., & Alvir, J. M. I. (2005). Developing cognitive-social-emotional competencies to enhance academic learning. *Psychology in the Schools, 42*, 405–418. https://doi.org/10.1002/pits.20066.

Lochman, J. E., & Wells, K. C. (2002). The Coping Power program at the middle-school transition: Universal and indicated prevention effects. *Psychology of Addictive Behaviors, 16*, S40–S54. https://doi.org/10.1037/0893-164X.16.4S.S40.

Luiselli, J. K., Putnam, R. F., Handler, M. W., & Feinberg, A. B. (2005). Whole. School positive behavior support: Effect on student discipline problems and academic performance. *Educational Psychology, 25*, 183–198. https://doi.org/10.1080/0144341042000301265.

Mantzicopoulos, P. Y., & Neurath-Pritchett, S. (1998). Transitional first-grade referrals: An analysis of school-related factors and children's characteristics. *Journal of Educational Psychology, 90*, 122–133. https://doi.org/10.1037/0022-0663.90.1.122.

Marion, M. (2003). *Guidance of young children*. Columbus: Merrill Prentice Hall.

Matheson, A. S., & Shriver, M. D. (2005). Training teachers to give effective commands: Effects on student compliance and academic behaviors. *School Psychology Review, 34*, 202–219.

McGinnis, J. C., Frederick, B. P., & Edwards, R. (1995). Enhancing classroom management through proactive rules and procedures. *Psychology in the Schools, 32*, 220–224. https://doi.org/10.1002/1520-6807(199507)32:3<220::AID-PITS2310320309>3.0.CO;2-4.

McGoey, K. E., & DuPaul, G. J. (2000). Token reinforcement and response cost procedures: Reading the disruptive behavior of preschool children with attention-deficit/hyperactivity disorder. *School Psychology Quarterly, 15*, 330–343. https://doi.org/10.1037/h0088790.

Moffitt, T. E., & Caspi, A. (2001). Childhood predictors differentiate life-course persistent and adolescence limited antisocial pathways among males and females. *Development and Psychopathology, 13*, 355–375. https://doi.org/10.1017/S0954579401002097.

Morris, A. S., Silk, J. S., Steinberg, L., Myers, S. S., & Robinson, L. R. (2007). The role of the family context in the development of emotion regulation. *Social Development, 16*(2), 361–388. https://doi.org/10.1111/j.1467-9507.2007.00389.x.

Nation, M., Crusto, C., Wandersman, A., Kumpfer, A., Seybolt, D., Morrissey-Kane, E., & Davino, K. (2003). What works in prevention – Principles of effective prevention programs. *American Psychologist, 58*, 449–456. https://doi.org/10.1037/0003-066X.58.6-7.449.

Nelson, G., Westhues, A., & MacLeod, J. (2003). A meta-analysis of longitudinal research on preschool prevention programs for children. *Prevention and Treatment, 6*, 1–25.

Prinz, R. J., & Sanders, M. R. (2007). Adopting a population-level approach to parenting and family support interventions. *Clinical Psychology Review, 27*, 739–749. https://doi.org/10.1016/j.cpr.2007.01.005.

Ramey, C. T., & Ramey, S. L. (2004). Early learning and school readiness: Can early intervention make a difference? *Merrill-Palmer Quarterly, 50*, 471–491. https://doi.org/10.1353/mpq.2004.0034.

Raver, C. C., Jones, S. M., Li-Grining, C., Zhai, F., Metzger, M. W., & Solomon, B. (2009). Targeting children's behavior problems in preschool classrooms: A cluster-randomized controlled trial. *Journal of Consulting and Clinical Psychology, 77*, 302–316. https://doi.org/10.1037/a0015302.

Robin, A., Schneider, M., & Dolnick, M. (1976). The turtle technique: An extended case study of self-control in the classroom. *Psychology in the Schools, 13*, 449–453. https://doi.org/10.1002/1520-6807(197610)13:4<449::AID-PITS2310130420>3.0.CO;2-W.

Rubin, K. H., & Rose-Krasnor, L. (1992). Interpersonal problem solving. In V. B. Van Hasselt & M. Hersen (Eds.), *Handbook of social development* (pp. 283–323). New York: Plenum.
Sanders, M. R., & Morawska, A. (2005). Can changing parental knowledge, dysfunctional expectations and attributions, and emotion regulation improve outcomes for children? In R. E. Tremblay, R. G. Barr, & R. V. De Peters (Eds.), *Encyclopedia on early childhood development*. Retrieved March 13, 2010, from www.excellence-earlychildhood.ca
Sebanc, A. N. (2003). The friedship features of preschool children: Lonks with prosocial behavior and aggression. *Social Development, 12*, 249–268. https://doi.org/10.1111/1467-9507.00232.
Severson, H. H., & Walker, H. M. (2002). Pro-active approaches for identifying children at risk for socio-behavioral problems. In K. L. Lane, F. M. Gresham, & T. E. O'Shaughnessy (Eds.), *Interventions for children with or at-risk for emotional and behavioral disorders* (pp. 33–54). Boston: Allyn & Bacon.
Severson, H. H., Walker, H. M., Hope-Doolittle, J., Kratochwill, T. R., & Gresham, F. M. (2007). Proactive, early screening to detect behaviorally at-risk students: Issues, approaches, emerging innovations, and professional practices. *Journal of School Psychology, 45*, 193–223. https://doi.org/10.1016/j.jsp.2006.11.003.
Sheridan, S. M., Hungelman, A., & Maughan, P. D. (1999). A contextualized framework for social skills assessment, intervention, and generalization. *School Psychology Review, 28*, 84–103.
Snow, K. L. (2006). Measuring school readiness: Conceptual and practical considerations. *Early Education and Development, 17*, 7–41. https://doi.org/10.1207/s15566935eed1701_2.
Snyder, H. (2001). Epidemiology of official offending. In R. Loeber & D. P. Farmington (Eds.), *Child delinquents: Development, intervention and service needs* (pp. 25–46). Thousand Oaks: Sage.
Spinrad, T. L., Eisenberg, N., Cumberland, A., Fabes, R. A., Valiente, C., Shepard, S. A., et al. (2006). Relation of emotion-related regulation to children's social competence: A longitudinal study. *Emotion, 6*, 498–510. https://doi.org/10.1037/1528-3542.6.3.498.
Ştefan, C. A., & Miclea, M. (2010). Prevention programs targeting emotional and social development in preschoolers: Current status and future directions. *Early Child Development and Care, 180*, 1103–1128. https://doi.org/10.1080/03004430902830263.
Ştefan, C. A., Bălaj, A., Porumb, M., Albu, M., & Miclea, M. (2009). Preschool screening for social and emotional competencies – Development and psychometric properties. *Cognition, Brain, Behavior. An Interdisciplinary Journal, 13*, 121–146.

Stifter, C. A., Spinrad, T., & Braungart-Rieker, J. (1999). Toward a developmental model of child compliance: The role of emotion regulation in infancy. *Child Development, 70*, 21–32. https://doi.org/10.1111/1467–8624.00003.

Strayer, J., & Roberts, W. (2004). Empathy and observed anger and aggression in 5-year-olds. *Social Development, 13*, 1–13. https://doi.org/10.1111/j.1467-9507.2004.00254.x.

Sutherland, K. S., Wehby, J. H., & Copeland, S. R. (2000). Effect of varying rates of behavior-specific praise on the on task behavior of students with emotional and behavioral disorders. *Journal of Emotional Disorders, 26*, 2–8. https://doi.org/10.1177/106342660000800101.

Swick, K. (2003). Communication concepts for strengthening family-school-community partnerships. *Early Childhood Education Journal, 30*, 275–280. https://doi.org/10.1023/A:1023399910668.

Taylor-Greene, S., Brown, D., Nelson, L., Longton, J., Gassman, T., Cohen, J., et al. (1997). School-wide behavioral support: Starting the year off right. *Journal of Behavioral Education, 7*, 99–112. https://doi.org/10.1023/A:1022849722465.

Trentacosta, C. J., Izard, C. E., Mostow, A. J., & Fine, S. E. (2006). Children's emotional competence and attentional competence in early elementary school. *School Psychology Quarterly, 21*, 148–170. https://doi.org/10.1521/scpq.2006.21.2.148.

Turner, K. M. T., & Sanders, M. R. (2006). Dissemination of evidence-based parenting and family support strategies: Learning from the Triple P – Positive Parenting Program system approach. *Aggression and Violent Behavior, 11*, 176–193. https://doi.org/10.1016/j.avb.2005.07.005.

van Lier, P. A. C., Vuijk, P., & Crijnen, A. A. M. (2005). Understanding mechanisms of change and development of antisocial behavior: The impact of a universal intervention. *Journal of Abnormal Child Psychology, 33*, 521–535. https://doi.org/10.1007/s10802-005-6735-7.

Walker, H. M., & Walker, J. E. (1991). *Coping with noncompliance in the classroom: A positive approach for teachers*. Austin: Pro-Ed Inc.

Webster-Stratton, C. (1999). *How to promote children's social and emotional competence*. London: Paul Chapman Publishing Ltd.

Webster-Stratton, C. (2000). *The Incredible Years Training Series*. Washington, DC: Office of Juvenile Justice and Delinquency Prevention.

Webster-Stratton, C., & Hammond, J. M. (1997). Treating children with early-onset conduct problems: A comparison of child and parent training interventions. *Journal of Consulting and Clinical Psychology, 65*, 93–109. https://doi.org/10.1037/0022-006X.65.1.93.

Webster-Stratton, C., & Taylor, T. (2001). Nipping early risk factors in the bud: Preventing substance abuse, delinquency, and violence in adolescence through interventions targeted at young children (0–8 years). *Prevention Science, 2*, 165–192. https://doi.org/10.1023/A:1011510923900.

Webster-Stratton, C., Reid, J. M., & Hammond, M. (2001). Preventing conduct problems, promoting social competence: A parent-teacher training partnership in Head Start. *Journal of Clinical Child Psychology, 30*, 283–302.

Webster-Stratton, C., Reid, J. M., & Hammond, M. (2004). Treating children with early-onset conduct problems: Intervention outcomes for parent, child, and teacher training. *Journal of Clinical Child and Adolescent Psychology, 33*, 105–124. https://doi.org/10.1207/S15374424JCCP3301_11.

Webster-Stratton, C., Reid, M. J., & Stoolmiller, M. (2008). Preventing conduct problems and improving school readiness: Evaluation of the Incredible Years teacher and child training programs in high-risk schools. *The Journal of Child Psychology and Psychiatry, 49*, 471–488. https://doi.org/10.1111/j.1469-7610.2007.01861.x.

Widen, S. C., & Russell, J. A. (2002). Gender and preschoolers' perception of emotion. *Merrill-Palmer Quarterly, 48*, 248–262. https://doi.org/10.1353/mpq.2002.0013.

Widen, S. C., & Russell, J. A. (2003). A closer look at preschoolers' freely produced labels for facial expressions. *Developmental Psychology, 39*, 114–128. https://doi.org/10.1037/0012-1649.39.1.114.

Youngstrom, E., Wolpaw, J. M., Schoff, K., Ackerman, B., & Izard, C. (2000). Interpersonal problem solving in preschool and first grade: Developmental change and ecological validity. *Journal of Clinical Child Psychology, 29*, 589–602. https://doi.org/10.1207/S15374424JCCP2904_11.

Zeman, J., Cassano, M., Perry-Parrish, C., & Stegall, S. (2006). Emotion regulation in children and adolescents. *Journal of Developmental Behavioral Pediatrics, 27*, 155–168. https://doi.org/10.1111/camh.12061_3.

Zubrick, S. R., Ward, K. A., Silburn, S. R., Lawrence, D., Williams, A. A., Blair, E., et al. (2005). Prevention of child behavior problems through universal implementation of a group behavioral family intervention. *Prevention Science, 6*, 176–193. https://doi.org/10.1007/s11121-005-0013-2.

CHAPTER 3

Assessing SEP Efficacy at the Classroom Level: Effects on Children's Social-Emotional Competencies and Behavior Problems

Introduction

Extensive empirical evidence supports the notion that children's maladaptive behaviors are the results of a complex interplay of risk factors (Fabes et al. 2006). Given the current knowledge concerning these risk factors, as well as increased calls to effectively address children's risk of mental health issues, professionals from the field of early education suggested that more resources should be directed towards designing and implementing prevention programs aimed at developing children's social-emotional competencies (Denham and Burton 2003; Izard 2002; Nelson et al. 2003). The choice of addressing children's risk of maladjustment through social-emotional learning is supported by the fact that deficient social-emotional competence development increases the risk of aggression and non-compliance, the behavioral markers of externalizing problems (Denham et al. 2001, 2003). Empirical evidence suggests that insufficiently developed abilities in recognizing emotions are associated with difficulties in anger regulation (Calkins and Dedmon 2000; Eisenberg et al. 2003; Gilliom et al. 2002), which in turn increases the risk of externalizing problems (Hill et al. 2006; Spinrad et al. 2004).

A number of evidence-based prevention programs have been developed with an explicit focus on high-risk children, such as those from low-income families (Conduct Problems Prevention Research Group [CPPRG] 1999a; Raver et al. 2009; Webster-Stratton et al. 2008), or those exhibiting clinical intensity externalizing problems (Webster-Stratton and Hammond

C. A. Ştefan, *Social-Emotional Prevention Programs for Preschool Children's Behavior Problems*,
https://doi.org/10.1007/978-3-319-74751-4_3

1997; Webster-Stratton and Reid 2003). Despite the need to provide support to children who are most in need of mental health services, some researchers argue that population level approaches, which target a relatively larger number of children and parents, might prove more beneficial for reaching those in need of such services (Conroy et al. 2008; Lopez et al. 2000).

Community-based interventions were initially designed as universal interventions targeting social-emotional competence development in both non-risk and at risk children (Domitrovich et al. 2010; Shure 1997; Shure and Spivak 1982). Such classroom-based interventions generally reported positive effects on children's social-emotional skills, but raised concerns over their inability to exert effects on high levels of externalizing problems (Stoolmiller et al. 2000). However, when teacher training was developed to support implementation of appropriate classroom management strategies (Filcheck et al. 2004), its addition to the classroom curriculum proved effective in reducing externalizing problems (CPPRG 1999b; Webster-Stratton et al. 2008). Also, some research suggested that classroom delivered content alone was rather ineffective when intervention outcomes were measured in home settings (Hughes et al. 2005). One potential explanation for this could be the fact that most universal interventions do not include parent training, thus reducing the probability of skill transfer. However, when parent training was included in community-based interventions (CPPRG 1999a) or was delivered for parents of high-risk or clinically referred children (Webster-Stratton et al. 2001, 2004), the results generally supported the notion that both parents and teachers reported significant improvement in children's behaviors at home, as well as in the classroom.

This analysis of the current status of community-based interventions suggests that highly effective interventions can be developed by including a multi-focused approach including a combination of child-, teacher-, and parent-focused activities (Webster-Stratton and Taylor 2001). Moreover, as suggested in Chap. 2, the Social-Emotional Prevention Program (SEP) was developed within a dual prevention delivery model, which aims to address the needs of both at risk and non-risk preschoolers (CPPRG 1999a, b). More precisely, it includes a universal prevention approach (i.e., targeting all children), and an indicated prevention approach (i.e., targeting children at risk of externalizing problems). The rationale supporting this approach is that delivering interventions just to children who are at risk does not address one main source of risk of externalizing problems, namely peers with similar deviant behaviors (Lochman and Wells 2002; van Lier et al. 2005). Children who are aggressive and non-compliant tend to preferentially establish friendships with peers exhibiting similar behaviors, which reinforce negative behavioral patterns (Dishion et al. 1999; Snyder et al. 2005). Therefore, when supporting behavioral change and skill development a universal approach attempting to change the social environment could be more effective in generating expected outcomes rather than exclusively focusing on children who are already at risk.

In a similar vein, the SEP was developed to deliver teacher training that attempts to reconcile classical approaches of classroom management with the emphasis on teachers' ability to appropriately deliver the contents of the classroom curriculum. Although the consultation format in which teachers were trained to implement the child-focused activities draws from previous interventions (Domitrovich et al. 2007; Kam et al. 2003), its approach is innovative because it explicitly focuses training on 2 aspects: (1) how to deliver the classroom curriculum; and (2) how to support skill development during daily teacher-child interactions. Thus, SEP offers not only structured, theory-driven teaching activities, but it also encompasses guidelines for supporting social-emotional learning in ecological contexts, as premises of effectively targeting children's needs.

Additionally, the inclusion of parent training in SEP is a relatively new approach in community-based interventions. Except for the *Triple P – Positive Parenting Program*, which includes only parent-focused activities (Turner and Sanders 2006), the SEP is to our knowledge the only prevention program which offers parents access to knowledge and strategies concerning preschoolers' social-emotional development within a multifocused prevention framework. Such approaches are more frequently implemented either for high-risk children (CPPRG 1999a), or for children with clinical intensity conduct problems (Webster-Stratton et al. 2001, 2004). In accordance with previous findings reported in the literature, parent training was introduced to secure the transfer of children's classroom acquired skills to parent-child interactions at home (Brotman et al. 2005; Hughes et al. 2005). Furthermore, skill transfer was expected to be supported by implementing a similar intervention rationale as in the teacher training: combining behavioral management strategies with coaching children's social-emotional development. This approach however, needed to attract a relatively large proportion of parents, which is less feasible when children are less likely to exhibit behavior problems (Prinz and Sanders 2007). In this respect, SEP included 4 parent training sessions, a shorter delivery format which had proved useful in previous community-based interventions aimed at preventing internalizing type problems (Dadds and Roth 2008; Izard et al. 2008).

The Current Study

The main aim of the current study was to evaluate SEP efficacy in developing children's social and emotional competencies, and reducing behavior problems. Previously reported findings on efficacy studies of community-based interventions showed that such interventions elicited increased teacher rated social-emotional skills (CPPRG 1999b; Domitrovich et al. 2007). The addition of teacher training in community-based interventions resulted in increased effectiveness in reducing teacher reported levels of externalizing problems (Domitrovich et al. 2007; Izard et al. 2008), as well as internalizing problems (Domitrovich et al. 2007; Raver et al. 2009). Also, parent training was shown to support skill transfer from the classroom to the parent-child interactions at home and significantly reduce levels of parent reported externalizing problems (Brotman et al. 2005; Raver et al. 2009). Based on these findings, the hypotheses were: (1) intervention group participants would show higher levels of child-reported and adult-reported (teacher/parent) social-emotional competencies compared to the control group children; and (2) intervention group children would exhibit significantly lower levels of behavior problems.

Method

Participants

Participants were selected from preschools in the urban area of Cluj-Napoca, a large town in the north-west of Romania. Two hundred and seventy-five parents were initially approached to provide consent for their child's participation in the study, and 204 agreed. Hence, 121 participants were allocated to the intervention condition, and 83 to the control group. Thirty-two out of the intervention participants (26%) and 14 from the control group (17%), did not take part in the postintervention assessment, thus generating normal attrition rates for this type of study (15–30%). The final sample included 89 children (42 boys and 47 girls) in the intervention group and 69 children (29 boys and 40 girls) in the control group with mean ages of 50.7 months (SD = .50), and 48.6 months (SD = .53), respectively. The sample was predominantly Romanian (87%), with the rest of the sample reflecting the typical ethnic background of the Romanian population: Hungarian, German, or Gipsy (total 13%). Thus some children came from households in which the primary spoken language was not Romanian, but their knowledge of the Romanian language was sufficient to perform the child-report tasks. Parents' level of education was employed as a measure of social-economic status (SES) as presented in Table 3.1, with 56.2% of intervention group children coming from high-SES families, 41.2% from moderate-SES families, and 3.6% from low-SES families, whereas 53.7% of control group children came from high-SES families, 42.2% from moderate-SES families, and 3.1% from low-SES families. Additional characteristics of the intervention and control group samples are presented in Table 3.1. Due to the underrepresentation of low-SES children, all subsequent analyses of children's risk status were performed

Table 3.1 Risk status and demographic factors for dropout and non-dropout participants from the intervention and control groups

	Final sample (N = 158)		*Dropout (N = 46)*	
	SEP (%)	*Control (%)*	*SEP (%)*	*Control (%)*
Gender (male)	47.2	42.0	50.1	44.6
SCBE externalizing problems <58[a]	21.3	17.4	12.5	14.3
SSRS behavior problems >5 girls/>6 boys[b]	22.4	20.3	21.9	21.4
PPI harsh/inconsistent parenting >3.03/>3.40[c]	44.8	50.7	56.3	42.9
Low and middle SES[d]	43.8	46.3	34.4	35.7
Minority status[e]	12.4	8.7	9.4	7.1
Single parent	13.5	14.5	12.5	14.3
Mother depression	2.2	2.9	–	–
Child diagnosed mental health problems	–	–	–	–

Note. SEP = Social-Emotional Prevention Program, *SCBE* = Social Competence and Behavior Evaluation, *SSRS* = Social Skills Rating System, *PPI* = Parent Practices Interview

[a]Cutoff score for SCBE Externalizing Problem scale computed for this sample using the split-half method

[b]Cutoff score for SSRS Behavior Problems scale determined on the basis of results obtained by the split-half method

[c]Risk determined by below cutoff scores for this sample on at least one of the Harsh Discipline and Inconsistent Discipline scales from PPI

[d]SES categories were established based on parents' level of education: low SES (less than high school), middle SES (high school graduate), and high SES (university/college degree)

[e]Minorities included Hungarian, German, or Gipsy children

by merging moderate- and low-risk children into a single category. This could be a consequence of the fact that the preschools selected for this study were situated in the city's metropolitan area, and therefore, the sample's composition might reflect SES distributions in these communities.

Design

The study was conducted in 5 sites, and in each site at least 2 classrooms were selected. This resulted in a total of 14 classrooms, with half of the classrooms in each site being randomly assigned to either the intervention or comparison condition. Hence, this was a partially randomized controlled trial, because randomization was not performed at the individual, but at the classroom level. For the purposes of this study, an intent-to-treat approach was employed for testing the intervention's efficacy, meaning that the analytic strategies were conducted with data from all participants who were available for postintervention assessment, even if they did not receive the full intervention dosage (attending a minimum of 75% of classroom activities and parent attendance in more than half of the 4 parent training sessions).

Procedure

Five preschools were selected to take part in this research, based on headmasters' willingness to accommodate program implementation. Administrative measures were taken at each implementation site to ensure that the SEP would be included as an optional curriculum activity. In early January 2009, parents from each classroom were asked to participate in a short meeting, in which the purpose and rationale of the research was presented to them. Each parent was given a pack containing the consent form and the questionnaires. They were asked to return the pack within the next week. Teachers were also requested to fill out their ratings of social-emotional development and behavior problems for those children for whom consent was provided by parents. The same children also participated in 2 testing sessions intended to evaluate their knowledge about emotions and problem-solving. During the 4 weeks prior to the SEP implementation, teachers from each classroom were invited to the teacher group workshops.

In the next step, the SEP was implemented beginning in February 2009 in intervention classrooms, whereas the control group classrooms received no intervention. The SEP was implemented in 7 classrooms with similar enrollment conditions for all children in terms of total number of hours spent in the classroom (8/day), classroom size (20–25 children), and curriculum requirements. As 2 teachers were assigned to each classroom, they were both responsible for implementing the classroom curriculum they participated in consultations prior to implementing each classroom intervention module. Weekly observations were carried out in all intervention classrooms and teachers were asked to conduct a lesson in the presence of the program's developer, who filled out fidelity checklists regarding SEP implementation. In all observed classrooms, the program's developer provided teachers with feedback regarding the conducted activities, and used these opportunities to emphasize central issues for the high-quality implementation of the classroom curriculum by discussing coaching of children's social-emotional skill development, as well as discipline related strategies for difficult behaviors which were observed during the classroom observations.

Also, parents were invited to attend 4 training sessions. Training sessions were conducted separately for parents in each intervention classroom. If requested, parents had the opportunity to participate not only in the group training, but also in individual training sessions. During the implementation, parents were asked to implement knowledge and strategies learned during the training as homework, and to monitor their use of discipline strategies.

The SEP program was implemented over 15 weeks from February to May 2009. Postintervention assessments were conducted during June 2009, and involved children, teachers and parents from both intervention and control groups. Follow-up measures were conducted in October 2009 (4-months postintervention). Note that follow-up data are not presented in this chapter.

Intervention

A detailed description of the child-, teacher-, and parent-focused interventions from the SEP was provided in Chap. 2.

Child, Teacher, and Parent Training Delivery and Attendance

The group workshops and one consultation were delivered by the developer of SEP 1 week before the implementation of the classroom curriculum. The classroom curriculum containing 5 modules and 37 classroom activities was implemented over a 15-week period by teachers. One week prior to each classroom intervention module targeting children's social-emotional skills, consultations were provided to teachers. These were intended to familiarize teachers with the objectives and contents of the activities, and to ensure consistency in implementing the activities. The 2 teachers from each of the 7 intervention classrooms alternated in implementing the activities on a weekly basis. Fidelity observations were conducted by the SEP developer in each classroom. Based on these checklists, it was apparent that teachers from all classrooms implemented more than 90% of the curriculum's activities. Teachers provided attendance rates for each child in their classroom, and these showed that only 8 children (9%) participated in less than 75% of the total number of activities.

Parents were invited to attend 4 group training sessions. The records concerning parental attendance indicated that 10 (11.5%) parents did not participate in any training session, 30 (34.5%) attended 1–2 sessions, and 47 (54.0%) took part in 3–4 sessions. Parents participating in at least 1 training session ($n = 69$) were 58 mothers, 8 fathers, and in 3 cases both mother and father attended. Also, to ensure compliance with the intervention, parents were asked to conduct a self-monitoring exercise after each training session. Among the parents who took part in 3–4 sessions, 36 (77%) returned 3–4 self-monitoring sheets, while 11 (23%) returned at least one self-monitoring sheet.

Measures

In this study, a multi-informant (teacher, parent, child), multi-method (questionnaire, experimental tasks) approach was employed in evaluating SEP efficacy. The child report measures included 2 tasks for measuring preschoolers' declarative knowledge about emotions and problem-solving. Parent and teacher rated questionnaires were used to assess preschoolers' social and emotional competencies, and behavior problems. Each questionnaire, except for those developed in Romania, was adapted from English to Romanian, and then a back translation was performed to ensure that all items' meaning was maintained.

Child Measures Children's emotion recognition was assessed with a modified version of the *Affective Knowledge Test* (AKT; Denham 1986). The original "puppet task" employed smiley-type facial features, which were replaced with an ecological set of stimuli depicting human faces. These were selected from the NimStim Face Stimulus database, based on the fact that previous research reported high agreement rates between children and adults concerning the emotions represented by these stimuli (Tottenham et al. 2002). The task was carried out according to the original AKT. First, children were asked to name happiness, anger, sadness, and fear (Expressive emotion recognition), and then, they were requested to recognize these emotions based on facial features (Receptive emotion recognition). Children were presented with a computerized version of the task. In the Expressive recognition task, children viewed 4, 14 x 14 cm cards with male or female faces depending on each child's gender, and were asked "how does he/she feel". In the Receptive recognition condition, all the cards were shown on the screen and the child was asked "which one feels happy/sad/fearful/angry". In both tasks the order of presenting the cards was counterbalanced across participants. Children's answers were scored based on the following criteria: 2 points for correctly identifying the emotion, 1 point for naming an emotion with a similar emotional valence as the target, and 0 points for incorrectly naming the emotion. The tasks were recorded with a *Sony DCR-SR3* camera, and 2 blind coders separately rated children's answers. Intraclass correlation coefficients (ICCs) using a 2-way random analysis in the Expressive recognition task ranged between .95 and .96 for happiness, .92 and .95 for anger, .87 and .90 for sadness, and .84 and .86 for fear. Conversely, indices for the receptive task varied between .95 and .96 for happiness, .94 and .95 for anger, 92 and .94 for sadness, and .91 and .93 for fear.

Children's knowledge about problem-solving skills was assessed with a modified version of the *Social Problem Solving Test* (SPST-R; Webster-Stratton 1990). From the initial task consisting of 13 vignettes, 5 were selected based on adults' ratings of most frequent potential conflict situations encountered by a preschooler: adult disapproval (#1), rejection from a friend (#2), toy access (#3), unjust treatment from another child (#4), and making a mistake (#5). Children were introduced to the vignettes and supporting colored drawings were used to illustrate the situation visually. Each child was asked to provide a solution to each situation "What would he/she do?" The answers were categorized as positive strategies (P) and negative strategies (N). Positive problem-solving strategies included apologizing, finding another toy/friend to play with, asking for help from an adult, etc.; negative problem-solving strategies included behaviors such as hitting, name calling, destroying a toy, or lying. Answers for each category could result in a score between 0 and 5. The task was recorded by a *Sony DCR-SR3* camera. ICCs ranged from .85 to .91 for positive problem-solving strategies, and from .81 to .86 for negative problem-solving strategies.

Teacher Measures Children's social-emotional competencies were first rated by teachers on 2 screening measures: the *Social Competence Screening for Preschoolers – Teacher Form* (SCS-T; Miclea et al. 2010) and the *Emotional Competence Screening for Preschoolers – Teacher Form* (ECS-T; Miclea et al. 2010). The SCS-T/2.5–4 includes 15 items assessing compliance to rules, interpersonal skills, and prosocial behaviors (e.g., "The child plays with more than 3 children at once"; "The child takes care of other children's toys"), whereas the ECS-T contains 10 items measuring emotion knowledge, emotionality, and emotion regulation (e.g., "The child recognizes that others feel happy, angry, sad, or afraid"; "The child is able to stay calm even in situations he/she does not know how to solve"). Responses for each item were coded on a 5-point Likert scale, where *1 = almost never* and *5 = almost always.* Previous reports of reliability and validity suggested that both scales exhibited appropriate psychometric properties (Ştefan et al. 2009). In the current study, ECS-T and SCS-T showed high internal consistency with Cronbach's α ranging from .93 at preintervention to .88 at postintervention, and from .91 at preintervention to .88 at postintervention, respectively.

Children's social competencies were also assessed by teachers based on the *Social Competence and Behavior Evaluation – Preschool Edition* (SCBE; LaFreniere and Dumas 1995). The total score on the Social Competence summary scale was computed by summing the scores from the 40 items from the 8 basic scales: Joyful, Secure, Tolerant, Integrated, Calm, Prosocial, Cooperative, Autonomous (e.g., "Children seek him/her out to play with them"; "Negotiates solutions to conflicts with other children"). Each item was coded on a 6-point Likert scale, where *0 = almost never* and *6 = almost always.* Cronbach's α for teacher rated social competencies ranged from .70 to .86, indicating good to high internal consistency.

Children were also assessed by teachers on measures of behavioral and emotional problems. The current study used teachers' ratings on the Externalizing Problems summary scale from SCBE (LaFreniere and Dumas 1995), which included 20 items from the following 4 basic scales: Angry, Aggressive, Egotistical, and Oppositional (e.g., "Bullies weaker children"; "Refuses to share toys"). Each item was evaluated on a 6-point Likert scale, where *0 = almost never* and *6 = almost always.* Final scores were reverse coded, meaning that a higher score on this scale corresponds to lower levels of behavior problems. The internal consistency was high with Cronbach's α ranging from .84 to .86. The cutoff scores for the Romanian sample were established using the split-half method (median – 1SD). Similar cutoffs were used for girls and boys, because unlike in the US normative sample, we found no gender differences on externalizing problems.

Teachers also rated children on the Internalizing Problems scale from SCBE (LaFreniere and Dumas 1995). This measure includes 20 items from 4 basic scales: Depressive, Anxious, Isolated, and Dependent (e.g., "Worries"; "Inactive, watchers other children play"). Each item was coded on a 6-point Likert scale, where *0 = almost never* and *6 = almost always.* Cronbach's α ranged between .83 and .87, suggesting that the internal consistency for this scale was high.

Parent Measures Parents also rated children's social-emotional competencies on 2 screening measures: the *Social Competence Screening for Preschoolers – Parent Form* (SCS-P; Miclea et al. 2010) and the *Emotional Competence Screening for Preschoolers – Teacher Form* (ECS-P; Miclea et al. 2010). The SCS-P scale includes 12 items assessing compliance to rules, interpersonal skills, and prosocial behavior (e.g., "The child easily accepts changes in game rules"; "The child shares his/her toys without being told"). Conversely, the ECS-P scale contains 14 items assessing emotion understanding, emotion expression, and emotion regulation (e.g., "The child recognizes that others feel happy, angry, sad, or afraid"; "The child shows patience until receiving attention or a reward"). Parents' answers on both scales were recorded on a 5-point Likert scale, where *1 = almost never* and *5 = almost always.* Previous studies showed that these measures show appropriate reliability and validity indices (Ştefan et al. 2009). In the current study, the SCS-P showed high internal consistency, with α-Cronbach coefficients ranging from .81 to .86. Similarly, the ECS-P showed good internal consistency, with Cronbach's α ranging from .71 to .74.

Parent also rated children's social skills with the Social Competence scale from the *Social Skills Rating System – Preschool (Parent Form)* (SSRS; Gresham and Elliott 1990). The Social Competence scale includes 4, 10-item subscales: Cooperation (e.g., "Helps you with household tasks without being asked"), Assertion (e.g., "Receives criticism well"), Responsibility (e.g., "Asks permission before using another family member's property"), and Self-control (e.g., "Controls temper in conflict situations with you"). Each item is rated on a 3-point Likert scale, measuring the frequency of a specific behavior, where *0 = never* and *2 = very often*. Internal consistency coefficients measured with Cronbach's α were high, and ranged between .85 and .87.

Parents also rated children on Externalizing problems with the Behavior Problem scale from the SSRS (Gresham and Elliott 1990). This scale comprises 10 items (e.g., "Argues with others", "Disturbs ongoing activities"), and answers are rated on a 3-point Likert scale, where *0 = never* and *2 = very often*. Internal consistency coefficients varied between .73 and .77, indicating good reliability. Cutoffs for the Romanian sample were computed with the split-half method. In this case, separate cutoffs were established for boys and girls, due to the fact that parents rated boys significantly higher on behavior problems compared to girls ($p < .01$).

RESULTS[1]

Attrition and Group Equivalence

First, children who remained in the project postintervention were compared to those who were not included in the final sample (intervention, $n = 32$; control, $n = 14$). These analyses were conducted on all relevant variables either using *t*, or χ^2 tests, which indicated that there were no significant differences between attrited and non-attrited participants. Socio-demographic characteristics and risk status for dropouts vs. non-dropouts are described in Table 3.1.

Children in the intervention and control groups did not differ significantly by age $t(156) = .77, p > .05$, gender, $\chi^2\ (1, N = 158) = .54, p > .05$, but there was a significant effect of socio-economic status, indicating that there were significantly fewer low-SES children compared to moderate- and high-SES children, $\chi^2\ (2, N = 158) = 9.94, p < .01$. Consequently, percentages for this risk category described in Table 3.1 were computed for moderate- and low-SES children combined. Comparisons on all other risk variables indicated that there were no significant group differences. Prior to the statistical analyses employed for testing the intervention's effectiveness, *t* tests were conducted on children's preintervention scores to establish potential group differences, but none of the results were significant. Pre- and postintervention means and standard deviations for the intervention and control groups are presented in Table 3.2.

HLM Analyses of SEP Effectiveness

Due to the fact that children were nested within classrooms, and there could be a potential effect of the shared environmental characteristics leading to inflated significance levels and incorrect inferences about the intervention's effects, the data analyses were performed employing hierarchical

Table 3.2 Means and standard deviations for intervention and control groups

	Preintervention				*Postintervention*			
	SEP		*Control*		*SEP*		*Control*	
Variable	*M*	*SD*	*M*	*SD*	*M*	*SD*	*M*	*SD*
AKT expressive	3.46	2.09	4.07	2.10	5.74	1.70	4.84	1.91
AKT receptive	5.15	2.24	5.52	2.64	7.09	1.57	6.43	2.07
Positive strategies	0.49	0.27	0.51	0.28	0.77	0.23	0.61	0.28
Negative strategies	0.04	0.09	0.04	0.08	0.01	0.05	0.04	0.09
SCS-T	55.18	9.79	56.42	9.41	61.12	8.68	58.16	8.55
ECS-T	44.43	7.43	44.70	6.28	49.16	6.11	46.07	5.70
SCBE social competence	111.22	33.89	112.88	33.83	129.38	24.74	120.29	26.07
SCBE externalizing problems	68.85	15.24	68.97	12.69	77.81	9.67	71.86	12.52
SCBE internalizing problems	69.84	12.32	68.13	9.28	75.58	8.71	70.42	8.98
SCS-P	43.25	6.30	43.80	6.04	47.75	4.69	46.07	4.74
ECS-P	44.43	7.53	44.70	6.28	49.16	6.11	46.07	5.70
SSRS social competence	49.74	8.63	51.68	7.93	55.28	6.83	53.75	7.85
SSRS behavior problems	3.42	2.07	3.13	1.94	2.22	1.54	2.67	1.75

Note. SEP = Social-Emotional Prevention Program, *AKT* = Affective Knowledge Test score, *SCS-T* = Social Competence Screening-Teacher score, *ECS-T* = Emotional Competence Screening-Teacher, *SCBE* = Social Competence and Behavior Evaluation score, *SCS-P* = Social Competence Screening-Parent score, *ECS-P* = Emotional Competence Screening-Parent score, *SSRS* = Social Skills Rating System score linear modeling (HLM) (Raudenbush and Bryk 2002). Taking into account children's clustering within classrooms, 2-level HLM analysis was conducted with children represented at Level 1 (within-class variance), and classrooms represented at Level 2 (between-class variance). Thirteen HLM models were estimated, 1 for each outcome variable. The HLM analyses were preceded by testing for significant preintervention differences between the means of the dependent variables, but no such differences were found. In each model, age, gender, and preintervention scores were entered at Level 1, while treatment was entered at Level 2 as a dummy-coded variable (1 = *intervention* and 0 = *control*). All predictor variables were grand mean centered (Bickel 2007). Due to differences in the homogeneity of variance of level 1 predictors for teacher rated externalizing and internalizing problems, the data were also analyzed with a non-parametric version of HLM based on assigning ranks to children's scores (Lloyd and Zumbo 2007). Effect sizes were computed as the mean difference between the intervention and control group divided by the pooled standard deviations (Cohen's *d*).

The final HLM models for performance on child-reported measures presented in Table 3.3 support the notion that SEP participation predicted higher gains in children's ability to name emotions, to recognize emotions, and to provide positive solutions for possible conflict situations compared to children from the control group. However, no significant reductions in negative problem-solving strategies were found between intervention and control group children. Also, peformance on outcome variables positively affected by the intervention was higher for girls compared to boys.

Statistically significant effects of SEP participation compared to the control group were found for teacher rated social competence evaluated either by SCS-T or SCBE, emotional competence, and externalizing problems. Conversely, the intervention did not exert effects on children's internalizing problems as indicated by the results in Table 3.4. However, significant rank differences were found in favor of intervention group children for both externalizing and internalizing problems, when the N-par difference analyses were conducted.

HLM analyses conducted on parental evaluations partially supported the notion that SEP participation would predict better developed social-emotional competencies compared to the control group condition. Data from Table 3.5 show that the results obtained for the SCS-P and the SSRS Social Competence scale were somewhat different, as parental evaluations of children's gains in social competencies from SSRS indicated that the intervention did not predict significant between group differences. Also, SEP participation predicted significant gains in children's emotional

Table 3.3 Student-classroom hierarchical linear modeling analyses: the effects of SEP on experimental task performance controlling for gender, age, and preintervention score

Fixed effect	*Est*	*SE*	*t*	*df*	*Cohen d*
AKT expressive					
Intercept	5.16	0.27	19.27***	12	
Gender	−0.64	0.27	−2.34*	13	
Age	−0.07	0.30	−0.22	13	
Preintervention AKT expressive	0.26	0.07	3.92**	13	
SEP intervention	0.91	0.31	2.93*	12	0.50
AKT receptive					
Intercept	6.65	0.27	24.35***	12	
Gender	−1.12	0.27	−4.24**	13	
Age	−0.17	0.28	−0.59	13	
Preintervention AKT receptive	0.20	0.06	3.63**	13	
SEP intervention	0.69	0.29	2.39*	12	0.36
Positive strategies					
Intercept	0.61	0.04	16.54***	12	
Gender	−0.03	0.04	−0.68	13	
Age	−0.01	0.03	−0.01	13	
Preintervention positive strategies	0.42	0.07	6.06***	13	
SEP intervention	0.17	0.04	3.91**	12	0.62
Negative strategies					
Intercept	0.05	0.01	3.61**	12	
Gender	0.01	0.01	0.01	13	
Age	−0.01	0.01	−0.74	13	
Preintervention negative strategies	0.27	0.06	4.81***	13	
SEP intervention	−0.03	0.02	−1.96†	12	

†$p < .10$, *$p < .05$, **$p < .01$, ***$p < .001$

competencies and significantly lower levels of aggressive and non-compliant behaviors compared to the control group condition. Additionally, gender predicted lower levels of behavior problems in girls compared to boys, which was not surprising given that separate cutoff points were established for boys and girls in this sample.

In order to further test the SEP efficacy in terms of "clinical significance," chi-square analyses were employed to test for changes in teacher SCBE, and parent SSRS ratings from pre- to postintervention in treatment and control classrooms. There was a postintervention decrease in the percentage of children with below cutoff scores on the SCBE from 21% (19 children) to 7% (6 children) in the intervention group, and from 17% (12 children) to 12% (8 children) in the control group. The differences between the groups were not significant preinterventinon,

Table 3.4 Student-classroom hierarchical linear modeling analyses: the effects of SEP on teacher's ratings controlling for gender, age, and preintervention score

Fixed effect	*Est*	*SE*	*t*	*df*	*Cohen d*
SCS-T					
Intercept	58.30	0.90	65.01***	12	
Gender	0.13	0.88	0.15	13	
Age	−0.79	0.93	−0.85	13	
Preintervention SCS-T	0.70	0.05	−14.70***	13	
SEP intervention	3.11	1.06	2.93*	12	0.34
ECS-T					
Intercept	46.95	0.92	51.09***	12	
Gender	−1.10	0.66	−1.66	13	
Age	−0.80	0.76	−1.05	13	
Preintervention ECS-T	0.56	0.05	11.30***	13	
SEP intervention	3.09	1.18	2.62*	12	0.52
SCBE social competence					
Intercept	121.51	2.34	51.98***	12	
Gender	−2.26	2.04	−0.17	13	
Age	−0.37	2.25	−1.11	13	
Preintervention SCBE social competence	0.65	0.03	19.54***	13	
SEP intervention	9.13	2.87	3.18**	12	0.36
SCBE externalizing problems					
Intercept	72.44	1.50	48.22***	12	
Gender	−1.78	1.24	−1.44	13	
Age	1.22	1.43	0.84	13	
Preintervention SCBE externalizing	0.55	0.05	11.79***	13	
SEP intervention	5.70	1.86	3.07*	12	0.53
SCBE internalizing problems					
Intercept	60.33	3.83	5.76***	12	
Gender	−2.13	1.31	−1.63	13	
Age	0.51	1.56	0.33	13	
Preintervention SCBE internalizing	0.16	0.05	3.16**	13	
SEP intervention	5.03	2.36	2.13†	12	

Fixed effect	*Est*	*SE*	*N-par test statistic*	*df*
SCBE externalizing problems				
Intercept	7.35	3.54	2.13*	12
Gender	−4.01	1.24	−1.45	13
Age	4.15	1.43	1.44	13
Preintervention SCBE externalizing	0.84	0.05	28.04***	13
SEP intervention	10.59	1.86	3.84***	12

(*continued*)

Table 3.4 (continued)

Fixed effect	*Est*	*SE*	*N-par test statistic*	*df*
SCBE internalizing problems				
Intercept	6.88	3.59	1.99*	12
Gender	0.19	2.88	0.07	13
Age	5.06	2.99	1.69	13
Preintervention SCBE internalizing	0.82	0.03	26.20***	13
SEP intervention	9.68	2.87	3.37***	12

†$p < .10$, *$p < .05$, **$p < .01$, ***$p < .001$

Note. Due to significant differences in homogeneity of variance in level 1 variables for SCBE Externalizing and Internalizing problems, the N-par difference statistic is also reported

Table 3.5 Student-classroom hierarchical linear modeling analyses: the effects of SEP on parent's ratings controlling for gender, age, and pretest score

Fixed effect	*Est*	*SE*	*t*	*df*	*Cohen d*
SCS-P					
Intercept	45.99	0.42	110.79***	12	
Gender	−0.29	0.47	−0.62	13	
Age	0.69	0.48	1.38	13	
Preintervention AKT expressive	0.61	0.04	16.14***	13	
SEP intervention	1.61	0.47	3.48**	12	0.36
ECS-P					
Intercept	46.19	0.65	70.64***	12	
Gender	−0.42	0.72	−0.59	13	
Age	0.32	0.73	0.43	13	
Preintervention AKT expressive	0.59	0.05	11.11***	13	
SEP intervention	3.03	0.74	4.09**	12	0.52
SSRS social competence					
Intercept	53.36	0.94	56.61***	12	
Gender	0.49	0.86	0.57	13	
Age	0.29	0.98	0.30	13	
Preintervention AKT expressive	0.61	0.05	11.54***	13	
SEP intervention	1.60	1.13	1.42	12	
SSRS behavior problems					
Intercept	2.50	0.16	15.97***	12	
Gender	0.49	0.18	2.79*	13	
Age	−0.12	0.18	−0.67	13	
Preintervention AKT expressive	0.58	0.04	13.42***	13	
SEP intervention	−0.45	0.17	−2.59*	12	−0.27

†$p < .10$, *$p < .05$, **$p < .01$, ***$p < .001$

χ^2 (1, N = 158) = 1.21, $p > .05$, but at postintervention children who had been exposed to SEP exhibited significantly lower rates of behavior problems compared to controls, χ^2 (1, N = 158) = 4.06, $p < .05$. Regarding parental ratings on the SSRS scale, the percentage of intervention group children at risk of externalizing problems dropped from 22% (20 children) to 9% (7 children), and from 20% (14 children) to 16% (11 children) in the comparison group. No significant preintervention differences were found between the intervention and control groups, χ^2 (1, N = 158) = .24, $p > .05$, but the number of high-risk children was significantly lower in the treatment group postintervention compared to the control group, χ^2 (1, N = 158) = 4.37, $p < .05$.

Discussion

Overall the data from this study on SEP efficacy at the classroom level suggest that the hypotheses put forward were largely supported. These results support the notion that SEP is an effective intervention strategy according to 3 assessment sources: children, teachers, and parents. The combined use of child, parent, and teacher reported measures represents an innovative approach to the efficacy assessment of community-based interventions, as most community-based interventions are only implemented as classroom curricula and outcome variables are rarely reported based on parent ratings of children's behaviors or on children's self-reported knowledge about emotions and problem-solving strategies. Moreover, these results concerning SEP efficacy are the first to suggest that a hybrid preventive approach combining universal and indicated interventions is effective for preschoolers, not only for school age children as previously reported in the literature (CPPRG 1999a, b).

The first hypothesis indicated that SEP participation was expected to improve intervention group children's social-emotional competencies compared to control group children. The results showed that in fact SEP intervention was associated with children's improved expressive and receptive emotion recognition, as well as with improved ability to offer positive, prosocial solutions to possible conflict situations (e.g., toy sharing, waiting, being compliant, etc.). These results mimic those obtained by other well-established prevention programs such as *The Incredible Years* (Webster-Stratton et al. 2008), *Emotion-Based Prevention Program* (EBP) (Izard et al. 2008), or *Pathways to Alternative Thinking Strategies* (PATHS) (Domitrovich et al. 2007). However, no significant SEP effects were found in terms of reducing children's negative problem-solving strategies. Results from indicated and selective prevention studies suggest that such effects are more commonly found in high-risk samples (Webster-Stratton and Hammond 1997; Webster-Stratton and Reid 2003). Therefore, the lack of intervention effects can be attributed to the fact that at risk children represented 10% of this study's sample, and changes in negative behaviors might be more difficult to observe in non-clinical samples such as the one employed in this study.

A rather unexpected finding for the child reported measures was a moderator effect of gender on both expressive and receptive emotion recognition. Based on data from the literature on children's emotion knowledge development, age and verbal abilities are highly correlated with performance on experimental tasks involving expressive emotion recognition (Bennett et al. 2005; Schultz et al. 2001), but not receptive emotion recognition. Furthermore, receptive emotion recognition seems to develop as a function of age at faster rates than expressive emotion recognition, and involves to a lesser extent children's vocabulary acquisitions (Widen and Russell 2002, 2003). Therefore, this unusual effect of gender suggests that girls are better at naming emotions, as well as recognizing them based on facial cues. One possible explanation is that girls may have better developed language abilities, which allow them to outperform boys on the expressive emotion recognition task, but this does not explain the effect on receptive recognition. Moreover, since in the current study a measure of verbal abilities was not employed, any inference regarding these effects should be made cautiously, and future studies might attempt to replicate these findings.

The results concerning SEP efficacy based on teacher ratings indicate that the first hypothesis was supported. SEP participation was associated with increased social-emotional competencies, which is in line with previously reported findings (Domitrovich et al. 2007; Webster-Stratton et al. 2001). However, it is noteworthy that these findings relied on combined measures of children's social-emotional competencies. Results from fundamental research indicated that while the 2 constructs are highly correlated (r = .50–.60), they are not identical (Roberts and Strayer 1996). Hence, one significant contribution of this study is related to the fact that it is the first to provide evidence of an intervention's efficacy employing separate measures of emotional and social competencies.

The SEP was also hypothesized to exert effects on reducing the levels of externalizing problems. According to the results, partial support was found for SEP efficacy on precursors of psychopathology. The presence of significant effects of children's externalizing problems was previously reported in community-based interventions for children from economically disadvantaged backgrounds (Izard et al. 2008; Raver et al. 2009), or clinically referred children (Webster-Stratton and Reid 2003). The results reported for the SEP as a hybrid approach are similar to those obtained by the developers of the Fast Track program for school aged children (CPPRG 1999b). Such outcomes could be explained by the fact that SEP as well as other prevention programs obtaining such effects combine classroom curriculum with both teacher and parent training, thus tackling a wider range of risk factors which increase children's risk of behavior problems. Furthermore, these outcomes provide indirect support for choosing to promote interactions between all the children in the classroom instead of separating at risk children by implementing additional pullout sessions. These results add to the already extant data indicating that non-exclusionary strategies are effective in reducing maladaptive behaviors (Dishion et al. 1999; Lochman and Wells 2002; van Lier et al. 2005).

Additionally, findings concerning statistical significance of intervention effects are backed up by the "clinical" relevance. More precisely, teacher ratings of behavior problems showed that more than half of the intervention group children who scored below the cutoff at baseline, were no longer at risk postintervention. This could also suggest that participation in the intervention accelerated a normative developmental outcome, because patterns of externalizing behavior tend to decrease by the time preschoolers reach the age of 5 (Hill et al. 2006; Owens and Shaw 2003).

In spite of this positive result obtained for externalizing problems, mixed intervention effects were found for internalizing problems. Selective and universal prevention programs found that children's anxiety and social isolation tend to diminish as a result of participating in interventions targeting behavior problems (Domitrovich et al. 2007; Raver et al. 2009). One possible explanation is that social skill training and teaching children strategies for friendship development (Calkins and Fox 2002), could be associated with lower levels of anxiety and isolation (Coplan et al. 2004; Warnes et al. 2005). As results indicated a marginally significant trend with HLM, and significant gains in rank with the N-par statistic, it could be inferred with some caution that the data add to the evidence that prevention programs designed to enhance especially children's social abilities can be to some extent used as a means of preventing internalizing problems (Dadds and Roth 2008).

The third source for gathering data about SEP efficacy was parents' ratings of children's social-emotional competencies and behavior problems. The data from this study offer contradictive evidence regarding the first hypothesis, because parents' evaluation of social skills showed significant gains when measured by SCS-P, but not by SSRS. A plausible explanation is that SSRS measured constructs are not similar to those of SCS-P, and SCS-P specifically measures social skills targeted by the SEP intervention. Therefore SCS-P might be more sensitive to detecting positive outcomes than SSRS. However, as expected significant intervention effects were found on parent rated emotional competencies. In relation to the second hypothesis, significant SEP effects were found for externalizing problems. Furthermore, similar to results from teacher ratings of externalizing problems, SEP participation was associated with a 50% reduction of below cutoff scores, suggesting that "clinical" significance was also obtained for parent ratings.

Taken together, these data provide indirect support to the notion that children's social-emotional competencies are enhanced, while aggressive and non-compliant behaviors are decreased as a result of parental involvement in the intervention. Previous community-based interventions showed that parent training as part of multifocused interventions is associated with better developed social-emotional competencies and reduced behavior problems in high-risk children (CPPRG 1999a; Webster-Stratton et al. 2001; Zubrick et al. 2005). This intervention is the first to show that parent training delivered to cover the intervention needs of both parents of at risk and low-risk children is in fact beneficial because it supports children's skill transfer.

One major concern regarding the parent training was its sustainability, because many community-based interventions previously reported difficulties in attracting parents of low-risk children (Prinz and Sanders 2007). SEP adopted a short, 4-session, group format and a hybrid approach for parents of both at risk and low-risk children with the explicit intent to ensure parental involvement irrespective of the baseline risk status. Parent attendance rates of 54% (65% of parents of at risk children and 40% of parents of low-risk children) suggest that the short format version of the training was important for attracting and keeping them involved. These findings provide additional support to the fact that short parent training delivered in prevention programs for internalizing problems can represent a successful intervention format for prevention programs aiming to decrease the risk of externalizing problems (Dadds and Roth 2008).

When comparing effect sizes obtained for SEP with those reported in other community-based programs such as The Incredible Years program (Webster-Stratton et al. 2001), EBP (Izard et al. 2008), and Fast Track (1999a, 2002), it is apparent that SEP exhibited small to moderate effect sizes (varying from .27 to .53), whereas other interventions exhibited moderate to large effect sizes (from .43 to .82) for measures of social-emotional competencies and behavior problems. These differences could be attributed to the fact that this sample included both at risk and low-risk children compared to effect sizes reported by other programs for predominantly high-risk samples.

Conclusions and Implications for Practice

The results obtained for SEP efficacy at the classroom level have several important implications for practitioners working in schools. First, effect sizes reported here for SEP, as well as those reported for other evidence-based interventions, build a strong case for the inclusion of a social-emotional learning curriculum in preschools. This might have important implications for children's mental health, but also for their long-term adjustment to school. Furthermore, consistent data suggesting that such approaches are in fact effective could be considered by policy makers as evidence of the sustainability and the practical utility of such undertakings. However, above all else, implementing school-based interventions grounded in empirical evidence supporting their efficacy would allow teachers and school counselors to put in place an approach which emphasizes a proactive, skill-building strategy for preventing negative outcomes, rather than reactive strategies, which sometime lead to labeling the child as "being" the problem.

Also, results from this study and other evidence-based interventions seem to indirectly support the notion that especially children who are at risk of behavior problems might be more inclined to respond positively to interventions which elicit changes in their environment (Lewis and Sugai 1999). It is also noteworthy that particularly in this age group children often manifest different behaviors depending on the adult who interacts with the child. For instance, some children might misbehave at home, but not at school, or *vice versa*. Given this characteristic, teacher-parent communication and direct parental involvement are paramount for a successful intervention. Involvement does not necessarily mean that parents need to invest a considerable amount of time and resources for participating in such programs. As indicated by results from this study, fairly consistent effects can be elicited with a short intervention format. In addition, it would be reasonable to assume, based on current results, that not only intervention format contributes to parents' engagement, but also the particular strategies taught to parents. SEP, as well as other programs for preschool children, rely on the assumption that teaching parents about discipline strategies is important, but to a certain extent is secondary to encouraging parents to teach their children about emotions, emotion regulation, or problem-solving.

Hence, based on these observations it could be that educating teachers and parents is essential for implementing successful interventions. Such efforts should consider: (1) emphasizing the fact that children are not the problem, only their behaviors can be seen as problematic; (2) raising awareness about the fact that children's behaviors reflect adults' ability to provide a nurturing environment; and (3) providing adults with meaningful strategies of supporting children's social-emotional development.

Furthermore, while it is obvious that in classroom-based interventions the most consistent changes can be seen in children who are at risk, it is also possible that children who are not actually at risk might benefit to some extent from participating in such interventions, at least in terms of improved competencies, if not in terms of reduced behavior problems. Consequently, the next chapter focuses on providing a more detailed response to the question about the extent to which universal interventions are actually effective in community settings.

Note

1. Text and tables from the Results and Discussion sections from the current chapter were previously published in: Ştefan, C. A., & Miclea, M. (2013). Effects of a multifocused prevention program on preschool children's competencies and behavior problems. *Psychology in the Schools*, *50*, 382-402. doi:10.1002/pits.21683 by ©Wiley Periodicals Inc., and their permission as copyright holders was obtained for the reuse of the material.

References

Bennett, D. S., Bendersky, M., & Lewis, M. (2005). Antecedents of emotion knowledge: Predictors of individual differences in young children. *Cognition and Emotion*, *19*, 375–396. https://doi.org/10.1080/02699930441000201.

Bickel, R. (2007). Multilevel regression growth models. In *Multilevel analysis for applied research* (pp. 285–329). New York: Guilford Publications.

Brotman, L. M., Gouley, K. K., Chesir-Teran, D., Dennis, T., Klein, R. G., & Shrout, P. (2005). Prevention for preschoolers at high risk for conduct problems: Immediate outcomes on parenting practices and child social competence. *Journal of Clinical Child and Adolescent Psychology, 34*, 724–734. https://doi.org/10.1207/s15374424jccp3404_14.
Calkins, S. D., & Dedmon, S. E. (2000). Psychological and behavioral regulation in two-year-old children with aggressive/destructive behavior problems. *Journal of Abnormal Child Psychology, 28*, 103–118. https://doi.org/10.1023/A:1005112912906.
Calkins, S. D., & Fox, N. A. (2002). Self-regulatory processes in early personality development: A multilevel approach to the study of childhood social withdrawal and aggression. *Development and Psychopathology, 14*, 477–498. https://doi.org/10.1017/S095457940200305X.
Conduct Problems Prevention Research Group. (1999a). Initial impact of the Fast Track prevention trial for conduct problems: I. The high risk sample. *Journal of Consulting and Clinical Psychology, 67*, 631–647. https://doi.org/10.1037/0022-006X.67.5.648.
Conduct Problems Prevention Research Group. (1999b). Initial impact of the fast track prevention trial for conduct problems: II. Classroom effects. *Journal of Consulting and Clinical Psychology, 67*, 648–657. https://doi.org/10.1037/0022-006X.67.5.648.
Conduct Problems Prevention Research Group. (2002). Evaluation of the first 3 years of the fast track prevention trial with children at high risk for adolescent conduct problems. *Journal of Abnormal Child Psychology, 30*, 19–35. https://doi.org/10.1023/A:1014274914287.
Conroy, M. A., Stichter, J. P., Daunic, A., & Haydon, T. (2008). Classroom-based research in the field of emotional and behavioral disorders: Methodological issues and future research directions. *Journal of Special Education, 41*, 209–222. https://doi.org/10.1177/0022466907310369.
Coplan, R. J., Prakash, K., O'Neil, K., & Armer, M. (2004). Do you "want" to play? Distinguishing between conflicted shyness and social disinterest in early childhood. *Developmental Psychology, 40*, 244–258. https://doi.org/10.1037/0012-1649.40.2.244.
Dadds, M. R., & Roth, J. H. (2008). Prevention of anxiety disorders: Results of a universal trial with young children. *Journal of Child and Family Studies, 17*, 320–335. https://doi.org/10.1007/s10826-007-9144-3.
Denham, S. A. (1986). Social cognition, social behavior, and emotion in preschoolers: Contextual validation. *Child Development, 57*, 194–201. https://doi.org/10.2307/1130651.
Denham, S. A., Blair, K. A., Schmidt, M. S., Blair, K., DeMulder, E., Caal, S., et al. (2003). Preschool understanding of emotions: Contributions to classroom anger and aggression. *Journal of Child Psychology and Psychiatry, 43*, 901–916. https://doi.org/10.1111/1469-7610.00139.

Denham, S. A., & Burton, R. (2003). *Social and emotional prevention and intervention programming for preschoolers.* New York: Kluwer Academic/Plenum Press.

Denham, S. A., Mason, T., Caverly, S., Schmidt, M., Hackney, R., Caswell, C., & DeMulder, E. (2001). Preschoolers at play: Co-socializers of emotional and social competence. *International Journal of Behavioral Development, 25,* 90–101. https://doi.org/10.1080/01650250143000067.

Dishion, T. J., McCord, J., & Poulin, F. (1999). When interventions harm: Peer groups and problem behaviors. *American Psychologist, 54,* 755–764. https://doi.org/10.1037/0003-066X.54.9.755.

Domitrovich, C. E., Cortes, R. C., & Greenberg, M. T. (2007). Improving young children's social and emotional competence: A randomized trial of the preschool "PATHS" curriculum. *The Journal of Primary Prevention, 28,* 67–91. https://doi.org/10.1007/s10935-007-0081-0.

Domitrovich, C. E., Bradshaw, C. P., Greenberg, M. T., Embry, D., Poduska, J. M., & Ialongo, N. S. (2010). Integrated models of school-based prevention: Logic and theory. *Psychology in the Schools, 47*(1), 71–88. https://doi.org/10.1002/pits.20452.

Eisenberg, N., Valiente, C., Morris, A. S., Fabes, R. A., Cumberland, A., & Reiser, M. (2003). Longitudinal relations among parental emotional expressivity, children's regulation, and quality of socioemotional function. *Developmental Psychology, 39,* 3–19. https://doi.org/10.1037/0012-1649.39.1.3.

Fabes, R. A., Gaertner, M. B., & Popp, T. K. (2006). Getting along with others: Social competence in early childhood. In K. M. D. Phillips (Ed.), *Handbook of early childhood development* (pp. 297–315). Malden: Blackwell Publishing.

Filcheck, H. A., McNeil, C. B., Greco, L. A., & Bernard, R. S. (2004). Using a whole-class token economy and coaching of teacher skills in a preschool classroom to manage disruptive behavior. *Psychology in the Schools, 4,* 351–361. https://doi.org/10.1002/pits.10168.

Gilliom, M., Shaw, D. S., Beck, J. E., Schonberg, M. A., & Lukon, J. L. (2002). Anger regulation in disadvantaged preschool boys: Strategies, antecedents, and the development of self-control. *Developmental Psychology, 38,* 222–235. https://doi.org/10.1037/0012-1649.38.2.222.

Gresham, F. M., & Elliott, S. N. (1990). *Social Skills Rating System.* Circle Pines: American Guidance Service.

Hill, A. L., Degnan, K. A., Calkins, S. A., & Keane, S. P. (2006). Profiles of externalizing behavior problems for boys and girls across preschool: The roles of emotion regulation and inattention. *Developmental Psychology, 42,* 913–928. https://doi.org/10.1037/0012-1649.42.5.913.

Hughes, J. N., Cavell, T. M., Meehan, B. T., Zhang, D., & Collie, C. (2005). Adverse school context moderates the outcomes of selective interventions for aggressive children. *Journal of Consulting and Clinical Psychology, 73,* 731–736. https://doi.org/10.1037/0022-006X.73.4.731.

Izard, C. E. (2002). Translating emotion theory and research into preventive interventions. *Psychological Bulletin, 128*, 796–824. https://doi.org/10.1037/0033-2909.128.5.796.

Izard, C. E., King, K. A., Trentacosta, C. J., Morgan, J. K., Laurenceau, J. P., Krauthamer-Ewing, E. S., & Finlon, K. J. (2008). Accelerating the development of emotion competence on Head Start children: Effects on adaptive and maladaptive behavior. *Development and Psychopathology, 20*, 369–397. https://doi.org/10.1017/S0954579408000175.

Kam, C.-M., Greenberg, M. T., & Walls, C. T. (2003). Examining the role of implementation quality in school-based prevention using the PATHS curriculum. *Prevention Science, 4*, 55–63. https://doi.org/10.1023/A:1021786811186.

LaFreniere, P. J., & Dumas, J. E. (1995). *Social competence and behavior evaluation* (Preschool ed.). Los Angeles: Western Psychological Services.

Lewis, T. J., & Sugai, G. (1999). Effective behavior support: A system approach to proactive schoolwide management. *Focus on Exceptional Children, 31*, 1–24.

Lloyd, J. E. V., & Zumbo, B. D. (2007). The non-parametric difference score: A workable solution for analysing two-wave change when the measures themselves change across waves. *Journal of Modern Applied Statistical Methods, 6*, 413–420. https://doi.org/10.22237/jmasm/1193889960.

Lochman, J. E., & Wells, K. C. (2002). The Coping Power program at the middle-school transition: Universal and indicated prevention effects. *Psychology of Addictive Behaviors, 16*, S40–S54. https://doi.org/10.1037/0893-164X.16.4S.S40.

Lopez, M. L., Tartullo, L. B., Forness, S. R., & Boyce, C. A. (2000). Early identification and intervention: Head Start's response to mental health challenges. *Early Education and Development, 11*, 265–282. https://doi.org/10.1207/s15566935eed1103_3.

Miclea, M., Bălaj, A., Porumb, M., Porumb, D., & Porumb, S. (2010). *PEDa: The developmental assessment platform for 3-6/7 year old children.* Cluj-Napoca: ASCR Publishing. https://doi.org/10.1002/jbmr.153.

Nelson, G., Westhues, A., & MacLeod, J. (2003). A meta-analysis of longitudinal research on preschool prevention programs for children. *Prevention and Treatment, 6*, 1–25.

Owens, E. B., & Shaw, D. S. (2003). Predictive growth curves of externalizing behavior across the preschool years. *Journal of Abnormal Child Psychology, 31*, 575–590. https://doi.org/10.1023/A:1026254005632.

Prinz, R. J., & Sanders, M. R. (2007). Adopting a population-level approach to parenting and family support interventions. *Clinical Psychology Review, 27*, 739–749. https://doi.org/10.1016/j.cpr.2007.01.005.

Raudenbush, S. W., & Bryk, A. S. (2002). *Hierarchical linear models: Applications and data analysis methods.* Thousand Oaks: Sage. https://doi.org/10.2466/pms.2002.94.2.671.

Raver, C. C., Jones, S. M., Li-Grining, C., Zhai, F., Metzger, M. W., & Solomon, B. (2009). Targeting children's behavior problems in preschool classrooms: A cluster-randomized controlled trial. *Journal of Consulting and Clinical Psychology, 77*, 302–316. https://doi.org/10.1037/a0015302.

Roberts, W., & Strayer, J. (1996). Empathy, emotional expressiveness, and prosocial behavior. *Child Development, 67*, 449–470. https://doi.org/10.1111/j.1467-8624.1996.tb01745.x.

Schultz, D., Izard, C. E., Ackerman, B. P., & Youngstrom, E. A. (2001). Emotion knowledge in economically disadvantaged children: Self-regulatory antecedents and relations to social difficulties and withdrawal. *Development and Psychopathology, 13*, 53–67. https://doi.org/10.1017/S0954579401001043.

Shure, M. B. (1997). Interpersonal cognitive problem-solving: Primary prevention of early high-risk behaviors in the preschool and primary years. In G. W. Albee & T. P. Gullotta (Eds.), *Primary prevention works* (pp. 167–188). Thousand Oaks: Sage.

Shure, M. B., & Spivak, G. (1982). Interpersonal problem-solving in young children: A cognitive approach to prevention. *American Journal of Community Psychology, 10*, 341–356. https://doi.org/10.1007/BF00896500.

Snyder, J., Schrepferman, L., Oeser, J., Patterson, G., Stoolmiller, M., Johnson, K., & Snyder, A. (2005). Deviancy training and association with deviant peers in young children: Occurrence and contribution to early-onset conduct problems. *Development and Psychopathology, 17*, 397–413. https://doi.org/10.1017/S0954579405050194.

Spinrad, T. L., Eisenberg, N., Harris, E., Hanish, L., Fabes, R. A., Kupanoff, K., et al. (2004). The relation of children's everyday nonsocial peer play behavior to their emotionality, regulation, and social functioning. *Developmental Psychology, 40*, 67–80. https://doi.org/10.1037/0012-1649.40.1.67.

Stoolmiller, M., Eddy, M., & Reid, J. B. (2000). Detecting and describing preventive intervention effects in a universal school-based randomized trial targeting delinquent and violent behavior. *Journal of Consulting and Clinical Psychology, 68*, 296–306. https://doi.org/10.1037//0022-006X.68.2.296.

Ştefan, C. A., Bălaj, A., Porumb, M., Albu, M., & Miclea, M. (2009). Preschool screening for social and emotional competencies – Development and psychometric properties. *Cognition, Brain, Behavior. An Interdisciplinary Journal, 13*, 121–146.

Tottenham, N., Borscheid, A., Ellertsen, K., Marcus, D. J., & Nelson, C. A. (2002, April). *Categorization of facial expressions in children and adults: Establishing a larger stimulus set*. Poster presented at the Cognitive Neuroscience Society annual meeting, San Francisco.

Turner, K. M. T., & Sanders, M. R. (2006). Dissemination of evidence-based parenting and family support strategies: Learning from the Triple P – Positive Parenting Program system approach. *Aggression and Violent Behavior, 11*, 176–193. https://doi.org/10.1016/j.avb.2005.07.005.

van Lier, P. A. C., Vuijk, P., & Crijnen, A. A. M. (2005). Understanding mechanisms of change and development of antisocial behavior: The impact of a universal intervention. *Journal of Abnormal Child Psychology, 33*, 521–535. https://doi.org/10.1007/s10802-005-6735-7.

Warnes, E. D., Sheridan, S. M., Geske, J., & Warnes, W. A. (2005). A contextual approach to the assessment of social skills: Identifying meaningful behaviors for social competence. *Psychology in the Schools, 42*, 173–187. https://doi.org/10.1002/pits.20052.

Webster-Stratton, C. (1990). Long-term follow-up of families with young conduct-problem children: From preschool to grade school. *Journal of Clinical Child Psychology, 19*, 1344–1349.

Webster-Stratton, C., & Hammond, M. (1997). Treating children with early-onset conduct problems: A comparison of child and parent training interventions. *Journal of Consulting and Clinical Psychology, 65*, 93–109. https://doi.org/10.1037/0022-006X.65.1.93.

Webster-Stratton, C., & Reid, J. M. (2003). Treating conduct problems and strengthening social and emotional competence in young children: The Dina Dinosaur Program. *Journal of Emotional and Behavioral Disorders, 2*, 130–143. https://doi.org/10.1177/10634266030110030101.

Webster-Stratton, C., Reid, J. M., & Hammond, M. (2001). Preventing conduct problems, promoting social competence: A parent-teacher training partnership in Head Start. *Journal of Clinical Child Psychology, 30*, 283–302. https://doi.org/10.1207/S15374424JCCP3003_2.

Webster-Stratton, C., Reid, J. M., & Hammond, M. (2004). Treating children with early-onset conduct problems: Intervention outcomes for parent, child, and teacher training. *Journal of Clinical Child and Adolescent Psychology, 33*, 105–124. https://doi.org/10.1207/S15374424JCCP3301_11.

Webster-Stratton, C., Reid, M. J., & Stoolmiller, M. (2008). Preventing conduct problems and improving school readiness: Evaluation of the Incredible Years teacher and child training programs in high-risk schools. *The Journal of Child Psychology and Psychiatry, 49*, 471–488. https://doi.org/10.1111/j.1469-7610.2007.01861.x.

Webster-Stratton, C., & Taylor, T. (2001). Nipping early risk factors in the bud: Preventing substance abuse, delinquency, and violence in adolescence through interventions targeted at young children (0–8 years). *Prevention Science, 2*, 165–192. https://doi.org/10.1023/A:1011510923900.

Widen, S. C., & Russell, J. A. (2002). Gender and preschoolers' perception of emotion. *Merrill-Palmer Quarterly, 48*, 248–262. https://doi.org/10.1353/mpq.2002.0013.

Widen, S. C., & Russell, J. A. (2003). A closer look at preschoolers' freely produced labels for facial expressions. *Developmental Psychology, 39*, 114–128. https://doi.org/10.1037/0012-1649.39.1.114.

Zubrick, S. R., Ward, K. A., Silburn, S. R., Lawrence, D., Williams, A. A., Blair, E., et al. (2005). Prevention of child behavior problems through universal implementation of a group behavioral family intervention. *Prevention Science, 6*, 176–193. https://doi.org/10.1007/s11121-005-0013-2.

CHAPTER 4

Assessing SEP Efficacy as a Function of Children's Risk Status: A Separate Evaluation of Indicated and Universal Intervention Levels

Introduction

As emphasized in Chap. 2, the Social-Emotional Prevention Program (SEP) was developed as a hybrid approach to developing social-emotional skills in children who are not at risk, as well as children who are at risk of behavior problems. This hybrid approach encompasses both a universal intervention and an indicated intervention component similar to the Fast Track prevention program (Conduct Problems Prevention Research Group [CPPRG] 1999a, b). Consequently, SEP implementation is grounded in the notion that different mechanisms support social-emotional learning in non-risk and at risk preschoolers, as detailed in Table 4.1.

First, children represent the main focus of universal interventions which are usually implemented as a *curriculum of classroom activities* (Webster-Stratton et al. 2001). In the context of SEP development the classroom intervention was designed for all children, irrespective of their risk status, based on research suggesting that added small group skill training for at risk children reinforces rather than discourages maladaptive behavioral patterns (Lochman and Wells 2002; van Lier et al. 2005). Therefore, SEP was consistent with the framework of the *Fast Track* program, but included the same approach for non-risk, as well as at risk children. This meant that SEP classroom intervention incorporated similar intervention strategies for both the universal and the indicated intervention level.

C. A. Ştefan, *Social-Emotional Prevention Programs for Preschool Children's Behavior Problems*,
https://doi.org/10.1007/978-3-319-74751-4_4

Table 4.1 SEP mechanisms underlying the universal and the indicated prevention strategies

SEP component	*Universal intervention (all children)*	*Indicated intervention (at risk children)*
Classroom curriculum	Classroom curriculum (social-emotional learning)	Classroom curriculum (social-emotional learning)
Teacher training	1. **Prevention strategies** for non-compliant and aggressive behaviors 2. Consultations for coaching social-emotional skills development	1. **Prevention and intervention strategies** for non-compliant and aggressive behaviors 2. Consultations for coaching social-emotional skills development
Parent training	1. Information about children's social-emotional development 2. **Prevention strategies** for non-compliant and aggressive behaviors 3. Coaching strategies for social-emotional skill development	1. Information about children's social-emotional development 2. **Prevention and intervention strategies** for non-compliant and aggressive behaviors 3. Coaching strategies for social-emotional skills development 4. Individual consultations at parents' request

Second, based on findings from the literature supporting the notion that classroom-based interventions alone failed to produce significant changes especially in at risk children's behavior problems (Domitrovich et al. 2007), SEP was also designed to address other contextual risk factors responsible for increasing children's risk. Teacher training as part of preventive programs for preschoolers exhibited positive effects on children's social-emotional skills (Domitrovich et al. 2007), whereas at risk children benefited in terms of lower levels of misconduct reported by either teachers or parents as a results of participating in the intervention (CPPRG 1999b; Filcheck et al. 2004; Raver et al. 2009). Hence, as in the case of the Fast Track program, SEP includes a teacher training component, but different intervention strategies are hypothesized to elicit changes in both non-risk and at risk children. Research uncovered that non-compliant and aggressive behaviors, which disrupt daily classroom activities are sometimes unwittingly reinforced by teachers through ineffective discipline strategies (Lewis and Sugai 1999). Given such findings, SEP training included behavioral management strategies which were expected to support prevention of non-risk children's behavior problems at the universal intervention level, and to reduce misconduct through teachers' effective use of both preventive and intervention strategies for children at risk, at the indicated intervention level. Furthermore, teacher training included consultations concerning SEP implementation in the classroom, as such strategies were found to support children's competence development (Kam et al. 2003). Given that this strategy was found effective in a sample of predominantly non-risk children targeted by a universal prevention program, SEP was designed with an explicit emphasis on teachers' skill building strategies meant to address the intervention needs of both non-risk, and at risk children. Hence, embedding a skill-building approach to developing children's social-emotional competence through coaching emotion regulation and prosocial behaviors in daily classroom interactions was expected to support learning of skills that would be essential for lowering levels of non-compliant and aggressive behaviors, especially in children who are at risk.

And third, besides the classroom curriculum and the teacher training, an additional strategy employed in multifocused interventions is represented by the parent training. This approach in the context of classroom-based interventions was supported by 2 categories of findings: (1) parent training supports the transfer and generalization of classroom acquired skills to parent-child interactions at home (Hughes et al. 2005); and (2) parental involvement in the intervention is consistently associated with lower levels of aggression and non-compliance in at risk children (Webster-Stratton et al. 2001, 2004). Consequently, unlike the Fast Track program which delivers parent training only to high-risk children as the target group of the indicated intervention (CPPRG 1999a), SEP was developed with the intention to reduce stigmatization and to offer relevant support to all parents (Dadds and Roth 2008). In this regard, SEP draws from the *Triple P – Positive Parenting Program* guidelines of a "minimally sufficient" framework for providing parents with the least amount of intervention needed in order to deflect children from a possible negative developmental trajectory towards conduct problems (Turner and Sanders 2006; Zubrick et al. 2005). Drawing from these intervention principles, SEP employs strategies such as informing parents about social-emotional development, prevention strategies for misbehavior, and coaching social-emotional development for parents of non-risk children as recipients of the universal intervention (Sanders and Morawska 2005), whereas parents of high-risk children as recipients of the indicated intervention are provided, in addition to these aforementioned strategies, with training intended to develop positive parenting strategies for effectively managing misbehavior. This approach was considered for parents of high-risk children, because the risk of resorting to harsh and/or inconsistent discipline strategies is higher among parents of children who frequently misbehave

(Chang et al. 2003; Dennis 2006). Moreover, parents were also offered the possibility of requesting individual training sessions for managing individual difficulties, and these were expected to be requested especially by parents of at risk children.

Establishing Target Groups for the SEP Indicated and Universal Intervention Levels

In prior research, risk status was usually determined either based on children's characteristics (i.e., parental or teachers' evaluations of social-emotional development and levels of externalizing problems) (Durlak and Wells 1998; Webster-Stratton et al. 2008), or based on background and/or social environment characteristics (i.e., delinquency and juvenile arrest rates in a given area, parental low socio-economic status) (CPPRG 1999a; Raver et al. 2009). Given that SEP provides a framework for addressing the intervention needs of both non-risk and at risk children, it would be important to establish the extent to which the hypothesized mechanisms of the universal and indicated intervention level are actually effective. As suggested in Chap. 2, the SEP was developed considering a corresponding screening system for determining risk status. The selected strategy was a multiple gate screening procedure, meaning that: (1) the first step consisted of employing a universal screener of children's social-emotional competence; and (2) the second step involved further investigating the risk of emotional and/or behavior problems with a second level screener (Severson and Walker 2002).

The screening system associated with SEP implementation encompasses 2 separate measures of children's social and emotional competencies (Ştefan et al. 2009). This choice was supported by empirical evidence from a number of studies showing that social and emotional competencies, although highly related constructs, include separate categories of behaviors as extensively discussed in Chap. 1 (Denham et al. 2001; Eisenberg et al. 2002). Moreover, poor development of these competencies has been predictive of externalizing problems (Calkins and Fox 2002; Denham et al. 2001, 2003; Eisenberg et al. 2005). An additional argument in favor of using this strategy is related to the fact that some studies indicated that parents tend to rate their children lower on externalizing problems (De Los Reyes and Kazdin 2005), as the convergence of questionnaire ratings and independent observations are in the small category $r = .27$ (Hinshaw et al. 1992). Thus, it is more likely that a method which emphasizes assessment of both skill development and conduct problems would provide a more accurate risk status assessment.

Previous research on the efficacy of preventive interventions for children relied on a similar 2-stage screening procedure in which risk status was established by employing a measure of skill development along with a measure of risk of behavior problems, resulting in 2 risk categories: high risk and low risk (Durlak and Wells 1998). The screening procedure employed in the current study allowed identifying 3 risk categories: high, moderate, and low. Children's *high-risk* status was derived based on the below cutoff scores (lowest 10th percentile) on the measures of social and emotional competence, and they were considered the target group for the indicated intervention (Miclea et al. 2010). Conversely, children who scored above the cutoff were further divided based on the norms in 2 separate categories: *moderate-risk* children scoring between the 11th and 33rd percentile on the screening measures, and *low-risk* children scoring above the 34th percentile. The inclusion of the moderate-risk group was established by taking into account prevalence reports from the United States and Australia cited by Prinz and Sanders (2007), indicating that up to one-third of all preschool children exhibit signs of behavior and emotional problems, which may result in adverse long-term outcomes. In other words, the moderate-risk group comprised children with normative development, but who long term could be at risk of maladjustment. Both moderate- and low-risk children were considered target groups of the universal intervention.

The Current Study

The current study's main aim was to evaluate SEP efficacy for the indicated (i.e., high-risk children), and the universal (i.e., moderate- and low-risk children) intervention levels. Children's risk status was established employing 2 parent and teacher reported screening measures. Based on teacher assessed social-emotional development, SEP efficacy was evaluated for outcomes related to children's classroom behaviors: social-emotional competencies, externalizing and internalizing problems. Conversely, based on parent rated social-emotional competencies, SEP efficacy was assessed in relation to children's social-emotional competencies and behavior problems, as well as their parents' discipline strategies and stress levels. The use of separate teacher and parent ratings for establishing children's risk status was supported by empirical data suggesting that parent and teacher ratings overlap in about 25% of cases in non-clinical samples (Achenbach et al. 2002), meaning that teachers' and parents' perceptions about children's behaviors are highly divergent for this age category. Consequently, given that children's behaviors are dependent upon the context and persons with whom they are interacting, separate ratings of classroom and home behaviors might be more suitable to detect potential behavioral changes as a result of SEP participation.

In both cases, data are presented separately for social and emotional competence screening risk status. Considering previously reported findings from the literature, results for the groups derived from social competence screening were expected to mirror results from the extant literature on the efficacy of early education programs; conversely, in terms of findings based on emotional competence screening, the results from this study are exploratory, but were expected to mirror to some extent results based on the social competence screening. Furthermore, the distinction between moderate- and low-risk children was intended to provide a more nuanced perspective on the universal intervention's efficacy, because moderate-risk children (and a to a lesser extent low-risk children) could benefit from participating in such preventive interventions delivered in the classroom.

More precisely, it was hypothesized that:

1. Intervention group children would show significantly improved social-emotional competencies compared to control group children. This hypothesis was supported by previous research suggesting that interventions aimed at developing social-emotional competencies lead to consistent improvements in terms of social and emotional competencies in both at risk and non-risk children (CPPRG 1999a; Domitrovich et al. 2007). However, based on previous findings supporting the notion that most consistent gains are made by high-risk children (Webster-Stratton 1998; Webster-Stratton et al. 2001), it was expected that the intervention's efficacy would decrease as a function of lower risk status.
2. High-risk intervention group children (but not moderate or low-risk children) would show significantly lower levels of behavior problems compared to control group counterparts. This expectation was supported by previous research showing that high-risk children exhibit significant changes in behavior problems as a result of participating to indicated interventions delivered in schools (Brotman et al. 2005; Webster-Stratton 1998).
3. Parents of high-risk intervention group children would report significantly increased use of appropriate discipline and praise, as well as decreased use of harsh and inconsistent parenting strategies and parental stress compared to parents of high-risk children from the control group. Previously reported findings from prevention programs indicated that parents of high risk children reported increased use of positive discipline (CPPRG 1999a; Webster-Stratton et al. 2001), as well as decreased levels of childrearing stress (Roberts et al. 2006), as a result of participating in school based prevention programs.

Method

Participants

Children A description of the sample's composition according to children's age, gender, and socio-economic status was presented in detail in Chap. 2. In the following, details are provided about children's distribution in the 3 risk categories (high, moderate, and low) according to teachers' and parents' assessment of social and emotional competence development. The screening procedure for social competencies based on teachers' assessment resulted in the following distributions: 16 high-risk, 34 moderate-risk, and 39 low-risk children in the intervention group, as well as 11 high-risk, 26 moderate-risk, and 32 low-risk children in the control group. Conversely, the screening for emotional competencies resulted in identifying 17 high-risk, 30 moderate-risk, and 42 low-risk children in the intervention group, and 12 high-risk, 22 moderate-risk, and 35 low-risk children in the control group. Demographic characteristics and additional risk status data are provided in detail in Table 4.2.

In case of parent rated social competencies, the obtained distribution across the 3 risk categories was as follows: 16 high-risk, 30 moderate-risk, and 43 low-risk children in the intervention group, as well as 12 high-risk, 24 moderate-risk, and 33 low-risk children in the control group. Conversely, risk categories based on screening of emotional competence development included 16 high-risk, 32 moderate-risk, and 41 low-risk children in the intervention group, and 11 high-risk, 26 moderate-risk, and 32 low-risk children in the control group. Screening measures were filled out predominantly by mothers (93.1% from the intervention group and 85.5% from the control group). Additionally, other risk characteristics of the samples are detailed in Table 4.3.

About 70–85% of children from the high-risk samples based on screening of social and emotional competencies, also scored in the high-risk category on the measures of behavior problems.

Teachers Twenty eight teachers participated in this study with a mean age of 41.29 (SD = 11.83) for intervention group teachers, and a mean age of 40.71 (SD = 11.32) for control group teachers. All teachers had at least 2 years' experience in preschool education, were college graduates, and had been working with children from their classroom for at least 6 months prior to the beginning of this study. Also, none of the teachers had previous experience with training and/or implementation of activities targeting social-emotional development.

Table 4.2 Demographic characteristics and risk status of intervention and control group children as a function of risk status and type of competence screening performed by teachers

	Social competence screening				*Emotional competence screening*			
Demographic and risk variables	**Intervention high risk**		**Control high risk**		**Intervention high risk**		**Control high risk**	
	M	*SD*	*M*	*SD*	*M*	*SD*	*M*	*SD*
Child age	49.06	2.79	49.33	4.52	49.33	2.93	49.46	4.29
Parent age	32.38	12.89	31.88	14.67	32.12	12.57	32.03	14.88
	%	*N*	%	*N*	%	*N*	%	*N*
Child gender (male)	63	10	64	7	63	10	67	8
Child risk	63	10	73	8	56	9	58	7
Parent ethnicity	19	3	18	2	19	3	17	2
Low/moderate SES	38	6	36	4	38	6	42	5
Single parent	6	1	9	1	13	2	8	1
Parent depression	6	1	–	–	6	1	–	–
Parent risk	63	10	55	6	75	12	67	8
	Intervention moderate risk		**Control moderate risk**		**Intervention moderate risk**		**Control moderate risk**	
	M	*SD*	*M*	*SD*	*M*	*SD*	*M*	*SD*
Child age	49.94	3.50	49.58	4.13	49.63	3.22	49.72	4.45
Parent age	31.44	13.45	32.21	15.44	31.89	13.17	32.16	14.68
	%	*N*	%	*N*	%	*N*	%	*N*
Child gender (male)	47	16	54	14	39	12	55	12
Child risk	26	9	23	6	26	8	23	5
Parent ethnicity	18	6	12	3	16	5	14	3
Low/moderate SES	44	15	35	9	45	14	32	7
Single parent	9	3	8	2	6	2	9	2
Parent depression	3	1	3	1	3	1	5	1
Parent risk	50	17	46	12	52	16	45	10
	Intervention low risk		**Control low risk**		**Intervention low risk**		**Control low risk**	
	M	*SD*	*M*	*SD*	*M*	*SD*	*M*	*SD*
Child age	48.69	3.62	49.97	2.68	48.73	3.76	49.70	2.59
Parent age	32.57	12.89	32.40	14.72	32.38	13.49	32.30	15.27
	%	*N*	%	*N*	%	*N*	%	*N*

(*continued*)

Table 4.2 (continued)

	Social competence screening				Emotional competence screening			
Child gender (male)	31	15	25	8	45	19	26	9
Child risk	6	3	3	1	12	5	9	3
Parent ethnicity	10	5	16	5	14	6	14	5
Low/moderate SES	43	21	41	13	52	22	40	14
Single parent	8	4	6	2	10	4	6	2
Parent depression	–	–	–	–	–	–	–	–
Parent risk	23	11	53	17	24	10	49	17

Table 4.3 Demographic characteristics and risk status of intervention and control group children as a function of risk status and type of competence screening performed by parents

	Social competence screening				*Emotional competence screening*			
Demographic and risk variables	**Intervention high risk**		**Control high risk**		**Intervention high risk**		**Control high risk**	
	M	*SD*	*M*	*SD*	*M*	*SD*	*M*	*SD*
Child age	48.80	3.38	49.44	3.90	49.55	3.07	49.15	3.86
Parent age	31.75	13.21	32.09	14.82	31.66	13.38	32.18	14.32
	%	*N*	%	*N*	%	*N*	%	*N*
Child gender (male)	69	11	58	7	75	12	64	7
Child risk	44	7	50	6	50	8	55	6
Parent ethnicity	25	4	17	2	19	3	18	2
Low/moderate SES	44	7	42	5	50	8	55	5
Single parent	13	2	8	1	6	1	–	–
Parent depression	13	2	8	1	6	1	–	–
Parent risk	69	11	50	6	56	9	64	7
	Intervention moderate risk		**Control moderate risk**		**Intervention moderate risk**		**Control moderate risk**	
	M	*SD*	*M*	*SD*	*M*	*SD*	*M*	*SD*
Child age	49.51	3.31	49.82	3.22	48.82	3.58	50.11	3.84
Parent age	32.12	12.55	32.44	14.13	32.47	12.89	31.94	15.20
	%	*N*	%	*N*	%	*N*	%	*N*
Child gender (male)	53	16	50	12	44	14	46	12

(*continued*)

Table 4.3 (continued)

	Social competence screening				*Emotional competence screening*			
Child risk	30	9	29	7	28	9	27	7
Parent ethnicity	13	4	13	3	16	5	15	4
Low/moderate SES	43	13	33	8	38	12	35	9
Single parent	7	2	4	1	6	2	8	2
Parent depression	–	–	4	1	3	1	4	1
Parent risk	50	15	63	15	53	17	58	15
	Intervention low risk		**Control low risk**		**Intervention low risk**		**Control low risk**	
	M	*SD*	*M*	*SD*	*M*	*SD*	*M*	*SD*
Child age	49.38	3.22	49.62	4.21	49.32	3.26	49.62	3.63
Parent age	32.52	13.47	31.96	15.63	32.26	12.96	32.88	15.29
	%	*N*	*%*	*N*	*%*	*N*	*%*	*N*
Child gender (male)	33	14	30	10	37	15	31	10
Child risk	9	4	–	–	10	4	–	–
Parent ethnicity	16	7	12	4	15	6	13	4
Low/moderate SES	51	22	39	13	54	22	38	12
Single parent	9	4	9	3	12	5	9	3
Parent depression	–	–	–	–	–	–	–	–
Parent risk	28	12	42	14	29	12	41	13

Parents The parent sample included 87 parents in the intervention, and 69 in the control group, with mean ages of 32.2 (SD = 6.56) and 34.1 (SD = 7.21), respectively. Details concerning parental demographic and risk status for each risk category are provided in Tables 4.2 and 4.3. Parental risk status was denoted by low socio-economic status (for more details, see Chap. 3), single parenting, previous diagnosis of parent depression, and/or below cutoff scores on harsh/inconsistent discipline and parent stress scales.

Design

For the purposes of this study a 2 × 3 quasi-experimental design was employed, with a between-subject variable (SEP intervention vs. control), and a within-subject variable (pre-, postintervention, and 3 months' follow-up). The randomization was conducted at the classroom level, and outcome assessment was performed in an *intent to treat* approach, meaning that scores for all children were included in the analyses, irrespective of whether they received or did not receive the full intended intervention dosage (i.e., participating in at least 75% of the classroom curriculum activities).

Procedures

Procedures for sample selection and SEP implementation were described in detail in the corresponding section from Chap. 3. Also, a detailed account of procedures for establishing risk status was provided in the Introduction section of this chapter.

Intervention

The SEP was delivered as a hybrid prevention program encompassing strategies for both indicated and universal intervention levels. The SEP was developed as a multifocused approach encompassing child-, teacher-, and parent-focused strategies, which were described in Chap. 2. Also, a more in-depth presentation of the objectives and of the activities is provided in Appendices 1, 2, and 3, which correspond to the 3 components of the intervention: the classroom curriculum, the teacher training, and the parent training.

Measures

To determine changes in children's behaviors in the classroom and at home, a multi-informant (teacher, child), multi-method (questionnaire, experimental tasks) approach was employed to assess the intervention's efficacy.

Children's Classroom Behaviors Children's classroom behaviors were assessed employing 2 separate measures of children's social-emotional competencies: the *Social Competence Screening for Preschoolers – Teacher Form* (SCS-T; Miclea et al. 2010) and the *Emotional Competence Screening for Preschoolers – Teacher Form* (ECS-T; Miclea et al. 2010). Children's social competencies, as well as externalizing and internalizing problems, were assessed using the *Social Competence and Behavior Evaluation – Preschool Edition* (SCBE; LaFreniere and Dumas 1995). Further details about the psychometric properties of these instruments and cutoff scores were provided in Chap. 3. Additionally, 2 direct measures of children's emotion recognition and problem-solving were employed: a modified version of the *Affective Knowledge Test* (AKT; Denham 1986), and a modified version of the *Social Problem Solving Test* (SPST-R; Webster-Stratton 1990). Further details on the reliability of these measures were provided in Chap. 3.

Children's Behaviors at Home The *Social Competence Screening for Preschoolers – Parent Form* (SCS-P; Miclea et al. 2010) and the *Emotional Competence Screening for Preschoolers – Parent Form* (ECS-P; Miclea et al. 2010) were employed as parental measures of children's social-emotional development. Children's social skills were also assessed by their parents using the Social Competence scale from the *Social Skills Rating System – Preschool (Parent Form)* (SSRS; Gresham and Elliott 1990). The Behavior Problem summary scale from the SSRS (Gresham and Elliott 1990) was used to evaluate parental perceptions of children's maladaptive behaviors. Further details about these instruments were provided in Chap. 3.

Parental Self-Reports of Discipline Strategies and Stress In this study a modified version of the *LIFT Parenting Practices Interview* (PPI; Webster-Stratton et al. 2001) was employed to assess parents' use of discipline strategies. The measure included 5 of the 7 initial scales: Harsh Discipline, Inconsistent Discipline, Appropriate Discipline, Positive Parenting, and Monitoring. A confirmatory factor analysis using a principal component analysis (PCA) was employed to establish factor loadings, and items loading below .30 on a particular factor were dropped. The Harsh Discipline scale comprised 12 items (e.g., "Slap or hit your child"), the Inconsistent Discipline scale included 9 items (e.g., "Threaten to punish him/her (but not really punish him/her)"), the Appropriate Discipline scale included 11 items (e.g., "Take away privileges (like TV, playing with friends)"), the Positive Parenting scale comprised 10 items (e.g., "I believe in using rewards to teach my child how to behave"), and the Monitoring included 7 items (e.g., "Giving children lots of free, unsupervised time helps them learn to be more responsible"). Each item was coded on a 7-point Likert scale, where *1 = strongly disagree* and *7 = strongly agree.* Cronbach's α ranged between .68 and .82, except for the Monitoring scale for which we obtained $\alpha = .39$. As a result, this scale was dropped from the analyses due to its low internal consistency. Cutoff points for the Harsh and Inconsistent Discipline scales were computed using the split-half method.

Parent stress ratings were obtained from the *Parent Stress Index-Short Form* (PSI-SF, Abidin 1995). This measure contains 3 basic scales comprised of 12 items each: Parental Distress (e.g., "Since having a child I fell that I am almost never able to do things that I like to do"), Childrearing Stress (e.g., "My child seems to cry or fuss more often than most children"), and Difficult Child (e.g., "My child turned out to be more of a problem than I had expected"). A Total Stress score is derived by summing the results from the basic scale, and this was the measure used in this study. Each item was scored on a 5-point Likert scale, where *1 = strongly disagree* and *5 = strongly agree*. The internal consistency was high, ranging from .86 to .91. The cutoff score for at risk parents was also obtained using the split-half method.

Training Delivery and Attendance

Information about the training delivery and attendance rates for children, teachers, and parents was presented in Chap. 3.

Results

Data Analysis Strategy

In the following sections, the data are presented in 2 separate sections: (1) the first section includes results for children's classroom behaviors, based on teachers' ratings of emotional and social competence, according to each intervention level: indicated (emotional competence and social competence high-risk groups) and universal (emotional competence and social competence moderate-/low-risk groups); while (2) the second section includes results for children's behaviors at home and parental discipline practices, based on parents' ratings of children's risk, according to each intervention level. Both sections report results concerning attrition and group equivalence, as well as results from the efficacy testing of SEP. Data analysis was performed employing mixed analysis of variance (ANOVA). The results are reported in terms of group by time interaction effect, followed by paired samples *t* tests to establish separate within group effects. For within group analyses, the significance level was adjusted using the Bonferroni correction for multiple comparisons. As a significant interaction effect only indicates within group differences, and does not provide specific information about between group differences, independent samples *t* tests were also conducted on postintervention and follow-up scores. Besides statistical significance, effect sizes were computed employing Cohen's *d*.

Results for Children's Classroom Behaviors

Attrition and Group Equivalence Differences between dropouts and non-drops on risk and demographic variables were examined using *t* and chi-square tests separately for intervention and control groups. No significant differences were found between dropouts and non-drops. Also, analyses comparing children who remained in the study postintervention with those who completed preintervention assessments, showed no significant differences in the number of dropouts from the intervention and control groups.

Analysis comparing the baseline equivalence of the participants included in this study indicated that there were no significant differences on any demographic and risk factor variables between the intervention and the control group. Also, analyses comparing the intervention and control group on risk factors within each risk category were conducted, and no significant differences were found between the groups, except for the percentage of high-risk parents from the low-risk groups. Specifically, there were significantly more control group children (48.6%) with at risk parents compared to intervention group children (26.2%) in the low-risk emotional competence group, $\chi^2(1, N = 81) = 6.32$, $p < .01$; and significantly more control group children (53.1%) with at risk parents compared to intervention group children (30.8%) in the low-risk social competence control group, $\chi^2(1, N = 67) = 3.01$, $p < .05$.

The analysis of low-risk children tested for possible effects of parental risk on teacher ratings and performance in the child report tasks. Multivariate analysis of variance (MANOVAs) were conducted (2 groups × 3 times × 2 parent risk) yielding a significant risk by group interaction effect immediately postintervention for externalizing problems in the low-risk social competence group, $F(1, 70) = 4.10$, $p < .05$, and in the low-risk emotional competence group, $F(1, 76) = 4.01$, $p < .05$. Subsequent analyses indicated that control group children with at risk parents were rated significantly lower by teachers on externalizing problems than intervention group children from the social competence low-risk group, $t(27) = 2.28$, $p < .05$, and similar significant differences were found for the emotional competence low-risk group, $t(26) = 2.37$, $p < .05$. At follow-up, these differences were no longer significant.

Baseline Equivalence Significant preintervention differences were found for the child-report tasks on expressive and receptive emotion recognition and problem-solving. For these variables, analyses of covariance (ANCOVAs) were conducted by entering preintervention data as covariates in order to establish group differences. For all other variables no significant preintervention differences were found.

Results for the Indicated Intervention Level

Social Competence Screening: The High-Risk Groups Descriptive statistics, values of time by group interaction effects, within group comparisons, and effect sizes are presented in Table 4.4. For the teacher rated social competence, intervention group children were rated significantly better on the SCS-T compared to control group children, $t(25) = 2.57$, $p < .05$. A similar effect was detected for the SCBE teacher-rated social-emotional competencies, $t(25) = 2.66$, $p < .05$. At follow-up, results confirmed that SEP effects were maintained for both the SCS-T, $t(25) = 2.32$, $p < .05$, and the SCBE, $t(25) = 2.16$, $p < .05$.
Conversely, independent samples *t* test indicated that intervention group children were rated significantly better by their teachers compared to control group children on the ECS-T, $t(25) = 2.29$, $p < .05$, and subsequent analysis revealed that the intervention's effects were maintained at follow-up, $t(25) = 2.60$, $p < .05$. Teachers also rated intervention group children significantly lower on levels of externalizing problems, $t(25) = 2.27$, $p < .05$, as well as on levels of internalizing problems compared to their control group counterparts, $t(25) = 3.05$, $p < .01$. For both measures, follow-up analyses confirmed that SEP effects were maintained, $t(25) = 3.08$, $p < .01$, and $t(25) = 3.45$, $p < .01$, respectively.

The presence of baseline significant differences between the intervention and control groups on all child report measures prompted the use of ANCOVAs. The results indicated that SEP participation was associated with significantly more recognized emotions, $t(25) = 2.10$, $p < .05$, significantly more positive problem-solving strategies, $t(25) = 2.56$, $p < .05$, as well as significantly less negative solutions, $t(25) = -2.12$, $p < .05$. ANCOVA covarying preintervention scores on follow-up data indicated that SEP effects were maintained for emotion recognition, $t(25) = 2.99$, $p < .01$, positive problem-solving strategies, $t(25) = 2.00$, $p < .05$, as well as negative problem-solving strategies, $t(25) = 2.99$, $p < .01$.

Table 4.4 Intervention effects on children's classroom behaviors and declarative knowledge for the high-risk social competence groups

	Preintervention		*Postintervention*		*Follow-up*		*Mixed ANOVA*	*Pre-post paired t test*		*Pre-FU paired t test*		*Cohen d*
Measures	*M*	*SD*	*M*	*SD*	*M*	*SD*		*INT*	*CTRL*	*INT*	*CTRL*	
SCS-T							5.16**	7.56***	2.27	9.73***	3.99**	0.96
Intervention	40.75	4.84	51.50	8.38	54.06	6.27						
Control	42.00	3.13	45.00	4.69	48.65	5.48						
ECS-T							10.46***	5.75***	1.61	10.01***	4.05**	0.90
Intervention	34.88	3.32	44.00	6.04	45.63	4.22						
Control	37.36	4.18	39.18	4.62	41.91	2.59						
SCBE social competence							4.15*	9.93***	3.67*	7.72***	3.41*	1.05
Intervention	71.50	18.55	102.86	15.11	114.31	14.78						
Control	68.45	18.14	87.27	14.72	103.18	10.21						
SCBE externalizing							3.77*	4.60**	1.29	4.28**	1.19	0.87
Intervention	63.19	14.40	73.50	10.61	78.50	13.74						
Control	59.18	12.14	62.91	13.66	62.64	12.24						
SCBE internalizing							8.24**	3.41*	0.53	4.75**	2.37	1.21
Intervention	63.13	13.66	71.81	9.57	78.00	5.89						
Control	59.73	6.08	60.00	8.22	67.27	9.48						
AKT expressive							9.60***	5.14***	1.84	6.73***	1.35	0.60
Intervention	2.44	2.00	5.50	1.71	6.06	1.61						
Control	4.09	1.81	5.00	1.73	4.73	1.42						

Positive problem-solving							6.54**	5.72***	1.37	5.18***	2.92†	0.64
Intervention	0.29	0.21	0.73	0.20	0.78	0.19						
Control	0.47	0.27	0.57	0.29	0.68	0.22						
Negative problem-solving							3.78*	−2.84†	1.00	−2.46†	−0.41	0.71
Intervention	0.10	0.13	0.01	0.05	0.01	0.05						
Control	0.07	0.12	0.08	0.13	0.05	0.09						

*$p < .05$, **$p < .01$, ***$p < .001$, †$p < .10$ statistically marginal effect

Emotional Competence Screening: The High-Risk Groups Descriptive statistics, values of time by group interaction effects, within group comparisons, and effect sizes are presented in Table 4.5. The results indicated that intervention group children were rated significantly higher than control group children on the ECS-T, $t(26) = 2.44$, $p < .05$. At follow-up, between group comparisons confirmed that the intervention's effect was maintained, $t(26) = 2.81$, $p < .01$.

Although a significant time by group interaction effect was found for the SCS-T, there was no significant difference between the intervention and the control group postintervention. Further analyses indicated that the difference became significant at follow-up, $t(26) = 2.03$, $p < .05$, but this effect cannot be attributed to the intervention. Teacher rated social-emotional competencies employing SCBE showed a marginally significant interaction effect, and therefore, no significant difference between intervention and control group children was found for this measure.

Also, intervention group children exhibited significantly less externalizing problems, $t(26) = 2.18$, $p < .05$, as well as significantly less internalizing problems, $t(26) = 3.02$, $p < .01$ compared to control group children. Analyses on follow-up scores showed that children from the intervention group were still rated lower compared to their control group counterparts on measures of externalizing problems, $t(26) = 3.35$, $p < .01$, and internalizing problems, $t(26) = 2.80$, $p < .01$.

Analysis of the data from the expressive task showed that the rate of improvement regarding the ability to correctly name emotions was significantly higher for the intervention group compared to the control group, $t(26) = 2.08$, $p < .05$. At follow-up, the intervention's effects were maintained, $t(26) = 3.08$, $p < .01$. However, no significant interaction effects were found for either positive or negative problem-solving strategies.

Results for the Universal Intervention Level

Social Competence Screening: The Moderate-Risk Groups Descriptive statistics, values of time by group interaction effects, within group comparisons, and effect sizes are presented in Table 4.6. The results indicated that intervention group children were rated significantly higher on the SCS-T, $t(58) = 2.42$, $p < .05$, as well as SCBE, $t(58) = 2.17$, $p < .05$. The intervention's effects were maintained at follow-up for both measures, namely the SCS-T, $t(58) = 2.30$, $p < .05$, and the SCBE, $t(58) = 2.82$, $p < .01$. Also, intervention group children were rated significantly better

Table 4.5 Intervention effects on children's classroom behaviors and declarative knowledge for high risk emotional competence groups

	Preintervention		*Postintervention*		*Follow-up*		*Mixed ANOVA*	*Pre-post paired t test*		*Pre-FU paired t test*		*Cohen d*
Measures	*M*	*SD*	*M*	*SD*	*M*	*SD*		*INT*	*CTRL*	*INT*	*CTRL*	
ECS-T							9.27***	7.81***	4.37**	11.60***	9.59***	0.97
Intervention	33.50	1.97	44.50	6.47	45.92	4.68						
Control	34.58	1.56	39.17	4.24	41.75	2.45						
SCS-T							7.96**	6.44***	2.29	8.61***	3.22†	
Intervention	43.75	6.77	54.19	8.57	55.69	7.20						
Control	46.33	6.44	49.50	7.38	50.58	5.60						
SCBE social competence							3.58†	9.47***	3.48*	8.41***	5.85***	
Intervention	77.69	22.28	106.88	15.00	116.75	13.19						
Control	84.92	20.39	101.00	20.35	112.25	18.91						
SCBE externalizing							11.16***	6.02***	1.56	7.57***	2.82†	0.86
Intervention	61.94	13.52	74.13	7.84	83.44	10.34						
Control	61.00	14.83	65.00	12.79	68.58	13.12						
SCBE internalizing							6.40**	4.39**	−0.07	4.58**	1.47	1.17
Intervention	61.06	14.41	73.31	7.26	77.06	7.42						
Control	65.33	7.23	65.50	6.05	69.50	7.87						
AKT expressive							10.46**	6.55***	4.10**	6.76***	3.19†	0.80
Intervention	2.38	1.96	5.75	1.53	6.19	1.52						
Control	3.33	1.50	4.58	1.38	4.50	1.31						
Positive problem-solving							2.97†	5.70***	1.51	7.66***	2.57†	

(*continued*)

Table 4.5 (continued)

Measures	*Preintervention*		*Postintervention*		*Follow-up*		*Mixed ANOVA*	*Pre-post paired t test*		*Pre-FU paired t test*		*Cohen d*
	M	*SD*	*M*	*SD*	*M*	*SD*		*INT*	*CTRL*	*INT*	*CTRL*	
Intervention	0.36	0.23	0.71	0.23	0.76	0.22						
Control	0.48	0.27	0.63	0.32	0.69	0.25						
Negative problem-solving							1.45	−2.15	0.00	−1.76	−1.00	
Intervention	0.07	0.11	0.01	0.05	0.01	0.05						
Control	0.03	0.08	0.03	0.08	0.02	0.06						

$^{*}p < .05$, $^{**}p < .01$, $^{***}p < .001$, $^{\dagger}p < .10$ statistically marginal effect

Table 4.6 Intervention effects on children's classroom behaviors and declarative knowledge for moderate-risk social competence groups

	Preintervention		*Postintervention*		*Follow-up*		*Mixed ANOVA*	*Pre-post paired t test*		*Pre-FU paired t test*		*Cohen d*
Measures	*M*	*SD*	*M*	*SD*	*M*	*SD*		*INT*	*CTRL*	*INT*	*CTRL*	
SCS-T							7.40**	7.14***	5.32***	9.16***	4.21**	0.58
Intervention	51.79	3.22	59.53	6.68	60.74	5.82						
Control	53.19	2.28	56.38	3.84	57.54	5.25						
ECS-T							4.30*	6.22***	4.80***	10.53***	4.60**	0.52
Intervention	41.41	3.77	47.21	5.60	50.09	4.87						
Control	41.58	4.29	44.73	3.77	46.73	6.02						
SCBE social competence							4.17**	7.90***	4.82***	9.19***	4.30**	0.56
Intervention	99.50	20.01	121.79	16.72	129.44	16.35						
Control	99.19	16.68	112.00	18.18	117.46	16.32						
SCBE externalizing							7.10**	5.59***	1.71	7.52***	3.99**	0.58
Intervention	65.38	14.61	76.38	10.19	80.82	9.68						
Control	67.42	14.49	70.19	11.12	74.85	11.34						
SCBE internalizing							3.97*	3.59*	1.43	4.09**	3.22**	0.52
Intervention	68.74	11.95	74.35	7.69	76.71	7.45						
Control	64.21	10.41	69.08	8.37	71.65	7.46						
AKT expressive							10.62***	7.63***	0.86	6.46***	1.52	0.83
Intervention	3.24	2.18	6.18	1.80	6.26	1.29						
Control	4.19	2.21	4.58	2.04	5.00	1.90						
Positive problem-solving							3.56*	6.37***	2.81†	7.92***	3.75**	0.62

(*continued*)

Table 4.6 (continued)

	Preintervention		*Postintervention*		*Follow-up*		*Mixed ANOVA*	*Pre-post paired t test*		*Pre-FU paired t test*		*Cohen d*
Measures	*M*	*SD*	*M*	*SD*	*M*	*SD*		*INT*	*CTRL*	*INT*	*CTRL*	
Intervention	0.51	0.29	0.78	0.25	0.81	0.20						
Control	0.47	0.28	0.61	0.30	0.68	0.30						
Negative problem-solving							$2.33^{\dagger}$	−1.38	1.71	−2.42	−0.25	
Intervention	0.03	0.07	0.01	0.05	0.00	0.00						
Control	0.04	0.09	0.07	0.11	0.02	0.07						

$^{*}p < .05$, $^{**}p < .01$, $^{***}p < .001$, $^{\dagger}p < .10$ statistically marginal effect

than control group children immediately postintervention on the ECS-T, $t(58) = 2.04$, $p < .05$, and these effects were still detectable at follow-up, $t(33) = 2.32$, $p < .05$.
Also, intervention group children were rated significantly lower by their teachers on externalizing problems, $t(58) = 2.24$, $p < .05$, as well as on internalizing problems, $t(58) = 2.46$, $p < .05$, compared to the control group children. At follow-up, the intervention's effects on externalizing problems $t(58) = 2.20$, $p < .05$, and internalizing problems $t(58) = 2.51$, $p < .05$, were maintained.

For the child-report tasks, the results indicated that intervention group children correctly named significantly more emotions compared to control group children postintervention, $t(58) = 3.22$, $p< .01$, and at follow-up, $t(58) = 2.92$, $p < .01$. Similar results were obtained for children's positive problem-solving, $t(58) = 2.39$, $p < .01$. Moreover, follow-up data showed that SEP participation was still associated with more positive problem-solving strategies suggesting that the intervention's effect was maintained, $t(58) = 2.03$, $p < .05$. No significant difference between groups was found for negative problem-solving strategies.

Social Competence Screening: The Low-Risk Groups Descriptive statistics, values of time by group interaction effects, within group comparisons and effect sizes are presented in Table 4.7. For teacher rated social competencies employing the SCS-T and the SCBE significant interaction effects were detected. However, independent samples *t* tests indicated there were no significant postintervention changes in ratings of children's competence in the intervention group compared to the control group ($ps > .05$). Conversely, intervention group children were rated significantly higher by their teachers compared to control group children on the ECS-T, $t(69) = 3.37$, $p < .05$. It is also notable that SEP effects were maintained as suggested by the follow-up analysis, $t(69) = 2.51$, $p < .05$.

On the SCBE teacher ratings of externalizing problems, intervention group children were assessed as exhibiting significantly lower levels of externalizing problems than control group children postintervention, $t(69) = 2.16$, $p < .05$. Subsequent analysis on follow-up data confirmed that the SEP effect on externalizing problems was maintained, $t(69) = 2.15$, $p < .05$. However, the presence of an immediate postintervention effect should be interpreted cautiously, because group risk status analyses showed that control group children with at risk parents were rated significantly lower on this measure compared to intervention group children with at risk parents. When considering this effect, only a marginally significant effect was found in favor of the intervention group ($p < .10$).

Table 4.7 Intervention effects on children's classroom behaviors and declarative knowledge for low-risk social competence groups

	Preintervention		*Postintervention*		*Follow-up*		*Mixed ANOVA*	*Pre-Post paired t test*		*Pre-FU paired t test*		*Cohen d*
Measures	*M*	*SD*	*M*	*SD*	*M*	*SD*		*INT*	*CTRL*	*INT*	*CTRL*	
SCS-T							5.98**	2.51†	0.20	2.48†	−1.82	
Intervention	64.05	5.01	66.46	6.13	66.66	5.43						
Control	64.00	6.71	64.13	6.37	62.19	7.06						
ECS-T							7.95**	3.03*	0.29	4.08**	1.45	0.80
Intervention	50.97	4.90	52.97	3.90	53.72	4.22						
Control	49.75	3.56	49.53	4.70	51.00	4.78						
SCBE social competence							11.21***	4.47***	−0.28	5.46***	−0.64	
Intervention	137.74	25.82	146.87	20.57	154.74	20.10						
Control	139.28	24.56	138.38	19.30	136.78	20.79						
SCBE externalizing							4.44*	3.37**	1.40	6.26***	5.18***	0.52
Intervention	75.36	14.29	80.95	8.09	86.28	8.13						
Control	73.72	8.81	76.28	11.53	82.16	7.95						
SCBE internalizing							4.37*	3.39**	2.51	4.74***	3.82**	
Intervention	73.77	10.77	78.21	8.69	80.64	6.20						
Control	72.00	7.56	74.69	6.37	76.94	6.39						
AKT expressive							0.59	3.55**	3.01*	5.45**	3.68**	
Intervention	4.08	1.90	5.46	1.55	6.08	1.44						
Control	3.97	2.15	5.00	1.90	5.44	1.98						

Positive problem-solving							4.66*	5.36***	1.72	3.68**	1.88	0.65
Intervention	0.57	0.26	0.78	0.24	0.78	0.28						
Control	0.55	0.30	0.61	0.28	0.66	0.27						
Negative problem-solving							0.43	−1.71	−1.67	−1.93	−1.00	
Intervention	0.03	0.08	0.01	0.04	0.01	0.03						
Control	0.03	0.07	0.01	0.04	0.02	0.07						

* $p < .05$, ** $p < .01$, *** $p < .001$, † $p < .10$ statistically marginal effect

The results also suggested that no significant group differences were found for the expressive emotion recognition task. However, intervention group children proposed significantly more positive problem-solving strategies than control group children, $t(69) = 2.72$, $p < .05$, and this trend was confirmed at follow-up, $t(69) = 2.07$, $p < .05$. Regarding negative problem-solving strategies, no significant interaction effect was found.

Emotional Competence Screening: The Moderate-Risk Groups

Descriptive statistics, values of time by group interaction effects, within group comparisons, and effect sizes are presented in Table 4.8. Analyses of teacher ratings showed that intervention group children were rated significantly higher than control group children on the ECS-T, $t(50) = 2.65$, $p < .01$. At follow-up, SEP effects were maintained as intervention group children obtained significantly higher scores compared to their control group counterparts on the ECS-T, $t(50) = 2.06$, $p < .05$. Ratings of social competence based on the screening showed a significant interaction effect, but only a marginally significant trend for postintervention scores on SCS-T. Similarly, for the SCBE significant group differences were found between intervention and control group children. Taken together, these results suggest that no significant SEP effects were found for these measures.

Intervention group children were rated by their teachers as exhibiting significantly lower levels of externalizing problems compared to control group children on the SCBE, $t(50) = 2.10$, $p < .05$, and the SEP effect was maintained at follow-up, $t(50) = 2.95$, $p < .01$. Although a significant time by group interaction effect was found for internalizing problems, there was no significant group difference, suggesting that the intervention did not exert effects on children's internalizing problems.

Also, intervention group children were able to name significantly more emotions compared to their control group counterparts, $t(50) = 3.01$, $p < .01$. The SEP effect on expressive emotion recognition was maintained at follow-up, $t(50) = 2.78$, $p < .01$. Also, the results indicated that intervention group children proposed significantly more prosocial strategies in managing potential conflict situations postintervention compared to control group children, both postintervention $t(50) = 3.36$, $p < .01$, and at follow-up, $t(50) = 3.10$, $p < .01$.

Table 4.8 Intervention effects on children's classroom behaviors and declarative knowledge for moderate-risk emotional competence groups

	Preintervention		*Postintervention*		*Follow-up*		*Mixed ANOVA*	*Pre-Post paired t test*		*Pre-FU paired t test*		*Cohen d*
Measures	*M*	*SD*	*M*	*SD*	*M*	*SD*		*INT*	*CTRL*	*INT*	*CTRL*	
ECS-T							7.46**	6.96***	2.39	11.67***	3.16**	0.92
Intervention	41.26	2.07	47.06	5.19	49.58	4.62						
Control	42.55	1.74	44.09	2.71	46.77	6.23						
SCS-T							6.60**	6.70***	5.43***	8.88***	3.36**	
Intervention	50.13	5.35	57.58	5.68	59.42	5.18						
Control	51.82	5.39	54.77	6.17	56.14	6.07						
SCBE social competence							1.47	5.94***	4.22**	5.59***	3.37**	
Intervention	99.13	21.96	119.65	17.55	125.42	25.99						
Control	97.59	28.01	109.55	23.17	115.27	17.11						
SCBE externalizing							10.25***	5.03***	−0.25	8.20***	2.60†	0.57
Intervention	64.77	15.24	73.61	12.63	79.00	10.14						
Control	65.95	13.38	65.55	15.34	69.18	14.08						
SCBE internalizing							3.23*	1.90	1.04	4.33***	3.59**	
Intervention	68.87	11.31	71.97	9.39	76.58	6.10						
Control	65.86	10.43	67.27	10.77	71.81	8.88						
AKT expressive							7.04***	7.22***	0.53	7.01***	1.29	0.82
Intervention	3.10	2.06	6.06	1.91	6.10	1.30						
Control	4.05	2.21	4.32	2.30	4.77	1.95						

(*continued*)

Table 4.8 (continued)

Measures	Preintervention		Postintervention		Follow-up		Mixed ANOVA	Pre-Post paired t test		Pre-FU paired t test		Cohen d
	M	SD	M	SD	M	SD		INT	CTRL	INT	CTRL	
Positive problem-solving							6.61**	6.42***	2.58†	6.41***	3.79**	0.99
Intervention	0.46	0.29	0.84	0.19	0.85	0.17						
Control	0.46	0.31	0.61	0.27	0.84	0.19						
Negative problem-solving							3.02*	8.38***	3.28*	8.71***	3.13*	
Intervention	0.04	0.09	0.01	0.04	0.00	0.00						
Control	0.04	0.10	0.07	0.12	0.04	0.08						

*$p < .05$, **$p < .01$, ***$p < .001$, †$p < .10$ statistically marginal effect

Emotional Competence Screening: The Low-Risk Groups Descriptive statistics, values of time by group interaction effects, within group comparisons, and effect sizes are presented in Table 4.9. Significant postintervention effects were obtained on the ECS-T, $t(75) = 2.99$, $p < .01$, which were maintained at follow-up, $t(75) = 2.45$, $p < .05$. Also, intervention group children were rated significantly higher compared to control group children on the SCS-T postintervention, $t(75) = 2.00$, $p < .05$, as well as at follow-up, $t(75) = 2.79$, $p < .05$. However, no significant difference was found between intervention and control group children on the SCBE ratings of social-emotional competence.

Although significant interaction effects were obtained for teacher rated externalizing and internalizing problems, the differences were only marginally significant in favor of the intervention group. Only at follow-up, were intervention group children rated by their teachers significantly lower on externalizing problems, $t(75) = 2.13$, $p < .05$, as well as internalizing problems than control group children, $t(75) = 3.04$, $p < .01$. However, these differences cannot be attributed to the intervention's efficacy.

For expressive emotion recognition, there were significantly more emotional displays correctly recognized by intervention group children compared to control group children, $t(50) = 2.01$, $p < .05$. At follow-up, the group difference was only marginally significant in favor of the intervention group ($p < .10$), indicating that the intervention's effect was not maintained. Also, postintervention group comparisons showed that intervention group children proposed significantly more positive problem-solving strategies compared to control group children, $t(50) = 3.34$, $p < .01$, but this effect was no longer significant at follow-up ($p > .05$).

Results for Children's Behaviors at Home and Parenting Practices

Attrition and Group Equivalence The analyses comparing children who remained in the project at follow-up with those who completed preintervention assessments showed no significant differences in the number of dropouts. Differences between dropouts and non-drops on risk and demographic variables were examined using *t* and chi-square tests separately for the intervention and the control group, and no significant differences were found. Analyses comparing the intervention and control group participants who remained in the study at follow-up yielded no significant differences on any demographic or risk factor variables. Further testing of group equivalence on demographic and risk factor variables was conducted within each risk category, but revealed that intervention and control groups did not differ significantly.

Table 4.9 Intervention effects on children's classroom behaviors and declarative knowledge for low-risk emotional competence groups

	Preintervention		*Postintervention*		*Follow-up*		*Mixed ANOVA*	*Pre-post paired t test*		*Pre-FU paired t test*		*Cohen d*
Measures	*M*	*SD*	*M*	*SD*	*M*	*SD*		*INT*	*CTRL*	*INT*	*CTRL*	
ECS-T							7.66**	2.88*	0.50	3.77**	1.69	0.68
Intervention	51.07	4.54	52.97	4.17	53.52	4.62						
Control	49.65	3.29	50.03	4.46	50.97	4.52						
SCS-T							4.76*	3.68***	0.87	3.93***	0.05	0.46
Intervention	63.05	5.25	66.24	6.41	66.69	5.65						
Control	62.71	7.33	63.26	6.67	62.66	7.06						
SCBE social competence							8.62**	5.03***	0.99	7.01***	0.52	
Intervention	131.60	29.22	142.98	20.75	152.24	21.03						
Control	131.20	29.73	134.46	22.50	133.49	20.69						
SCBE externalizing							4.97*	3.84**	2.12	7.21***	4.56***	
Intervention	74.33	13.90	80.76	8.08	85.88	8.17						
Control	71.85	11.85	76.20	12.46	81.11	11.42						
SCBE internalizing							5.07**	3.34**	2.90*	4.91***	4.10***	
Intervention	73.45	10.42	77.57	8.17	80.86	5.65						
Control	70.77	8.89	74.17	6.71	76.69	6.38						
AKT expressive							3.21*	4.57***	2.01	6.13***	3.17*	0.45
Intervention	3.95	2.05	5.69	1.35	6.19	1.52						
Control	4.26	2.16	4.94	1.91	5.49	4.94						

Positive problem-solving							8.62**	4.51***	1.46	3.07*	2.88*	0.75
Intervention	0.59	0.25	0.77	0.25	0.76	0.28						
Control	0.49	0.28	0.57	0.28	0.66	0.27						
Negative problem-solving							0.71	−1.69	−0.24	−2.67†	−2.67†	
Intervention	0.03	0.08	0.01	0.04	0.00	0.00						
Control	0.03	0.08	0.03	0.10	0.01	0.03						

*$p < .05$, **$p < .01$, ***$p < .001$, †$p < .10$ statistically marginal effect

Baseline Equivalence For all outcome variables, independent samples *t* tests were performed on preintervention scores to determine baseline equivalence. The results indicated that there were significant preintervention differences on expressive emotion recognition in the high-risk social competence group and on the ECS-P in the low-risk emotional competence group. Where parental behaviors were concerned, preintervention significant differences were found for appropriate discipline in the high-risk emotional competence group. For these measures, ANCOVAs covarying preintervention on postintervention and follow-up data, were employed for establishing SEP efficacy.

Results for the Indicated Intervention

Social Competence Screening: The High-Risk Groups Descriptive statistics, values of time by group interaction effects, within group comparisons, and effect sizes are presented in Tables 4.10 and 4.11. The results for parent rated social skills suggest that intervention group children improved significantly compared to their control group counterparts on the SCS-P, $t(26) = 2.21$, $p < .05$, as well as on the SSRS, $t(26) = 2.01$, $p < .05$. Follow-up group differences were still in favor of the intervention group on both measures of children's competencies, $t(26) = 2.26$, $p < .05$, and $t(26) = 2.10$, $p < .05$, respectively.
For externalizing problems, there was only a marginally significant difference in favor of the intervention group postintervention ($p < .10$). However, when the difference was computed for children whose parents attended the intervention, the intervention group scored significantly lower on externalizing problems than the control group, $t(18) = -2.04$, $p < .05$.

Results for children's emotion knowledge were established employing ANCOVA, and the outcome indicated that intervention group children outperformed control group children, $t(26) = 2.14$, $p < .05$. Also, the SEP effect was maintained at follow-up, $t(26) = 3.70$, $p < .01$. Conversely, results for problem-solving strategies showed that intervention group children provided significantly more prosocial answers compared to control group children immediately postintervention, $t(26) = 2.01$, $p < .05$, and at follow-up, $t(26) = 2.18$, $p < .05$.

In relation to parent outcomes, intervention group parents reported employing significantly more often appropriate discipline strategies, positive parenting strategies, and significantly less inconsistent discipline strategies from pre- to postintervention. However, there were no significant

Table 4.10 Intervention effects on children's behaviors at home and declarative knowledge for high-risk social competence groups

	Preintervention		*Postintervention*		*Follow-up*		*Mixed ANOVA*	*Pre-post paired t test*		*Pre-FU paired t test*		*Cohen d*
Measures	*M*	*SD*	*M*	*SD*	*M*	*SD*		*INT*	*CTRL*	*INT*	*CTRL*	
SCS-P							5.04**	9.62***	6.18***	9.59***	6.53***	0.85
Intervention	35.12	1.59	41.44	2.68	44.38	3.12						
Control	35.33	1.37	39.25	2.45	41.50	3.61						
SSRS social competence							8.64***	8.60***	5.23**	6.51***	5.14**	0.77
Intervention	40.44	6.32	50.56	4.56	55.12	4.68						
Control	43.00	4.26	47.17	4.22	50.92	5.92						
ECS-P							3.51*	8.11***	2.03	8.91***	7.00***	
Intervention	46.88	4.92	52.00	4.31	54.00	3.90						
Control	47.92	4.32	50.08	5.63	53.25	5.31						
SSRS behavior problems							8.56**	−5.91***	−1.17	−6.14***	−1.54	
Intervention	5.00	1.67	3.06	1.39	2.38	1.41						
Control	4.42	1.88	4.08	1.44	3.75	1.60						
AKT expressive emotion recognition							7.56**	4.28***	0.62	5.62***	0.54	0.55
Intervention	2.63	2.33	5.69	2.21	6.06	1.48						
Control	4.08	2.07	4.42	2.39	4.33	1.61						

(*continued*)

Table 4.10 (continued)

	Preintervention		*Postintervention*		*Follow-up*		*Mixed ANOVA*	*Pre-post paired t test*		*Pre-FU paired t test*		*Cohen d*
Measures	*M*	*SD*	*M*	*SD*	*M*	*SD*		*INT*	*CTRL*	*INT*	*CTRL*	
Positive problem-solving strategies							4.52*	4.50**	0.53	6.85***	1.10	0.75
Intervention	0.38	0.31	0.68	0.22	0.79	0.30						
Control	0.44	0.29	0.49	0.28	0.56	0.26						
Negative problem-solving strategies							2.51†	−2.15	−1.00	−1.77	−1.00	
Intervention	0.07	0.11	0.01	0.05	0.01	0.05						
Control	0.04	0.11	0.06	0.11	0.03	0.08						

*$p < .05$, **$p < .01$, ***$p < .001$, †$p < .10$ statistically marginal effect

Table 4.11 Intervention effects on discipline and stress for children's parents from the high-risk social competence groups

	Preintervention		*Postintervention*		*Follow-up*		*Mixed ANOVA*	*Pre-post paired t test*		*Pre-FU paired t test*		*Cohen d*
Measures	*M*	*SD*	*M*	*SD*	*M*	*SD*		*INT*	*CTRL*	*INT*	*CTRL*	
Harsh discipline							1.57	−1.52	0.49	−1.98	−0.12	
Intervention	2.68	0.50	2.54	0.46	2.50	0.40						
Control	2.59	0.70	2.64	0.72	2.58	0.67						
Inconsistent discipline							5.97**	−3.07*	0.82	−3.35*	0.70	
Intervention	3.10	0.73	2.76	0.57	2.77	0.58						
Control	3.06	0.88	3.14	0.99	3.15	0.85						
Appropriate discipline							6.91**	4.77**	0.86	5.55***	0.92	
Intervention	4.24	0.75	4.76	0.73	4.78	0.70						
Control	4.61	0.80	4.68	0.76	4.72	0.76						
Positive parenting							3.19*	3.06*	0.49	2.95*	0.41	
Intervention	5.70	0.63	6.04	0.60	6.03	0.57						
Control	5.65	0.54	5.69	0.43	5.69	0.42						
Parent stress							1.38	−1.31	−0.30	−2.54†	−0.51	
Intervention	74.13	14.44	69.93	14.06	66.25	13.69						
Control	75.50	9.44	74.67	11.12	74.00	11.29						

*$p < .05$, **$p < .01$, ***$p < .001$, †$p < .10$ statistically marginal effect

differences ($ps > .05$) between the intervention and comparison groups immediately postintervention or at follow-up on any of these measures. No significant changes were found for harsh discipline or parent stress ($ps > .05$).

Emotional Competence Screening: The High-Risk Groups Descriptive statistics, values of time by group interaction effects, within group comparisons, and effect sizes are presented in Tables 4.12 and 4.13. Intervention group children were evaluated significantly higher by their parents than control group children on the ECS-P, $t(25) = 2.00$, $p < .05$. Analysis on follow-up scores showed that the intervention's effects on emotional competencies were maintained, $t(25) = 2.16$, $p < .05$. However, no significant intervention effects were detected on the SCS-P and the SSRS.

For parent rated externalizing problems, no significant group differences were found. However, when the difference was computed only for children whose parents attended the intervention the difference was significant, $t(20) = -2.49$, $p < .05$. At follow-up, again the group difference was maintained for those children whose parents attended 3 or more parent training sessions, $t(20) = -2.36$, $p < .05$.

Results for children's ability to name emotions suggested that significant pre- to postintervention effects were found for intervention group children, but their progress was only marginally significant ($p < .10$) compared to the control group. When similar analyses were performed for children's use of positive problem-solving strategies, the results suggested that intervention group children generated significantly more positive problem-solving strategies compared to control group children, $t(25) = 2.15$, $p < .05$. However, at follow-up the difference in favor of the intervention group was only marginally significant ($p < .10$), indicating that the intervention did not maintain its effects. No significant intervention effect was found on negative problem-solving strategies.

For parent related outcomes no significant group differences were obtained for any of the measures of parental discipline or stress ($ps > .05$). Although the intervention did not exert effects in terms of between group difference, it is noteworthy that pairwise comparisons suggested that postintervention the frequency of inconsistent discipline strategies has significantly ($p> .05$) decreased compared to preintervention for intervention group parent. Also, intervention group parents were found to use significantly ($ps < .05$) more praise and rewards for appropriate behavior from pre- to postintervention.

Table 4.12 Intervention effects on children's behaviors at home and declarative knowledge for high-risk emotional competence groups

	Preintervention		*Postintervention*		*Follow-up*		*Mixed ANOVA*	*Pre-post paired t test*		*Pre-FU paired t test*		*Cohen d*
Measures	*M*	*SD*	*M*	*SD*	*M*	*SD*		*INT*	*CTRL*	*INT*	*CTRL*	
ECS-P							9.32**	8.92***	6.89***	13.29***	8.86***	0.85
Intervention	43.06	2.17	50.06	3.60	52.25	2.67						
Control	43.82	2.27	47.36	2.73	49.73	2.97						
SCS-P							0.72	5.44***	4.89**	7.60***	5.27**	
Intervention	39.64	5.59	44.44	4.16	46.38	4.77						
Control	40.18	5.72	44.27	5.14	45.45	5.84						
SSRS social competence							0.67	4.81**	2.01	4.92**	2.08	
Intervention	45.50	10.01	52.94	6.60	55.19	5.60						
Control	46.82	6.87	52.18	10.58	53.27	11.12						
SSRS externalizing							5.05*	−8.54***	−5.24**	−9.91***	−3.54*	
Intervention	5.68	1.14	3.44	1.52	2.63	1.15						
Control	5.36	1.43	4.36	1.63	3.64	1.69						
AKT expressive							4.86*	4.27**	1.27	4.55**	1.89	
Intervention	2.31	2.15	5.31	1.45	5.62	1.45						
Control	3.27	2.24	4.27	1.27	4.55	1.37						
Positive problem-solving							3.93*	5.41***	0.61	5.53***	0.94	0.80
Intervention	0.43	0.27	0.77	0.22	0.76	0.25						
Control	0.49	0.34	0.56	0.30	0.60	0.18						
Negative problem-solving							0.20	−1.90	−0.55	−2.27	−1.50	
Intervention	0.05	0.09	0.01	0.05	0.00	0.00						
Control	0.05	0.09	0.04	0.08	0.02	0.06						

$^{*}p < .05$, $^{**}p < .01$, $^{***}p < .001$, $^{\dagger}p < .10$ statistically marginal effect

Table 4.13 Intervention effects on discipline and stress for children's parents from the high-risk emotional competence groups

	Preintervention		*Postintervention*		*Follow-up*		*Mixed ANOVA*	*Pre-post paired t test*		*Pre-FU paired t test*		*Cohen d*
Measures	*M*	*SD*	*M*	*SD*	*M*	*SD*		*INT*	*CTRL*	*INT*	*CTRL*	
Harsh discipline							2.89†	−1.07	0.11	−2.16	0.71	
Intervention	2.70	0.67	2.59	0.52	2.45	0.57						
Control	2.52	0.54	2.53	0.73	2.58	0.66						
Inconsistent discipline							7.20**	−3.10*	1.19	3.32*	0.78	
Intervention	3.22	0.86	2.88	0.60	2.80	0.57						
Control	2.70	0.71	2.83	0.97	2.78	0.84						
Appropriate discipline							4.94*	3.47*	0.36	4.07**	0.32	
Intervention	4.49	0.66	4.84	0.67	4.86	0.69						
Control	4.91	0.44	4.94	0.57	4.94	0.50						
Positive parenting							3.64*	3.16*	0.27	3.37*	0.19	
Intervention	5.70	0.63	6.04	0.60	6.03	0.57						
Control	5.65	0.54	5.69	0.43	5.69	0.42						
Parent stress							3.22†	−1.52	0.22	−2.89†	0.98	
Intervention	77.06	18.13	75.25	13.55	67.43	12.08						
Control	66.91	11.91	67.67	15.38	70.45	16.96						

$^{*}p < .05$, $^{**}p < .01$, $^{***}p < .001$, $^{\dagger}p < .10$ statistically marginal effect

Results for the Universal Intervention

Social Competence Screening: The Moderate-Risk Groups Descriptive statistics, values of time by group interaction effects, within group comparisons, and effect sizes are presented in Tables 4.14 and 4.15. The intervention group children were rated significantly higher on social skills in comparison to the control group children on the SCS-P, $t(52) = 2.60$, $p < .05$. Moreover, parent ratings on this measure of social competence were still significantly higher for intervention group children at follow-up, $t(52) = 2.07$, $p < .05$, indicating that the SEP effect was maintained. Similar results were found for the SCBE, suggesting that intervention group children were rated significantly higher on social-emotional competencies compared to control group children, $t(52) = 2.04$, $p < .05$. Subsequent analysis on follow-up data confirmed the maintenance of the intervention's effects, $t(52) = 2.51$, $p < .05$. However, no significant intervention effects were found on children's externalizing or internalizing problems ($p > .05$).

Postintervention comparisons indicated that intervention group children correctly named significantly more emotions than control group children, $t(52) = 2.74$, $p < .01$, and generated significantly more positive problem-solving strategies than control group children, $t(52) = 2.04$, $p < .05$. At follow-up, SEP participation was still associated with improved emotion recognition in intervention group children compared to those from the control group, $t(52) = 3.33$, $p < .01$, whereas the SEP effect on positive problem-solving was not maintained, as group differences were only marginally significant ($p < .10$). No significant effect of SEP participation was obtained for negative problem-solving strategies.

Intervention group parents improved significantly from pre- to postintervention on measures of positive parenting and showed significantly lower levels of stress. However, the differences between the intervention and control groups were marginally significant (*p*s < .10).

Follow-up data indicated that intervention group parents did not use more praise and rewards for their children's positive behaviors, but reported significantly less stress compared to control group parents, $t(52) = 2.87$, $p < .01$. However, this result cannot be considered a direct effect of the intervention.

Table 4.14 Intervention effects on children's behaviors at home and declarative knowledge for moderate-risk social competence groups

Measures	*Preintervention*		*Postintervention*		*Follow-up*		*Mixed ANOVA*	*Pre-post paired t test*		*Pre-FU paired t test*		*Cohen d*
	M	*SD*	*M*	*SD*	*M*	*SD*		*INT*	*CTRL*	*INT*	*CTRL*	
SCS-P							5.64**	11.20***	6.93***	16.09***	5.86***	0.76
Intervention	40.40	1.25	46.37	2.67	47.83	2.73						
Control	41.00	1.38	44.54	2.43	46.08	3.75						
SSRS social competence							12.08***	7.69***	3.13*	9.06***	3.41**	0.57
Intervention	46.16	5.21	53.47	5.28	55.43	5.83						
Control	48.37	4.82	50.79	4.09	51.79	4.55						
ECS-P							10.88***	6.72***	3.12*	10.42***	2.97†	
Intervention	50.10	4.14	54.97	3.30	57.33	3.19						
Control	51.79	5.02	53.75	4.01	54.42	3.49						
SSRS behavior problems							2.14†	−7.43***	−2.44†	−6.53***	−4.74***	
Intervention	4.26	1.70	2.76	1.40	2.06	1.41						
Control	4.08	1.72	3.29	1.55	2.63	1.38						
AKT expressive emotion recognition							4.28*	4.00***	1.10	5.17***	1.59	0.75
Intervention	3.73	2.02	5.60	1.67	6.07	1.44						
Control	3.79	2.17	4.29	1.83	4.54	1.93						
Positive problem-solving strategies							3.70*	4.10**	1.64	4.05**	3.79**	0.55
Intervention	0.53	0.28	0.74	0.25	0.78	0.22						
Control	0.47	0.26	0.57	0.36	0.66	0.27						
Negative problem-solving strategies							2.81†	−2.83†	0.75	−3.22*	0.70	
Intervention	0.06	0.10	0.01	0.05	0.01	0.04						
Control	0.03	0.07	0.07	0.18	0.03	0.07						

*$p < .05$, **$p < .01$, ***$p < .001$, †$p < .10$ statistically marginal effect

Table 4.15 Intervention effects on discipline and stress for children's parents from the moderate-risk social competence groups

Measures	*Preintervention* *M*	*SD*	*Postintervention* *M*	*SD*	*Follow-up* *M*	*SD*	*Mixed ANOVA*	*Pre-post paired t test* *INT*	*CTRL*	*Pre-FU paired t test* *INT*	*CTRL*	*Cohen d*
Harsh discipline							1.74	−1.09	−0.60	−2.42†	−0.29	
Intervention	2.35	0.61	2.26	0.49	2.14	0.45						
Control	2.64	0.91	2.62	0.90	2.64	0.90						
Inconsistent discipline							2.53†	−2.95†	0.61	−2.69†	−1.19	
Intervention	2.87	0.84	2.64	0.83	2.57	0.72						
Control	2.89	0.83	2.93	0.83	2.80	0.82						
Appropriate discipline							0.08	2.31†	1.84	2.21†	2.56†	
Intervention	4.49	0.73	4.68	0.60	4.73	0.43						
Control	4.29	0.65	4.43	0.68	4.50	0.57						
Positive parenting							7.04**	4.03**	−0.34	5.63***	−0.21	
Intervention	5.50	0.65	5.77	0.53	5.86	0.52						
Control	5.52	0.64	5.47	0.66	5.50	0.61						
Parent stress							4.77**	−3.56**	−0.05	−3.83**	1.65	
Intervention	67.97	18.14	62.00	14.80	60.33	13.35						
Control	70.83	18.62	70.71	19.95	71.46	15.09						

*$p < .05$, **$p < .01$, ***$p < .001$, †$p < .10$ statistically marginal effect

Social Competence Screening: The Low-Risk Groups Descriptive statistics, values of time by group interaction effects, within group comparisons, and effect sizes are presented in Tables 4.16 and 4.17. No significant SEP effects were found for the SCS-P, SSRS, ECS-P, behavior problems rated on the SSRS, and problem-solving strategies ($ps > .05$). However, intervention group children correctly named significantly more emotional displays than control group children, $t(74) = 2.24$, $p < .05$, but at follow-up the group difference was no longer significant ($p > .05$). Parent related outcomes suggested that intervention group parents reported employing more appropriate discipline strategies, as well as more positive parenting strategies, but the differences compared to the control group were only marginally significant ($p < .10$).

Emotional Competence Screening: The Moderate-Risk Groups Descriptive statistics, values of time by group interaction effects, within group comparisons, and effect sizes are presented in Tables 4.18 and 4.19. Immediately postintervention, parents evaluated intervention group children significantly higher on emotional competence compared to the control group children, $t(56) = 2.39$, $p < .05$. Analysis on follow-up scores indicated that SEP participation was still associated with positive outcomes, as intervention group parents rated their children as more emotionally competent than parents of the control group children, $t(56) = 3.45$, $p < .01$. No significant group differences were found for the SCS-P, but on the SSRS intervention group children were rated higher on their social skills compared to control group counterparts, $t(56) = 2.08$, $p < .05$. However, the difference was no longer significant at follow-up.

Also, a significant reduction in intervention group children's externalizing problems compared to control group children was found as a result of the intervention, $t(56) = -2.98$, $p < .01$. At follow-up, intervention group children were rated significantly lower on externalizing problems compared to the control group, $t(56) = -3.97$, $p < .01$. This suggested that the SEP effect on externalizing problems was maintained.

Intervention group children named significantly more emotions correctly compared to control group children, $t(56) = 2.09$, $p < .05$. Conversely, children's performance on the problem-solving task suggested that those from the intervention group were able to generate significantly more positive problem-solving strategies than control

Table 4.16 Intervention effects on children's behaviors at home and declarative knowledge for low-risk social competence groups

Measures	*Preintervention*		*Postintervention*		*Follow-up*		*Mixed ANOVA*	*Pre-post paired t test*		*Pre-FU paired t test*		*Cohen d*
	M	*SD*	*M*	*SD*	*M*	*SD*		*INT*	*CTRL*	*INT*	*CTRL*	
SCS-P							1.71	3.79**	0.97	3.70**	2.27†	
Intervention	48.44	4.08	50.58	3.94	50.86	3.96						
Control	49.39	4.27	49.19	3.58	51.21	2.90						
SSRS social competence							0.51	2.81†	0.96	3.48**	2.36†	
Intervention	55.70	6.63	58.56	6.78	60.19	7.71						
Control	57.42	7.35	58.70	8.45	60.61	7.70						
ECS-P							4.14**	3.80**	1.29	7.09***	2.20	
Intervention	54.95	5.00	57.09	4.19	59.28	4.84						
Control	56.03	5.62	56.91	4.53	57.70	4.68						
SSRS behavior problems							1.54	−3.21**	−0.82	−3.63**	−1.44	
Intervention	2.26	1.76	1.58	1.40	1.40	1.15						
Control	1.85	1.33	1.64	1.43	1.48	1.18						
AKT expressive emotion recognition							7.25**	6.82***	2.07	7.82***	3.26**	0.51
Intervention	3.44	1.99	5.84	1.48	6.14	1.44						
Control	4.27	2.07	4.97	1.90	5.64	1.64						
Positive problem-solving strategies							1.87	6.13***	1.83	6.60***	2.89†	
Intervention	0.53	0.26	0.76	0.27	0.78	0.26						
Control	0.55	0.29	0.66	0.24	0.71	0.25						
Negative problem-solving strategies							0.72	−0.50	−0.80	1.00	−0.50	
Intervention	0.01	0.05	0.01	0.04	0.01	0.03						
Control	0.03	0.07	0.05	0.11	0.02	0.07						

*$p < .05$, **$p < .01$, ***$p < .001$, †$p < .10$ statistically marginal effect

Table 4.17 Intervention effects on discipline and stress for children's parents from the low-risk social competence groups

	Preintervention		*Postintervention*		*Follow-up*		*Mixed ANOVA*	*Pre-post paired t test*		*Pre-FU paired t test*		*Cohen d*
Measures	*M*	*SD*	*M*	*SD*	*M*	*SD*		*INT*	*CTRL*	*INT*	*CTRL*	
Harsh discipline							1.74	−1.09	−0.60	−2.42†	−0.29	
Intervention	2.46	0.65	2.40	0.56	2.29	0.59						
Control	2.46	0.65	2.62	0.90	2.64	0.90						
Inconsistent discipline							1.80	−2.11	0.62	−1.80	−0.67	
Intervention	2.67	0.94	2.54	0.75	2.54	0.67						
Control	2.81	0.87	2.86	0.79	2.80	0.82						
Appropriate discipline							9.96***	4.13***	0.71	5.54***	0.34	
Intervention	4.56	0.82	4.87	0.76	4.95	0.70						
Control	4.83	0.89	4.76	0.89	4.80	0.84						
Positive parenting							3.37*	3.29***	0.78	4.21***	1.29	
Intervention	5.66	0.55	5.84	0.42	5.87	0.41						
Control	5.55	0.68	5.61	0.59	5.65	0.59						
Parent stress							1.37	−1.16	−1.01	−1.75	0.22	
Intervention	61.19	13.69	59.67	10.32	58.47	10.31						
Control	58.45	11.79	56.67	12.06	59.03	14.02						

*$p < .05$, **$p < .01$, ***$p < .001$, †$p < .10$ statistically marginal effect

Table 4.18 Intervention effects on children's behaviors at home and declarative knowledge for moderate-risk emotional competence groups

	Preintervention		*Postintervention*		*Follow-up*		*Mixed ANOVA*	*Pre-post paired t test*		*Pre-FU paired t test*		*Cohen d*
Measures	*M*	*SD*	*M*	*SD*	*M*	*SD*		*INT*	*CTRL*	*INT*	*CTRL*	
ECS-P							9.56***	10.85***	4.16**	2.12***	5.35***	0.63
Intervention	50.06	1.57	55.18	2.57	57.09	3.09						
Control	50.76	1.36	53.40	3.09	54.36	2.87						
SCS-P							4.60*	7.99***	6.97***	9.35***	4.93***	
Intervention	40.41	4.67	45.66	3.44	47.63	3.38						
Control	40.50	3.77	43.77	4.19	44.85	3.54						
SSRS social competence							10.27***	9.18***	2.93†	8.51***	3.73**	0.54
Intervention	46.00	6.68	53.34	4.92	55.53	6.12						
Control	48.15	6.79	50.54	5.35	52.42	6.31						
SSRS externalizing							4.97**	−5.64***	−1.31	−6.86***	−3.38**	
Intervention	4.12	1.76	2.67	1.47	1.94	1.12						
Control	4.32	1.86	3.88	1.61	3.28	1.46						
AKT expressive							3.80*	4.57***	1.60	4.13**	1.67	0.41
Intervention	3.36	2.37	5.64	1.90	5.48	1.75						
Control	4.08	1.89	4.80	2.18	4.76	1.76						
Positive problem-solving							3.90*	4.98***	1.67	5.04***	3.22*	0.68
Intervention	0.51	0.29	0.77	0.21	0.80	0.22						
Control	0.50	0.24	0.59	0.31	0.67	0.28						
Negative problem-solving							2.27	−2.05	0.65	−2.89†	−1.05	
Intervention	0.05	0.11	0.01	0.05	0.00	0.00						
Control	0.04	0.09	0.06	0.11	0.02	0.07						

$^{*}p < .05$, $^{**}p < .01$, $^{***}p < .001$, $^{\dagger}p < .10$ statistically marginal effect

Table 4.19 Intervention effects on discipline and stress for children's parents from the moderate-risk emotional competence groups

	Preintervention		*Postintervention*		*Follow-up*		*Mixed ANOVA*	*Pre-post paired t test*		*Pre-FU paired t test*		*Cohen d*
Measures	*M*	*SD*	*M*	*SD*	*M*	*SD*		*INT*	*CTRL*	*INT*	*CTRL*	
Harsh discipline							2.49†	−2.12	0.02	−2.46†	0.23	
Intervention	2.50	0.54	2.35	0.48	2.31	0.40						
Control	2.69	0.87	2.69	0.79	2.70	0.84						
Inconsistent discipline							3.83*	−3.49**	0.49	2.75*	0.14	
Intervention	2.95	0.85	2.70	0.80	2.65	0.69						
Control	3.00	0.87	3.03	0.86	2.98	0.86						
Appropriate discipline							3.51*	3.44**	0.83	3.37**	1.17	
Intervention	4.42	0.81	4.80	0.68	4.81	0.51						
Control	4.46	0.93	4.52	0.83	4.57	0.75						
Positive parenting							3.64*	3.16*	0.27	3.37*	0.19	
Intervention	5.45	0.69	5.74	0.59	5.78	0.56						
Control	5.55	0.65	5.69	0.43	5.69	0.42						
Parent stress							3.49*	−4.00**	−2.41	−3.12*	−2.75†	
Intervention	67.25	14.78	62.31	13.46	61.59	13.07						
Control	66.91	11.91	69.15	17.19	66.08	15.65						

$^{*}p < .05$, $^{**}p < .01$, $^{***}p < .001$, $^{\dagger}p < .10$ statistically marginal effect

group children, $t(56) = 2.49$, $p < .05$. However, the intervention's effect was not maintained, as the difference between the intervention and control group was no longer significant at follow-up for both measures of children's declarative knowledge about emotions and problem-solving.

Intervention group parents reported employing significantly less inconsistent strategies, as well as significantly more appropriate discipline and positive parenting strategies from pre- to postintervention. However, there were no significant postintervention differences between intervention and control group parents.

Emotional Competence Screening: The Low-Risk Groups Descriptive statistics, values of time by group interaction effects, within group comparisons, and effect sizes are presented in Tables 4.20 and 4.21. Because significant preintervention differences were found for the ECS-P, ANCOVA was employed to determine possible group differences. There was no significant group effect on postintervention results for emotional competence ratings ($p > .05$). Similarly, no significant group differences were found on parent ratings of children's social skills and externalizing problems.

Significant differences in children's knowledge about emotions and problem-solving strategies were obtained. As expected, the intervention group performed significantly better on the expressive emotion recognition task compared to control group children, $t(71) = 2.14$, $p < .05$, and also on the problem-solving task, $t(71) = 2.79$, $p < .01$. However, in both cases, the group differences were no longer significant at follow-up.

Within group differences were found for parent reported appropriate discipline strategies and positive parenting, suggesting that intervention group parents relied more on such strategies after participating in the intervention. However, significant postintervention differences were found for the intervention group compared to control group parents only for positive parenting, $t(71) = 2.13$, $p < .05$. However, this difference was no longer significant at follow-up ($p > .05$).

Table 4.20 Intervention effects on children's behaviors at home and declarative knowledge for low-risk emotional competence groups

Measures	*Preintervention*		*Postintervention*		*Follow-up*		*Mixed ANOVA*	*Pre-post paired t test*		*Pre-FU paired t test*		*Cohen d*
	M	*SD*	*M*	*SD*	*M*	*SD*		*INT*	*CTRL*	*INT*	*CTRL*	
ECS-P							6.05**	2.36†	−0.38	7.98***	0.65	
Intervention	56.80	2.89	57.90	3.87	59.82	3.23						
Control	58.28	3.59	58.03	4.09	58.72	3.87						
SCS-P							3.22*	5.26***	1.18	5.19***	2.76†	
Intervention	47.05	5.11	50.17	4.54	50.46	4.23						
Control	48.06	5.41	48.78	4.48	50.72	3.62						
SSRS social competence							3.58*	3.42**	0.89	4.49***	1.57	
Intervention	53.95	7.28	57.93	7.23	60.20	7.51						
Control	56.09	7.74	57.00	8.02	57.88	6.60						
SSRS externalizing							7.14**	−3.85**	−2.19	−7.20***	5.80***	
Intervention	2.60	1.85	1.80	1.47	1.24	1.22						
Control	1.91	1.38	1.78	1.52	1.63	1.10						
AKT expressive							3.67*	5.74***	1.87	6.36***	3.10*	0.47
Intervention	3.92	1.78	5.90	1.54	6.17	1.55						
Control	4.19	2.18	5.03	2.10	5.78	1.90						
Positive problem-solving							4.75*	6.79***	3.64**	5.73***	4.07**	0.65
Intervention	0.52	0.27	0.80	0.26	0.82	0.24						
Control	0.47	0.30	0.63	0.26	0.71	0.27						
Negative problem-solving							0.27	−2.22	−1.00	−2.40†	−0.81	
Intervention	0.02	0.07	0.01	0.03	0.00	0.00						
Control	0.04	0.09	0.03	0.08	0.03	0.08						

*$p < .05$, **$p < .01$, ***$p < .001$, †$p < .10$ statistically marginal effect

Table 4.21 Intervention effects on discipline and stress for children's parents from the low-risk emotional competence groups

	Preintervention		*Postintervention*		*Follow-up*		*Mixed ANOVA*	*Pre-post paired t test*		*Pre-FU paired t test*		*Cohen d*
Measures	*M*	*SD*	*M*	*SD*	*M*	*SD*		*INT*	*CTRL*	*INT*	*CTRL*	
Harsh discipline							2.84†	−0.56	0.05	−2.34†	1.04	
Intervention	2.34	0.64	2.31	0.55	2.18	0.58						
Control	2.26	0.65	2.26	0.67	2.36	0.63						
Inconsistent discipline							1.00	−1.65	0.33	−1.39	−0.65	
Intervention	2.55	0.85	2.45	0.73	2.45	0.66						
Control	2.85	0.89	2.88	0.79	2.78	0.79						
Appropriate discipline							4.57*	4.24***	0.01	5.00***	0.65	
Intervention	4.52	0.81	4.76	0.74	4.89	0.67						
Control	4.62	0.82	4.62	0.84	4.69	0.80						
Positive parenting							4.11*	3.04*	0.44	4.42***	1.10	0.52
Intervention	5.73	0.51	5.90	0.40	5.95	0.36						
Control	5.58	0.67	5.62	0.65	5.65	0.63						
Parent stress							2.44†	−0.29	0.12	−2.06	0.91	
Intervention	60.27	13.84	58.41	10.55	56.93	10.41						
Control	59.28	13.03	59.56	16.60	61.81	15.46						

*$p < .05$, **$p < .01$, ***$p < .001$, †$p < .10$ statistically marginal effect

Discussion

The current study's main aim was to assess the efficacy of a community-based intervention prevention program for preschool children comprising both an indicated and universal intervention framework for enhancing preschoolers' social-emotional competencies and preventing behavior problems. Hence, SEP efficacy was assessed at the indicated intervention level targeting high-risk children, and at the universal intervention level targeting moderate- and low-risk children. For each intervention, results were obtained on 2 types of outcomes: outcomes related to children's classroom behaviors, and outcomes related to children's behaviors at home as well as parenting strategies/parental stress. Classroom behaviors were reported based on the results of the teacher rated screeners, whereas children's behaviors at home correspond to the parent rated screeners. In both cases, 2 different classification criteria were employed, namely separate screening of social and emotional competence.

It is noteworthy that the decision to derive separate risk status was indirectly supported by the fact that only about 50–60% of the children in this sample received overlapping high-risk evaluations on both types of skills from teachers and parents, respectively. Such results are in accordance with data suggesting that emotional and social competencies exhibit relatively large correlation coefficients, but are not overlapping constructs (Denham et al. 2003; Izard et al. 2001). Additionally, as expected most of the high-risk children, irrespective of the adult rater or the type of screening employed, were boys (60–70%), as they tend to be more consistently evaluated as difficult by both teachers and parents (Chaplin et al. 2005).

Moreover, between 70% and 85% of children scoring at risk on these screeners received similar below cutoff ratings on the teacher rated measure of externalizing problems (SCBE), whereas only 65–75% of children were rated by their parents as at risk on the behavior problem scale (SSRS). This finding is consistent with reports from the literature suggesting that parents tend to rate their children lower on externalizing problems than teachers (De Los Reyes and Kazdin 2005). Therefore, assessing children's risk of underdeveloped social-emotional competencies could be particularly useful, mainly because parents might underrate their child's risk of behavior problems. Also, these results are highly similar to those of Achenbach et al. (2002), who found that the correlation between teacher and parent ratings of externalizing behaviors is quite low. In this study, overlapping teacher and parent ratings of risk based on social and emotional competence screening occurred in 30–35% of the cases, mirroring the results obtained by Achenbach et al. (2002), and suggesting that these informants hold different perspectives on children's adaptive and maladaptive behaviors.

SEP Efficacy on Children's Classroom Behaviors

Indicated Intervention Effects As previously discussed, findings on SEP efficacy for the high-risk group based on teachers' ratings of social and emotional competencies provide evidence about the indicated intervention's outcomes in relation to classroom behaviors. As expected, the results from the social competence high-risk group were consistent with the hypothesis that children who were exposed to SEP will exhibit significant gains in social-emotional development compared to control group children. These results are also in line with previous findings indicating that at risk children are the most likely to benefit in terms of skill development from the exposure to a multifocused intervention strategy (Raver et al. 2009; Webster-Stratton et al. 2001, 2008). Conversely, when emotional competencies were used as the measure of high-risk status, SEP participation was associated with significant improvements in children's emotional competencies, but not in their social competencies. One possible explanation is that deficient emotional competencies could have a more damaging effect on children's ability to adapt to social interactions. From an ontogenetic point of view, emotions develop earlier and the socialization of emotions is fundamental for children's ability to exhibit socially acceptable behaviors (Eisenberg et al. 1998a, b). On the other hand, previous studies showed that the most consistent predictor of adequate social functioning is children's ability to regulate emotions (Eisenberg et al. 2000, 2003). Emotion regulation is improved when children are able to recognize emotions, and in turn, adequate emotion regulation exerts effects on how emotions are expressed (Denham et al. 2002, 2012). Given that the measure of emotional competence employed in this study did not differentiate between these domains of emotional competence, it is possible that improvements in emotion regulation might not have been consistent enough to generate changes in social behaviors for these high-risk children. Another possible explanation is that significant improvements occurred for emotion regulation strategies, but these might require longer time intervals in order to elicit effects on children's social skills.

A second category of outcomes was related to children's self-reported ability to name emotions and to problem-solve. For the social competence high-risk group the results were similar to previously reported improvements in declarative knowledge following exposure to community-based interventions, as SEP intervention group children were able to name significantly more emotions, as well as to use significantly more positive problem-solving strategies for potential conflict situations (Webster-Stratton et al. 2008). Also, results from the high-risk group are the first to suggest that a significant reduction occurs for the use of negative problem-solving strategies as a result of the intervention, results which were previously found only in clinically referred preschoolers (Webster-Stratton and Hammond 1997; Webster-Stratton and Reid 2003). Interestingly, the results for the emotional competence high-risk group showed that the intervention group children only improved in terms of their ability to correctly name emotions, but not regarding their problem-solving strategies. This result mimics those obtained for this risk category on teacher ratings of social and emotional competencies. Taken together, the similarity of these findings provides further support to the initial interpretation according to which interventions might affect social and emotional competencies to some extent independently from each other, and therefore, intervention's efficacy in terms of emotional competence does not guarantee progress in terms of social competence development.

Teacher rated externalizing problems showed that the intervention was effective in reducing the frequency of behavior problems in high-risk groups derived based on both social and emotional competence screening, thus confirming the second hypothesis of this study. Although consistent intervention effects were found on children's externalizing problems in early intervention programs with clinically referred children (Webster-Stratton and Hammond 1997; Webster-Stratton et al. 2001), these findings are among the few that show the potential of classroom delivered interventions to produce positive outcomes for high-risk preschoolers. Other studies found similar effects either in the context of added small group training (CPPRG 1999a), or in school-aged children (CPPRG 1999a; Lochman and Wells 2002). Consequently, these results indirectly support the notion that high-risk preschoolers do not necessarily require additional small group training and that the reduction in externalizing problems can be successfully achieved by ensuring that teachers are prepared to effectively manage children's misbehaviors (CPPRG 1999a; Domitrovich et al. 2007; Webster-Stratton et al. 2008). Hence, the first potential mechanism which could be inferred as responsible for SEP efficacy is related to the classroom management strategies taught during teacher training, which placed particular emphasis on increasing the use of positive discipline strategies (e.g., rule setting, establishing logical consequences for misbehavior, timeout) known to be associated with lower levels of children's misconduct (Filcheck et al. 2004). Furthermore, a second potential mechanism is related to the inclusion of consultations to ensure high-quality implementation of the SEP classroom curriculum. Although this strategy was reported as successful in reducing levels of externalizing problems in an universal prevention program (Domitrovich et al. 2007), these results provide support the notion that such strategies could be effective in indicated interventions as well. It is also noteworthy that this result could be associated with the fact that SEP teacher consultations encompassed skill building strategies and that the classroom curriculum required assisting children during daily interactions to exercise their social-emotional competencies. In fact, previously reported findings suggest that coaching children is an essential intervention component which can contribute to reduced levels of behavior problems (Bear et al. 2000; Howes 2000). However, future studies should separately compare the effects of the classroom curriculum and components of teacher training (classroom management and consultations), in order to better understand mechanisms that are responsible of changes in high-risk children's behavior problems.

Increasing empirical evidence suggests that interventions aimed at preventing externalizing problems can be useful when it comes to internalizing problems, as similar child related risk factors are predictive of both types of problems. More precisely, internalizing problems are associated with low levels of emotion regulation of sadness and fear, and avoidance of social interactions (Hay et al. 2004; Spinrad et al. 2004). Results from both the social and emotional competencies high-risk groups concur with those previously reported suggesting that high-risk children from the intervention group exhibit significantly lower levels of negative emotionality (sadness and fear) and isolation as a result of interventions aimed at reducing externalizing problems (Raver et al. 2009). Such findings are unsurprising, as research suggests that similar developmental cascades are involved in increasing children's risk of both externalizing and internalizing type problems from preschool to adolescence (Bornstein et al. 2010; Burt et al. 2008), and hence, such difficulties tend to cooccur (Angold et al. 1999).

Universal Intervention Effects The results for the universal intervention level for classroom behaviors correspond to the moderate- and low-risk groups derived from teachers' ratings of social and emotional competence.

Concerning data from the moderate-risk groups, it is important to note that they largely mirrored the results from the high-risk groups, except for the fact that effect sizes were consistently in the medium range. Consequently, the results are in accordance with the first hypothesis suggesting that the intervention's efficacy decreases as a function of risk. More precisely, in the social competence moderate-risk group significant gains were detected in both the social and the emotional competence domain as a result of SEP participation, which is consistent with previous results reported from community-based interventions (CPPRG 1999b; Domitrovich et al. 2007). On the other hand, the moderate-risk emotional competence group again showed significant gains on the measure, but a delayed follow-up effect for social competencies. Furthermore, results for the low-risk social competence and low-risk emotional competence groups suggest that SEP efficacy concerning social-emotional development is less consistent when compared to other risk categories.

Indirect support for the presence of different effects on social and emotional competencies was provided by results from the child-report tasks. Data concerning children's ability to correctly name emotions indicated that children from the moderate-risk intervention group performed significantly better than the control group; such findings are similar to those reported for universal interventions (Domitrovich et al. 2007). Also, this is the first universal intervention to report significant increases in children's knowledge of positive problem-solving strategies, given that such measures were previously employed only in assessing intervention outcomes for high-risk children (Webster-Stratton 1998). The moderate-risk emotional competence risk group exhibited similar improvements to the moderate social competence risk group for emotion recognition and problem-solving, indicating that in fact progress in terms of declarative knowledge might occur at faster rates than such knowledge is transferred to behaviors observed by teachers in the classroom. Where the low-risk social and emotional competence groups were concerned, the results indicated postintervention improvements in declarative knowledge, but these were no longer maintained at follow-up, suggesting that there might be a "ceiling" effect as both intervention and control group children's performance significantly improved at follow-up. This is in line with research suggesting that by the time children turn 5, they are able to correctly recognize all of the basic emotions included in the AKT (Widen and Russell 2003), and they are probably more inclined to offer constructive solutions to conflicts as a result of exposure to social expectations in this regard (Youngstrom et al. 2000).

This study is also the first to report that non-risk children, from the social and the emotional competence moderate-risk groups, exhibited lower levels of externalizing problems as a result of SEP participation compared to control group children. A possible explanation for this rather unexpected result might be age related. Research on children's externalizing profiles suggested that between the ages of 3 and 5 all children irrespective of whether they exhibit one or more risk factors tend to manifest significant reductions in aggressive and non-compliant behaviors (Hill et al. 2006). Therefore, it is possible that the intervention might act as a trigger for accelerating an already occurring developmental trend. However, in line with the second hypothesis, children from the low-risk social and the low-risk emotional competence did not improve on measures of externalizing problems. Regarding the findings for the low-risk social competence group, it is noteworthy that differences between the intervention and control groups on parent risk factors affected postintervention evaluations of externalizing problems. This effect is explained by studies which indicate that inappropriate parenting practices are highly predictive of children's aggressive and non-compliant behaviors (Chang et al. 2003; Dennis 2006). Additionally, SEP related outcomes for internalizing problems mimicked those for externalizing problems, indicating that reductions in externalizing problems can contribute to lowering levels of internalizing type behaviors.

SEP Efficacy on Children's Behaviors at Home and Parenting Practices

Indicated Intervention Effects Findings on SEP efficacy for the high-risk group based on parents' ratings of social and emotional competencies provide evidence about the indicated intervention's outcomes in relation to children's behaviors at home and parenting practices. Results from the high-risk social competence group partially confirmed the first hypothesis, and were in line with previous research suggesting that parents perceive improvements in their children's acquired social competencies as a result of participation in either selective (CPPRG 1999a) or indicated prevention programs (Webster-Stratton et al. 2008). However, the results suggest that improvements were only found on this measure, but not regarding parental ratings of children's emotional competence development, for which only a within group trend was detected.

However, more consistent SEP effects were found for children's declarative knowledge about emotions and problem-solving strategies. Although previous research employed such measurements for testing the efficacy of community-based interventions for low SES children (Webster-Stratton et al. 2008), these results are the first to provide insights into children's gains in emotion recognition in the context of an indicated intervention. However, no such effects were found for negative problem-solving strategies (aggression, non-compliance, and isolation/avoidance). This might be a consequence of the fact that participants in this study were not children with early-onset conduct disorders for whom such outcomes were more consistently reported (Webster-Stratton and Hammond 1997; Webster-Stratton and Reid 2003).

In accordance with the second hypothesis, SEP participation was associated with significant reductions in children's aggressive and non-compliant behaviors. Parents reported reductions in high-risk children's externalizing behaviors, but a significant effect was in fact obtained only for those children, whose parents attended at least 75% of the intervention sessions. These results mimicked those from prevention programs targeting at risk children, which suggest that significant group differences are not detectable in community samples, because effects are visible mainly when taking into account parental attendance (Webster-Stratton 1998; Webster-Stratton et al. 2001).

Where the emotional competence high-risk group is concerned, the results mirrored those obtained for the social competence high-risk group. The results showed significant gains in parent rated emotional competencies, but not in parent rated social competencies. Conversely, the SEP was associated with improved emotion knowledge and social problem-solving. Also, the data showed that significantly lower levels of aggression and non-compliance were reported for those children whose parents attended the minimal required intervention participation. Interestingly, the results would suggest that although both social competence high-risk children and emotional competence high-risk children exhibited improved emotion knowledge and problem-solving, parents reported improvements only for the target competence. Hence, it could be that either longer timelines are needed for knowledge to be transferred to observable skills or that longer time intervals are required to transfer skills from the classroom to parent-child interactions at home (Lewis and Sugai 1999).

Data on parenting practices indicated that no significant group differences were found, but rather there were significant within group trends for intervention group parents. In the social competence high-risk group, contrary to the proposed hypothesis, no changes were found in relation to harsh parenting, which is considered the most robust predictor of children's behavior problems (Bradley and Corwyn 2007; Snyder et al. 2005). Because harsh parenting is highly associated with maternal depression (Chronis et al. 2007), low SES parents (Curtner-Smith et al. 2006), as well as clinical intensity child behavior problems (Gutermuth-Anthony et al. 2005), it is possible that intervention effects are less likely in samples such as the one from this study with relatively fewer parental risk factors. A similar explanation could be applied to the lack of intervention effects on parent stress levels, which is also more frequently associated with multiple risk sources (Gutermuth-Anthony et al. 2005).

Significant trends for inconsistent parenting strategies were found for social competence high-risk children, reflecting significant changes towards consistency in disciplining from their parents, which have also been reported in other community-based prevention programs (CPPRG 1999a). Since high-risk groups from this study included more boys, such results might be a consequence of the fact that in normative samples parents tend to be more inconsistent in their disciplining strategies in relation to boys (Kim et al. 2005). Previously reported improvements for appropriate parenting and increased use of praise were more consistently reported in parents of children with early onset behavior problems (Webster-Stratton and Hammond 1997) or those targeted by selective interventions (Webster-Stratton et al. 2001). The presence of a significant trend within the high-risk social competence group could be explained by the fact that indicated interventions might actually exert effects by boosting protective factors such as appropriate discipline and positive parenting (Brotman et al. 2005). For the emotional competence high-risk intervention group, trends concerning parental practices were similar to those found for the social competence high-risk group.

Overall the results for the high-risk groups based on screening of social and emotional competencies seem to suggest that SEP intervention was generally effective. It is noteworthy that short format parent training was able to attract relatively high parent attendance rates, and specifically, as expected based on previous reports, parents of high-risk children were more likely to attend SEP parent training (68% high risk vs. 53 moderate risk vs. 38% low risk) (Prinz and Sanders 2007). Also, there seems to be a relationship between parent participation in the training sessions and the intervention's efficacy on children's behaviors at home, because effect sizes decreased as a function of children's lower risk status and lower parent attendance rates. Furthermore, one of the main concerns in SEP development was to provide parents with a sustainable intervention program, which would not stigmatize parents by delivering the training only to high-risk children's caregivers. As suggested by Kazdin and Wassell (1999) parents are more likely to attend such interventions if they believe that they are suitable for their needs. In the case of SEP, parent training was developed as a combination of information about children's social-emotional development and coaching, on the one hand, and behavior management on the other hand (Sanders and Morawska 2005; Turner and Sanders 2006). However, as previously discussed in the context of classroom behaviors, future studies might disentangle the exact contribution of each intervention component to changes in high-risk children's behaviors at home.

Universal Intervention Effects Results for the universal intervention concerning children's behaviors at home and parenting practices were obtained from the moderate- and low-risk groups derived by parent ratings of social and emotional competencies. Findings from the social competence moderate-risk group are in consensus with previous results reported by Domitrovich et al. (2007) from a universal intervention, suggesting that parents observed improved social skills at home after their children participated in a classroom-based intervention. An interesting pattern of results emerged for the moderate-risk group which showed consistent improvements in terms of better developed social and emotional competencies, whereas the high-risk group only improved in terms of social competencies. These data suggest that in fact parents observed the most consistent gains in terms of social-emotional development for moderate-risk children rather than high-risk children, contrary to the initially proposed hypothesis. Conversely, SEP was not related to increases in social-emotional competencies for low-risk children.

In a similar vein to parent reports, children's performance on self-reported tasks suggested that for the moderate-risk category, intervention group children exhibited improved expressive emotion recognition and used more positive problem-solving strategies compared to control group children. These data are the first child reported outcomes in a community-based intervention, as the other similar findings were previously found in samples of children with diagnosed conduct problems (Webster-Stratton and Hammond 1997), or from low-income families (Webster-Stratton et al. 2008). Conversely, no significant intervention effects were found for these tasks for the low-risk social competence group. Moreover, the results obtained for the moderate- and low-risk emotional competence group were similar to those for the moderate- and low-risk social competence groups. Taken together these results would suggest that: (1) moderate-risk children are the main beneficiaries of the universal intervention; and (2) moderate-risk children exhibit more consistent improvements in social-emotional competencies based on parent ratings compared to high-risk children. Therefore, it is possible that skill transfer from the classroom to parent-child interactions at home might occur at faster rates for this risk category compared to high-risk children. Additionally, the SEP was intended to provide parents of non-risk children with the opportunity to learn more about how to support their children's skill building process, which could be the mechanism responsible for these outcomes.

Interestingly, an unexpected effect emerged for the moderate emotional competence group, for which SEP participation was associated with decreased externalizing problems compared to control group children. One possible interpretation is that assessment of emotional competencies might constitute a more accurate evaluation of children's behavior problems from the parents' perspective. Lack of behavioral control or anger outbursts are more easily observed by parents than the extent to which children properly interact with same-age peers, for which they would require more consistent access to observing group play. However, another equally plausible explanation is that this effect might be an artifact, and future studies will need to confirm the presence of such an effect.

Based on findings reported in the literature suggesting that positive discipline strategies are more consistently employed by parents of high-risk children (Brotman et al. 2005), it is unsurprising that outcome measures for parental self-reported discipline strategies and stress indicated no significant SEP effects for the universal intervention. Although the parent training did not exert significant between group effects on parental behaviors, the results support the notion that significant within group trends obtained for positive parenting strategies suggest that in some instances community-based universal interventions actually work in terms of boosting protective factors such as appropriate discipline and positive parenting, rather than decreasing harsh and/or inconsistent parenting strategies (Brotman et al. 2005). However, as previously discussed it would be important to compare the relative effect of each intervention strategy in order to determine which intervention component is more effective in eliciting changes in parental behaviors.

Conclusions and Implications for Practice

The results from this efficacy study, which assessed SEP effects depending on children's risk status, suggest some interesting implications for practice. First, it seems that screening practices for establishing risk status should be linked to the content of a given prevention program so that it can more accurately detect changes in children's behaviors (Essex et al. 2009; Severson et al. 2007). In relation to this, it must be emphasized that simply screening children for delayed social-emotional competencies is meaningless, unless there are specific remedial/preventive steps which can be implemented in school settings to take action when difficulties are signaled by these assessments. Second, implementing universal screeners such as the ones employed in this study might prove effective for at least 2 reasons: (1) they emphasize children's skills acquisition, not their negative behaviors which could make them less susceptible to parents' social desirability; and (2) they help prevent children being labeled as "bad" or "difficult" by focusing on their strengths, as well as the potential for improvement, rather than focusing on misbehaviors. Third, because teachers' and parents' evaluation of risk seems to be more divergent than convergent, and because children behave differently depending on context, it could be that separate ratings performed by teachers and parents would provide a more specific answer as to how interventions elicit changes in the classroom and at home. Hence, it could be important for practitioners to consider screening for children's social-emotional development as a first step in detecting risk, involving both teachers and parents in their evaluation, as well as implementing specific prevention programs emphasizing social-emotional learning.

The findings from SEP implementation suggest rather different outcomes of indicated and universal interventions in community-based settings. Although as previously suggested by the literature, intervention related changes in classroom behaviors are more evident for high-risk children, the current data pointed out that moderate-risk children might also benefit from such interventions, albeit not to the same extent as the high-risk category. This outcome is further supported by the findings on children's behaviors at home. In this case, children from the moderate-risk category exhibited even more consistent behavioral changes than those from the high-risk group. Therefore, practitioners working in schools might take into account this evidence which points out that the percentage of children in a given classroom for whom preventive interventions work is not reduced to the 5–10% who are at risk, but are effective for approximately 30% of children.

Moreover, based on the findings reported in this chapter, it is apparent that parental involvement in the intervention increases as a function of children's risk status: parents who perceive their children as more exposed to risk are more likely to attend and be engaged in parent training. This means that in ecological settings a naturally self-selection process seems to occur, in which parents choose to participate depending on children's risk. Therefore, singling out parents and providing intervention only to those whose children are at risk might actually be counterproductive. It would be more effective to employ inclusive strategies and attempt to implement training strategies which at the content level reflect the needs of a broader category of parents.

Given that the findings from this chapter address SEP efficacy at the risk group level, it is important to further investigate whether SEP actually elicits changes at the individual level. Although much less employed for testing school-based interventions, single-subject designs might be an important tool for understanding how fast and when preventive programs elicit behavioral change.

References

Abidin, R. R. (1995). *Parenting stress index: Professional manual* (3rd ed.). Odessa: Psychological Assessment Resources, Inc.

Achenbach, T. M., Dumenci, L., & Rescorla, L. A. (2002). Ten-year comparisons of problems and competencies for national samples of youth: Self, parent, and teacher reports. *Journal of Emotional and Behavioral Disorders, 10*, 194–203. https://doi.org/10.1177/10634266020100040101.

Angold, A., Costello, E. J., & Erkanli, A. (1999). Comorbidity. *Journal of Child Psychology and Psychiatry, 40*, 57–87. https://doi.org/10.1111/1469-7610.00424.

Bear, G. G., Webster-Stratton, C., Furlong, M. J., & Rhee, S. (2000). Preventing aggression and violence. In K. M. Minke & G. G. Bear (Eds.), *Preventing school problems-promoting school success* (pp. 1–69). Bethesda: NASP.

Bornstein, M. H., Hahn, C.-S., & Haynes, O. M. (2010). Social competence, externalizing, and internalizing behavioral adjustment from early childhood through early adolescence: Developmental cascades. *Development and Psychopathology, 22*, 717–735. https://doi.org/10.1017/S0954579410000416.

Bradley, R. H., & Corwyn, R. F. (2007). Externalizing problems in the fifth grade: Relations with productive activity, maternal sensitivity, and harsh parenting from infancy through middle childhood. *Developmental Psychology, 43*, 1390–1401. https://doi.org/10.1037/0012-1649.43.6.1390.

Brotman, L. M., Gouley, K. K., Chesir-Teran, D., Dennis, T., Klein, R. G., & Shrout, P. (2005). Prevention for preschoolers at high risk for conduct problems: Immediate outcomes on parenting practices and child social competence. *Journal of Clinical Child and Adolescent Psychology, 34*, 724–734. https://doi.org/10.1207/s15374424jccp3404_14.

Burt, K. B., Obradović, J., Long, J. D., & Masten, A. S. (2008). The interplay of social competence and psychopathology over 20 years: Testing transactional and cascade models. *Child Development, 79*, 359–374. https://doi.org/10.1111/j.1467-8624.2007.01130.x.

Calkins, S. D., & Fox, N. A. (2002). Self-regulatory processes in early personality development: A multilevel approach to the study of childhood social withdrawal and aggression. *Development and Psychopathology, 14*, 477–498. https://doi.org/10.1017/S095457940200305X.

Chang, L., Schwartz, D., Dodge, K. A., & McBride-Chang, C. (2003). Harsh parenting in relation to child emotion regulation and aggression. *Journal of Family Psychology, 17*, 598–606. https://doi.org/10.1037/0893-3200.17.4.598.

Chaplin, T. M., Cole, P. M., & Zahn-Waxler, C. (2005). Parental socialization of emotion expression: Gender differences and relations to child adjustment. *Emotion, 5*, 80–88. https://doi.org/10.1037/1528-3542.5.1.80.

Chronis, A. M., Lahey, B. B., Pelham, W. E., Jr., Hall Williams, S. H., Baumann, B. L., Kipp, H., et al. (2007). Maternal depression and early positive parenting predict future conduct problems in young children with attention-deficit/hyperactivity disorder. *Developmental Psychology, 43*, 70–82. https://doi.org/10.1007/s10826-005-9016-7.

Conduct Problems Prevention Research Group. (1999a). Initial impact of the Fast Track prevention trial for conduct problems: I. The high risk sample. *Journal of Consulting and Clinical Psychology, 67*, 631–647. https://doi.org/10.1037/0022-006X.67.5.648.

Conduct Problems Prevention Research Group. (1999b). Initial impact of the Fast Track prevention trial for conduct problems: II. Classroom effects. *Journal of Consulting and Clinical Psychology, 67*, 648–657. https://doi.org/10.1037/0022-006X.67.5.648.

Curtner-Smith, M. E., Culp, A. M., Culp, R., Scheib, C., Owen, K., Tilley, A., et al. (2006). Mothers' parenting and young economically disadvantaged children's relational and overt bullying. *Journal of Child and Family Studies, 15*, 181–193. https://doi.org/10.1007/s10826-005-9016-7.

Dadds, M. R., & Roth, J. H. (2008). Prevention of anxiety disorders: Results of a universal trial with young children. *Journal of Child and Family Studies, 17*, 320–335. https://doi.org/10.1007/s10826-007-9144-3.

De Los Reyes, A., & Kazdin, A. E. (2005). Informant discrepancies in the assessment of childhood psychopathology: A critical review, theoretical framework, and recommendations for further study. *Psychological Bulletin, 131*, 483–509. https://doi.org/10.1037/0033-2909.131.4.483.

Denham, S. A. (1986). Social cognition, social behavior, and emotion in preschoolers: Contextual validation. *Child Development, 57*, 194–201. https://doi.org/10.2307/1130651.

Denham, S., Mason, T., Caverly, S., Schmidt, M., Hackney, R., Caswell, C., & DeMulder, E. (2001). Preschoolers at play: Co-socializers of emotional and social competence. *International Journal of Behavioral Development, 25*, 90–101. https://doi.org/10.1080/016502501143000067.

Denham, S. A., Blair, K. A., Schmidt, M. S., Blair, K., DeMulder, E., & Caal, S. (2002). Preschool understanding of emotions: Contributions to classroom anger and aggression. *Journal of Child Psychology and Psychiatry, 43*, 901–916. https://doi.org/10.1111/1469-7610.00139.

Denham, S. A., Blair, K. A., DeMulder, E., Levitas, J., Sawyer, K., Auerbach-Major, S., & Quinnan, P. (2003). Preschool emotional competence: Pathway to social competence? *Child Development, 74*, 238–256. https://doi.org/10.1111/1467-8624.00533.

Denham, S. A., Bassett, H. H., Way, E., Mincic, M., Zinsser, K., & Graling, K. (2012). Preschoolers' emotion knowledge: Selfregulatory foundations, and predictions of early school success. *Cognition and Emotion, 26*, 667–679. https://doi.org/10.1080/02699931.2011.602049.

Dennis, T. (2006). Emotional self-regulation in preschoolers: The interplay of child approach reactivity, parenting, and control capacities. *Developmental Psychology, 42*, 84–97. https://doi.org/10.1037/0012-1649.42.1.84.84.

Domitrovich, C. E., Cortes, R. C., & Greenberg, M. T. (2007). Improving young children's social and emotional competence: A randomized trial of the preschool "PATHS" curriculum. *The Journal of Primary Prevention, 28*, 67–91. https://doi.org/10.1007/s10935-007-0081-0.

Durlak, J. A., & Wells, A. M. (1998). Evaluation of indicated preventive intervention (secondary prevention) mental health programs for children and adolescents. *American Journal of Community Psychology, 26*, 775–802. https://doi.org/10.1023/A:1022162015815.

Eisenberg, N., Spinrad, T. L., & Cumberland, A. (1998a). Parental socialization of emotion. *Psychological Inquiry, 9*, 241–273.

Eisenberg, N., Spinrad, T. L., & Cumberland, A. (1998b). The socialization of emotion: Reply to commentaries. *Psychological Inquiry, 9*, 317–333.

Eisenberg, N., Fabes, R. A., Guthrie, I. K., & Reiser, M. (2000). Dispositional emotionality and regulation: Their role in predicting quality of social functioning. *Journal of Personality and Social Psychology, 78*, 136–157. https://doi.org/10.1037/0022-3514.78.1.136.

Eisenberg, N., Fabes, R. A., Guthrie, I. K., & Reiser, M. (2002). The role of emotionality and regulation in children's social competence and adjustment. In L. Pulkinnen & A. Caspi (Eds.), *Paths to successful development: Personality in the life course* (pp. 46–70). Cambridge: Cambridge University Press.

Eisenberg, N., Valiente, C., Morris, A. S., Fabes, R. A., Cumberland, A., & Reiser, M. (2003). Longitudinal relations among parental emotional expressivity, children's regulation, and quality of socioemotional function. *Developmental Psychology, 39*, 3–19. https://doi.org/10.1037/0012-1649.39.1.3.

Eisenberg, N., Sadovsky, A., Spinrad, T. L., Fabes, R. A., Losoya, S. H., Valiente, C., et al. (2005). The relations of problem behavior status to children's negative emotionality, effortful control, and impulsivity: Concurrent relations and prediction of change. *Developmental Psychology, 42*, 193–211. https://doi.org/10.1037/0012-1649.41.1.193.

Essex, M. J., Kraemer, H. C., Slattery, M. J., Burk, L. R., Boyce, W. T., Woodward, H. R., & Kupfer, D. J. (2009). Screening for childhood mental health problems: Outcomes and early identification. *Journal of Child Psychology and Psychiatry, 50*, 562–570. https://doi.org/10.1111/j.1469-7610.2008.02015.x.

Filcheck, H. A., McNeil, C. B., Greco, L. A., & Bernard, R. S. (2004). Using a whole-class token economy and coaching of teacher skills in a preschool classroom to manage disruptive behavior. *Psychology in the Schools, 4*, 351–361. https://doi.org/10.1002/pits.10168.

Gresham, F. M., & Elliott, S. N. (1990). *Social skills rating system*. Circle Pines: American Guidance Service.

Gutermuth-Anthony, L., Anthony, B. J., Glanville, D. N., Naiman, D. Q., Waandres, C., & Shaffer, S. (2005). The relationship between parenting stress, parenting behavior and preschoolers' social competence and behavior problems in the classroom. *Infant and Child Development, 14*, 133–154. https://doi.org/10.1002/icd.385.

Hay, D. F., Payne, A., & Chadwick, A. (2004). Peer relations in childhood. *Journal of Child Psychology and Psychiatry, 45*, 84–108. https://doi.org/10.1046/j.0021-9630.2003.00308.x.

Hill, A. L., Degnan, K. A., Calkins, S. A., & Keane, S. P. (2006). Profiles of externalizing behavior problems for boys and girls across preschool: The roles of emotion regulation and inattention. *Developmental Psychology, 42*, 913–928. https://doi.org/10.1037/0012-1649.42.5.913.

Hinshaw, S. P., Han, S. S., Erhardt, D., & Huber, A. (1992). Internalizing and externalizing behavior problems in preschool children: Correspondence among parent and teacher ratings and behavior observations. *Journal of Clinical Child Psychology, 21*, 143–150. https://doi.org/10.1207/s15374424jccp2102_6.

Howes, C. (2000). Social-emotional classroom climate in child care, child-teacher relationships and children's second grade peer relations. *Social Development, 9*, 191–204. https://doi.org/10.1111/1467-9507.00119.

Hughes, J. N., Cavell, T. M., Meehan, B. T., Zhang, D., & Collie, C. (2005). Adverse school context moderates the outcomes of selective interventions for aggressive children. *Journal of Consulting and Clinical Psychology, 73*, 731–736. https://doi.org/10.1037/0022-006X.73.4.731.

Izard, C. E., Fine, S., Schultz, D., Mostow, A., Ackerman, B., & Youngstrom, E. (2001). Emotion knowledge as a predictor of social behaviour and academic competence in children at risk. *Psychological Science, 12*, 18–23. https://doi.org/10.1111/1467-9280.00304.

Kam, C.-M., Greenberg, M. T., & Walls, C. T. (2003). Examining the role of implementation quality in school-based prevention using the PATHS curriculum. *Prevention Science, 4*, 55–63. https://doi.org/10.1023/A:1021786811186.

Kazdin, A. E., & Wassell, G. (1999). Barriers to treatment participation and therapeutic change among children referred for conduct disorder. *Journal of Clinical Child Psychology, 28*, 160–172. https://doi.org/10.1037/0022-006X.69.2.262.

Kim, H.-J., Arnold, D. H., Fisher, P. H., & Zeljo, A. (2005). Parenting and preschoolers' symptoms as a function of child gender and SES. *Child and Family Behavior Therapy, 27*, 23–41. https://doi.org/10.1300/J019v27n02_03.

LaFreniere, P. J., & Dumas, J. E. (1995). *Social competence and behavior evaluation* (Preschool ed.). Los Angeles: Western Psychological Services.

Lewis, T. J., & Sugai, G. (1999). Effective behavior support: A system approach to proactive schoolwide management. *Focus on Exceptional Children, 31*, 1–24.

Lochman, J. E., & Wells, K. C. (2002). The Coping Power program at the middle-school transition: Universal and indicated prevention effects. *Psychology of Addictive Behaviors, 16*, S40–S54. https://doi.org/10.1037/0893-164X.16.4S.S40.

Miclea, M., Bălaj, A., Porumb, M., Porumb, D., & Porumb, S. (2010). *PEDa: The developmental assessment platform for 3–6/7 year old children.* Cluj-Napoca: ASCR Publishing.

Prinz, R. J., & Sanders, M. R. (2007). Adopting a population-level approach to parenting and family support interventions. *Clinical Psychology Review, 27*, 739–749. https://doi.org/10.1016/j.cpr.2007.01.005.

Raver, C. C., Jones, S. M., Li-Grining, C., Zhai, F., Metzger, M. W., & Solomon, B. (2009). Targeting children's behavior problems in preschool classrooms: A cluster-randomized controlled trial. *Journal of Consulting and Clinical Psychology, 77*, 302–316. https://doi.org/10.1037/a0015302.

Roberts, C., Mazzucchelli, T., Studman, L., & Sanders, M. R. (2006). Behavioral family intervention for children with developmental disabilities and behavioral problems. *Journal of Clinical Child and Adolescent Psychology, 35*, 180–193. https://doi.org/10.1207/s15374424jccp3502_2.

Sanders, M. R., & Morawska, A. (2005). Can changing parental knowledge, dysfunctional expectations and attributions, and emotion regulation improve outcomes for children? In R. E. Tremblay, R. G. Barr, & R. DeV Peters (Eds.), *Encyclopedia on early childhood development.* Retrieved March 13, 2010, from www.excellence-earlychildhood.ca

Severson, H. H., & Walker, H. M. (2002). Pro-active approaches for identifying children at risk for socio-behavioral problems. In K. L. Lane, F. M. Gresham,

& T. E. O'Shaughnessy (Eds.), *Interventions for children with or at-risk for emotional and behavioral disorders* (pp. 33–54). Boston: Allyn & Bacon.

Severson, H. H., Walker, H. M., Hope-Doolittle, J., Kratochwill, T. R., & Gresham, F. M. (2007). Proactive, early screening to detect behaviorally at-risk students: Issues, approaches, emerging innovations, and professional practices. *Journal of School Psychology, 45*, 193–223. https://doi.org/10.1016/j.jsp.2006.11.003.

Snyder, J., Cramer, A., Afrank, J., & Patterson, G. R. (2005). The contributions of ineffective discipline and parental hostile attributions of child misbehavior to the development of conduct problems at home and school. *Developmental Psychology, 41*, 30–41. https://doi.org/10.1037/0012-1649.41.1.30.

Spinrad, T. L., Eisenberg, N., Harris, E., Hanish, L., Fabes, R. A., Kupanoff, K., Ringwald, S., & Holmes, J. (2004). The relation of children's everyday nonsocial peer play behavior to their emotionality, regulation, and social functioning. *Developmental Psychology, 40*, 67–80. https://doi.org/10.1037/0012-1649.40.1.67.

Ştefan, C. A., Bălaj, A., Porumb, M., Albu, M., & Miclea, M. (2009). Preschool screening for social and emotional competencies – Development and psychometric properties. *Cognition, Brain, Behavior. An Interdisciplinary Journal, 13*, 121–146.

Turner, K. M. T., & Sanders, M. R. (2006). Dissemination of evidence-based parenting and family support strategies: Learning from the Triple P – Positive Parenting Program system approach. *Aggression and Violent Behavior, 11*, 176–193. https://doi.org/10.1016/j.avb.2005.07.005.

van Lier, P. A. C., Vuijk, P., & Crijnen, A. A. M. (2005). Understanding mechanisms of change and development of antisocial behavior: The impact of a universal intervention. *Journal of Abnormal Child Psychology, 33*, 521–535. https://doi.org/10.1007/s10802-005-6735-7.

Webster-Stratton, C. (1990). Long-term follow-up of families with young conduct-problem children: From preschool to grade school. *Journal of Clinical Child Psychology, 19*, 1344–1349.

Webster-Stratton, C. (1998). Preventing conduct problems in Head Start children: Strengthening parent competencies. *Journal of Consulting and Clinical Psychology, 66*, 715–730. https://doi.org/10.1037/0022-006X.66.5.715.

Webster-Stratton, C., & Hammond, M. (1997). Treating children with early-onset conduct problems: A comparison of child and parent training interventions. *Journal of Consulting and Clinical Psychology, 65*, 93–109. https://doi.org/10.1037/0022-006X.65.1.93.

Webster-Stratton, C., & Reid, J. M. (2003). Treating conduct problems and strengthening social and emotional competence in young children: The Dina Dinosaur Program. *Journal of Emotional and Behavioral Disorders, 2*, 130–143. https://doi.org/10.1177/10634266030110030101.

Webster-Stratton, C., Reid, J. M., & Hammond, M. (2001). Preventing conduct problems, promoting social competence: A parent-teacher training partnership in Head Start. *Journal of Clinical Child Psychology, 30*, 283–302. https://doi.org/10.1207/S15374424JCCP3301_11.

Webster-Stratton, C., Reid, J. M., & Hammond, M. (2004). Treating children with early-onset conduct problems: Intervention outcomes for parent, child, and teacher training. *Journal of Clinical Child and Adolescent Psychology, 33*, 105–124. https://doi.org/10.1207/S15374424JCCP3301_11.

Webster-Stratton, C., Reid, M. J., & Stoolmiller, M. (2008). Preventing conduct problems and improving school readiness: Evaluation of the Incredible Years teacher and child training programs in high-risk schools. *The Journal of Child Psychology and Psychiatry, 49*, 471–488. https://doi.org/10.1111/j.1469-7610.2007.01861.x.

Widen, S. C., & Russell, J. A. (2003). A closer look at preschoolers' freely produced labels for facial expressions. *Developmental Psychology, 39*, 114–128. https://doi.org/10.1037/0012-1649.39.1.114.

Youngstrom, E., Meltzer Wolpaw, J., Kogos, J. L., Schoff, K., Ackerman, B., & Izard, C. (2000). Interpersonal problem solving in preschool and first grade: Developmental change and ecological validity. *Journal of Clinical Child Psychology, 29*, 589–602. https://doi.org/10.1207/S15374424JCCP2904_11.

Zubrick, S. R., Ward, K. A., Silburn, S. R., Lawrence, D., Williams, A. A., Blair, E., et al. (2005). Prevention of child behavior problems through universal implementation of a group behavioral family intervention. *Prevention Science, 6*, 176–193. https://doi.org/10.1007/s11121-005-0013-2.

Check for updates

CHAPTER 5

Assessing SEP Efficacy at the Individual Level: A Multiple Baseline Evaluation of Changes in Observed Classroom Behaviors

Introduction

Research conducted on preschool age children supports the notion that poorly developed social-emotional competencies place children at increased risk of behavior problems (Denham et al. 2001; Hastings et al. 2000). As extensively discussed in Chap. 1, child risk factors interact with environmental factors, which might lead to increased difficulties in children's social adjustment (Fabes et al. 2006). Children's low social-emotional competencies were consistently associated with either adult-child interactions characterized by ineffective support offered for developing age-appropriate social-emotional skills, or ineffective discipline strategies (Dennis 2006; Filcheck et al. 2004). Besides increased risk of behavior problems, research has uncovered that children with persistent behavior problems are in the long term more likely to be at risk of several other problems such as poor academic performance and school dropout (Mantzicopoulos and Neurath-Pritchett 1998; Trentacosta et al. 2006), social adjustment problems in relation to both adults and peers (Wahler 1997), increased likelihood of clinical referrals in middle childhood, and engaging in substance abuse and delinquency during adolescence (Trentacosta et al. 2006). Moreover, given that misconduct in the form of aggression and non-compliance tends to exhibit a relatively stable pattern from preschool to adolescence (Eisenberg et al. 1999, 2000; Mendez et al. 2002), researchers directed their attention toward translating knowledge about risk into effective

C. A. Ştefan, *Social-Emotional Prevention Programs for Preschool Children's Behavior Problems*,
https://doi.org/10.1007/978-3-319-74751-4_5

interventions, focused on deflecting children from such negative developmental trajectories (Nation et al. 2003; Nelson et al. 2003). In this context, previous research was focused on 2 types of interventions: (1) preventive interventions in community-based settings aimed at children who are at risk or exhibit no risk; and (2) individualized interventions mainly aimed at children with clinical intensity behavior problems.

Community-Based Interventions as Preventive Strategies for Children at Risk

Preventive interventions are usually delivered within schools in community settings, as part of an effort to reach a large number of children and parents in need of psychological services (Conroy et al. 2008). Such interventions take the form of either universal interventions targeting non-risk children or indicated interventions targeting children who are at risk of behavior problems. From a methodological point of view, establishing the efficacy of such interventions is based on comparing intervention and control group outcomes at different time points (Morgan and Morgan 2008). Chapters 3 and 4 provided an overview of SEP efficacy in the context of a partially randomized controlled trial employing this type of research design. The obtained results were consistent with previous research suggesting that interventions which consider including a wider range of intervention strategies aiming to target the complex interplay between both individual (i.e., poor social-emotional skills) and interpersonal (i.e., adults' behavioral management strategies, communication style) risk factors exhibit more consistent effects of lowering children's risk of conduct problems (Ştefan and Miclea 2010; Webster-Stratton and Taylor 2001).

Hence, results from community-based interventions suggested that universal interventions are associated with significant postintervention improvements in terms of children's social-emotional development (Domitrovich et al. 2007; Kam et al. 2003). However, classroom curriculum delivery alone was ineffective in addressing non-compliant and aggressive behaviors. Therefore, targeting additional risk factors was found to increase such interventions' efficacy in at risk children's behavior problems. For instance, teacher training and consultations for supporting the implementation of the classroom curriculum for social-emotional development were associated with better outcomes of at risk children (Domitrovich et al. 2007, 2009). Conversely, improved behavioral outcomes and transfer of children's skills from the classroom to home interactions were found when parents were also included as a target group of the intervention (Hughes et al. 2005; Webster-Stratton et al. 2001). Taken together, these results suggest that community-based interventions which include multi-component approaches are in fact promising strategies for lowering not only children's risk of behavior problems (Conduct Problems Prevention Research Group [CPPRG] 1999a, b; Raver et al. 2009; Webster-Stratton et al. 2008), but also in changing teachers' and parents' ineffective discipline strategies and enhancing their ability to employ positive discipline strategies (Webster-Stratton et al. 2001, 2004).

Individualized Interventions as Strategies for Preventing Escalation of Clinically Significant Conduct Problems

Whereas efficacy testing of community-based interventions relies on intervention versus control group comparisons, research on clinically-referred children is performed by comparing a participant's baseline scores against postintervention scores. Such single-subject designs were consistently employed in assessing the efficacy of intervention strategies for a wide range of clinical intensity problems such as conduct disorders, attention-deficit and hyperactivity disorder (ADHD), autism, etc. (Gmeider and Kratochwill 1998; Fenstermacher et al. 2006; Loftin et al. 2008). Compared to designs grounded in group comparisons which provide a perspective on intervention mechanisms which elicit changes in broadly defined competencies, the major benefit of single-subject designs is related to the fact that they permit an in-depth assessment of an intervention's effect on a given behavior. This allows a more refined interpretation of how specific intervention strategies affect the person rather than the group (Dunlap et al. 2006).

Single-subject designs were most often employed in applied behavioral analysis with the intention to disentangle the relative contributions of environmental variables (e.g., teacher behaviors, instructional components, parental behaviors or changes in physical environment) to reductions in observed frequency of children's externalizing type behaviors (Gunter et al. 1998; Stichter et al. 2004). Research on children referred for conduct problems suggests that in fact strategies which are employed as part of community-based interventions are responsible for eliciting changes in children's behaviors. For example, group social skills training was found to exert effects in terms of increased levels of adaptive behaviors such as cooperation and sharing, or on task behaviors, as well as reduced levels of aggression and non-compliance (Chandler et al. 1999; Conroy et al. 2005; Lane et al. 2003).

On a related note, social skills training methods were also assessed in combination with teacher training in behavioral management. Hence, besides training children, adding consultations conducted with teachers by program providers aimed at increasing teachers' ability to implement behavior contracts/contingency contracts and corrective feedback for misbehaviors, had positive effects by increasing children's involvement in school related tasks, compliance and prosocial behaviors (Ducharme et al. 2010; Fairbanks et al. 2007).

Conversely, parental skill training for effective praise and corrective teaching resulted in improved parental behavior management skills, and significant changes in children's compliant behaviors (Marchant et al. 2004; Ducharme et al. 2002). In another study attempting to train parents in delivering effective instructions, using positive reinforcements for children's appropriate behaviors, and response-cost procedures for inappropriate behaviors, found that children displayed significantly less-frequent aggressive and non-compliant behaviors, while parents showed a significant reduction in employing ineffective discipline strategies (Ducharme and DiAdamo 2005).

The Current Study

In light of the above presented results, it can be inferred that group and single-subject designs provide answers concerning a particular intervention's efficacy at different levels: if intervention vs. control group designs help researchers define strategies that work in general for a relatively larger number of children, single-subject designs provide evidence supporting the efficacy of particular intervention strategies in eliciting changes in certain types of behaviors. As suggested by the reviewed evidence from single-subject designs, these were generally employed for children who have diagnosed behavioral disorders. Consequently, with the exception of Lees and Ronan (2008) who employed a similar methodology for testing the effects of the Incredible Years program on children with ADHD and their mothers, no other research has previously focused on this type of methodology in the context of community-based interventions. Therefore, for the purposes of this study, the Social-Emotional Prevention Program's (SEP) efficacy was evaluated specifically in the context of children at risk of behavior problems with the emphasis on changes in their classroom behaviors. Furthermore, based on previous research suggesting that intervention strategies employed for clinically referred children are similar to those employed in community-based settings, the second objective of this study was to examine the extent to which patterns of intervention effects in group interventions for at risk children are different from those obtained in individualized interventions.

Method

Participants

A detailed description of the selection process of participants from the intervention and control groups was provided in Chaps. 3 and 4. From the 121 intervention group children, participants in this efficacy study were selected based on the following criteria: (1) below cutoff scores on teacher rated emotional and social competencies; (2) below cutoff scores on teacher rated externalizing problems; (3) child attendance to at least 75% of the classroom curriculum activities; and (4) their parents attending at least 3 out of 4 parent training sessions. A total of 9 ($n = 9$) participants from 7 different classrooms met the above described criteria. Four children were excluded from the sample because additional risk factors were identified, namely above cutoff scores on harsh and/or inconsistent discipline strategies. From the final analyses 1 child was excluded due to low classroom attendance levels, and 1 due to his mother's low attendance in the parent training. The final sample included 3 children ($n = 3$) from 3 different classrooms: a 42-month-old girl (Oana), and 2 boys (Rareş and Alex) who were 52-months-old and 43-months-old respectively, at the beginning of the intervention. Their risk characteristics are described in Table 5.1. Rareş came from a middle socio-economic status family (parents were high-school graduates), while Oana and Alex came from high SES backgrounds (parents were university graduates).

Design

In order to evaluate SEP efficacy at the individual level a non-concurrent multiple baseline design (MBD) was employed (Watson and Workman 1981). Non-concurrent designs include a series of A–B (baseline-intervention) replications in which the baseline length is predetermined,

Table 5.1 Participant risk assessments based on teacher evaluations

Participant	*Teacher rated emotional and social competence*		*Teacher rated externalizing problems – SCBE*[b]
	ECS-T[a]	*SCS-T*[a]	
Oana	36[c]	46[c]	52[c]
Rareş	34[c]	44[c]	52[c]
Alex	31[c]	44[c]	45[c]

Note: *ECS-T* = emotional competence screening-teacher, *SCS-T* = social competence screening-teacher, *SCBE* = social competence behavior evaluation

[a]Cutoff score for the externalizing problem (< 56) scale was obtained using a cutoff established at the 10th percentile of the norms

[b]Cutoff scores based on Romanian norms for ECS-T (< 37) and SCS-T (< 47)

[c]Below cutoff score on the measured construct

unlike in concurrent designs in which baseline timeframes become more prolonged with the addition of new participants (Carr 2005; Christ 2007). However, in ecological settings one must consider that participants become available at a given time point, and longer baselines are impossible to handle in such circumstances (Freeman and Mash 2007). In non-concurrent designs, participants are randomly assigned to a particular baseline length, and although this type of design does not provide the degree of experimental control which is usually encountered in concurrent designs, this type of design was chosen due to its sensitivity to the ecological context in which SEP was implemented. Observation of children's classroom behaviors were conducted during 4 phases: baseline, intervention, maintenance, and follow-up.

Procedures

Procedures for including children and their parents in this study were described in detail in Chaps. 3 and 4. Also, exclusion and inclusion criteria were presented in the participants section of this chapter. After selection of the participants, 5 children were observed in their classrooms by 3 undergraduate female students (later 2 participants were dropped from the final analyses due to low attendance rates to the intervention). Observations were conducted during 4 phases (baseline, intervention, maintenance, and follow-up), in 3 different settings. Teachers were unaware which child was observed, because it was important to prevent adults from unwittingly making changes to their own behaviors in relation to these children, which could implicitly influence the outcomes of the observations.

Classroom observers were trained as follows: (1) they were asked to learn behavioral definitions for each of the observed behaviors; (2) after being tested for the definitions, they practiced on videotapes the data collection procedure; and (3) videotaped behaviors were individually scored, results were compared, and eventual discrepancies between coding was discussed. Training continued until the observers reached an 80% agreement rate. In each classroom, observations were conducted once or twice a week for 2 hours using a paper and pencil method for collecting the data. Observers were blind to the intervention phases and the intervention's content. Each observation session took place during morning classroom activities. The observation sessions were also recorded, and reliability checks were conducted by the program's developer on half of the observation sessions for each participant.

Children selected to take part in this study were randomly assigned to 1 of the 3 *baseline* (no intervention) lengths including 2, 3, or 4 weeks, with 2 observations conducted each week. In the next phase, namely the *intervention* phase, observations were scheduled to take place once a week as follows: 4 observations for the first intervention phase, 3 for the second, and 4 for the third and fourth phases. Intervention phases were linked to the timeline of particular intervention modules from the SEP classroom curriculum, as follows: (1) during the first 4 weeks teachers implemented the activities from the compliance to rules and emotion recognition modules (first to fourth week); (2) the next intervention phase lasted 3 weeks during which time teachers covered the contents of the emotion regulation module (fifth to seventh week); (3) the next phase was associated with the problem-solving module from the classroom curriculum (eighth to the eleventh week); and (4) the final 4 weeks corresponded to the cooperative play module (twelth to fifteenth week). In the *maintenance phase* one observation session was conducted per week, and data corresponding to this phase were gathered beginning with the fifth, eighth, and twelfth week respectively. For the last intervention module, no maintenance phase was evaluated. *Follow-up* observations were conducted 4 months after the intervention was removed; the observers recorded behaviors during 4 weekly observation sessions. Classroom observations were conducted after the end of data gathering on child, parent, and teacher reported measures.

Intervention

SEP encompasses child, teacher, and parent focused activities, which were described in Chap. 2. Also, a detailed specification of the intervention's objectives and of the implemented activities can be found in Appendices 1, 2 and 3, which correspond to each of the 3 intervention components.

Measures

Screening Measures Children's risk status was established using 2 separate screening measures of social and emotional competencies development: the *Social Competence Screening for Preschoolers – Teacher Form* (SCS-T; Miclea et al. 2010) and the *Emotional Competence Screening for Preschoolers – Teacher Form* (ECS-T; Miclea et al. 2010). Teachers also rated children on the Externalizing Problems summary scale from *Social Competence and Behavior Evaluation* (SCBE; LaFreniere and Dumas 1995). The Harsh and Inconsistent Discipline scales from the *LIFT Parenting Practices Interview* (PPI; Webster-Stratton et al. 2001) were used to evaluate parent risk. More details on the reliability, validity, and cutoff points of these measures can be found in Chaps. 3 and 4.

Outcome Measures During classroom observations, data were collected for each participant on 4 classroom behaviors, which are defined and described in Table 5.2. Participants were rated on the frequency of positive and negative behaviors. Positive behaviors included compliance to teacher's requests, adequate responses to frustrating events, prosocial behaviors, and cooperative play. Conversely, negative behaviors referred to non-compliance to teacher's requests, inadequate responses to frustrating events, aggressive behaviors, and isolated play. For each observed behavior a frequency score was computed as follows: the total number of positive behaviors was divided by the sum of positive and negative behaviors, and the result was multiplied by 100.

Interobserver agreement was computed for 50% of the observation sessions. Video recordings were obtained by using 2 Sony DCR-SR3 cameras, which were placed unobtrusively in the classrooms. The agreement rate between observers was obtained using the following formula: the number of agreements, divided by the number of agreements plus disagreements, multiplied by 100. For compliance, interobserver agreement varied between 91% and 94% for compliance; 82–84% for frustration tolerance; 88–92% for prosocial behaviors; and 85–90% for cooperative play.

Table 5.2 Description of positive and negative child behaviors observed in the classroom

	Definition	*Observations*
Observed positive behavior		
1. Compliance with teacher's requests	Performing the requested behavior (e.g., the child performs the behavior without further prompting from the teacher; says "yes" when asked to do something, and follows though the promise)	Requests from the teacher might include behaviors during classroom activities (e.g., remaining seated, staying on task, speaking when asked to), playing activities (e.g., gathering toys, stop playing when asked to), or during transitions
2. Adequate responses to frustrating events	Reorienting attention or seeking help from the teacher when denied access to a toy or not being allowed to play in a group of children Waiting patiently when the teacher cannot answer immediately to his/her requests	These behaviors can be observed both during classroom activities and play sessions
3. Prosocial behaviors	Sharing toys with other children Responding positively when another child makes a request for a toy Offering to help or comfort a child when something bad happens to him/her (e.g., falling or being hit) Taking turns in playing with a toy Asking for permission to play with another child's toy	These behaviors can be observed during play sessions
4. Cooperative play	Playing in a group of children and using verbal exchanges with other play-mates (e.g., "You are … and I am going to be …", "Let's build a train") Inviting other children to join him/her in playing Approaching a group of children and blending into the game Making an overt request to play with other children (e.g., "Can I come and play with you?")	If a child begins a play session involved in group play, it is recorded as cooperative play; the cooperative play is recorded only once, if the child does not change his/her behavior during the play session

(*continued*)

Table 5.2 (continued)

	Definition	*Observations*
Observed negative behavior		
1. Non-compliance with teacher's requests	Refusing to perform the behavior requested by the teacher (e.g., the child ignores the teacher's request, and continues to do something else; says "no" when asked to do something)	If a child does not comply with a request and the teacher directs the same request to him/her again this is recorded as a separate behavior
2. Inadequate responses to frustrating events	Crying or temper tantrum when asked to do something, or being denied access to a toy	These behaviors can be observed both during classroom activities and play sessions
	Trying to get the teacher's attention with repeated requests	
3. Aggressive behaviors	Physical aggression (e.g. hitting, slapping, biting, scratching, or throwing objects)	These behaviors can be observed during play sessions
	Grabbing a toy without obtaining permission	
	Intruding in other children's play without permission	
	Destroying other children's toys	
4. Isolated play	Playing alone and/or playing without exhibiting verbal exchanges with another child	If a child begins a play session involved in isolated play, it is recorded as such only once

Treatment Integrity and Attendance Rates

In the current study, the children included in the final sample participated in at least 75% of the classroom activities, and their parents in at least 3 out of 4 parent training sessions.

Results[1]

Analysis Strategy

The traditional approach to single-subject designs employs visual inspection of the graphed data (Kazdin 1982). One major criticism of visual analysis came from research indicating that interrater reliability indices were rather low (.55–.62) (Gibson and Ottenbacher 1988). Consequently, specific quantitative methods for interpreting data from single-subject designs were developed (Nourbakhsh and Ottenbacher 1994).

Data analysis for this study involved interpretation of: (1) mean shift computed as the difference between baseline and intervention means; (2) variability assessed using the 2 standard deviation method (2 SD), which indicates that significant changes in performance are associated with the presence of 2 consecutive data points outside the 2 SD deviation range (Nourbakhsh and Ottenbacher 1994); (3) level changes were interpreted using the percentage of non-overlapping data (PND), a non-parametric method indicating the percentage of data points from the intervention phase which fall above or below the highest score from the baseline (Scruggs et al. 1987); (4) trend changes were evaluated using the *C* statistic, a time-series analysis method which is best suited to small data sets containing as few as 8 observations (Tryon 1982), and polynomial contrasts, *a priori* planned comparisons, were computed using univariate ANOVAs to test for possible significant linear, quadratic, or cubic trends in the data sets; and (5) degree of serial dependency in the data, an inherent characteristic of single-subject studies, in which observations are thought to be dependent, was assessed using the Lag1 autocorrelation (Borckhardt et al. 2008).

Observed Classroom Behaviors

Participant 1 For Oana the data show that positive mean shifts, and significant variability and level changes, were obtained during the maintenance phase of the intervention for compliance and tolerance frustration as indicated in Table 5.3. Time-series analyses employing the *C* statistic presented in Table 5.4 revealed the presence of a significant intervention-maintenance, as well as a significant maintenance-follow-up, trend for compliance and tolerance frustration, while for cooperative play a significant baseline to intervention trend was obtained ($ps < .01$).

Preplanned ANOVA comparisons were conducted and confirmed the presence of a significant linear trend from intervention to maintenance for compliance, $t(11) = 3.67, p < .01$ depicted in Fig. 5.1, and a similar significant trend for frustration tolerance, $t(7) = 2.32, p < .05$, which can be seen in Fig. 5.2. No significant changes in trend occurred for prosocial behaviors, but due to the presence of a significant baseline trend for cooperative play possible effects were tested on baseline observations. A significant linear effect was detected for the last data set, $t(12) = 2.91, p < .05$, suggesting that the data pattern changed at the same time the intervention for developing prosocial behaviors began as indicated in Fig. 5.4.

Participant 2 The presence of a postintervention effect on compliance was sustained by a positive mean shift, as well as significant changes in variability and level. These changes were also present in the maintenance phase for frustration tolerance and prosocial behaviors, but not for cooperative play as indicated in Table 5.3. These data were supported by the presence of a significant baseline-intervention trend for compliance, as well as significant intervention-maintenance trends for frustration tolerance and prosocial behaviors ($p < .01$), as indicated in Table 5.4.

The following baseline-intervention contrasts indicated that there was a significant shift in the data immediately postintervention for compliance, $t(6) = 4.19, p < .01$ presented in Fig. 5.1, a significant linear trend for frustration tolerance in the maintenance phase $t(6) = 2.50, p < .05$ depicted in Fig. 5.2, and also a significant linear trend for prosocial behaviors in the maintenance phase, $t(5) = 2.66, p < .05$, presented in Fig. 5.3.

Participant 3 A positive mean shift and significant changes in variability and slope level took place in the maintenance phase for all observed behaviors as indicated in Table 5.3. The *Z* score of the *C* statistic presented in Table 5.4 confirmed the presence of a significant trend in the intervention

Table 5.3 Means, standard deviations, mean shift, variability changes, level changes, and autocorrelations for observed behaviors

	Mean (range)	*Standard deviations*	*Mean shift*	*2 SD*	*PND (%)*	*r(lag 1)*
Participant 1						
Compliance with rules						
Baseline	26.75 (17–38)	8.96				0.17
Intervention	32.00 (20–50)	13.14	5.25	NS	25	−0.45
Maintenance	50.33 (33–67)	11.27	23.58	S	78	−0.17
Follow-up	95.75 (83–100)	8.50	71.00	S	100	−0.42
Frustration tolerance						
Baseline	22.63 (0–50)	16.94				0.55
Intervention	27.67 (0–50)	25.42	5.04	NS	0	−0.59
Maintenance	66.67 (33–100)	23.07	44.04	S	67	0.11
Follow-up	85.50 (67–100)	17.06	61.87	S	100	−0.66
Prosocial behaviors						
Baseline	24.00 (0–50)	15.45				0.01
Intervention	42.67 (33–50)	8.74	18.67	NS	0	−0.35
Maintenance	55.67 (50–67)	9.81	31.67	NS	25	−0.33
Follow-up	86.75 (67–100)	16.19	62.75	S	100	−0.78*
Cooperative play						
Baseline	34.64 (0–67)	18.30				0.42
Intervention	72.33 (50–100)	25.42	37.67	NS	33	−0.48
Follow-up	71.00 (50–100)	20.93	36.36	NS	25	−0.11
Participant 2						
Compliance to rules						
Baseline	42.20 (33–50)	7.56				−0.13
Intervention	65.00 (57–71)	7.21	22.80	S	100	0.12
Maintenance	66.89 (56–78)	8.30	24.69	S	100	−0.54*
Follow-up	69.00 (60–80)	10.15	26.80	S	100	−0.59
Frustration tolerance						
Baseline	33.75 (0–60)	28.26				−0.03
Intervention	42.33 (0–67)	36.83	8.58	NS	25	−0.66
Maintenance	77.86 (50–100)	18.68	44.11	S	86	0.46
Follow-up	78.33 (70–80)	4.89	44.58	S	100	−0.17
Prosocial behaviors						
Baseline	28.45 (7–57)	14.45				0.05
Intervention	40.00 (30–57)	14.80	11.15	NS	0	0.16
Maintenance	62.50 (53–70)	7.89	34.05	S	75	0.09
Follow-up	75.50 (60–100)	17.45	47.05	S	100	−0.10

(*continued*)

Table 5.3 (continued)

	Mean (range)	*Standard deviations*	*Mean shift*	*2 SD*	*PND (%)*	*r(lag 1)*
Cooperative play						
Baseline	71.57 (50–85)	10.07				0.13
Intervention	75.50 (67–80)	6.14	4.07	NS	0	−0.38
Follow-up	91.25 (80–100)	10.31	36.36	S	50	0.15
Participant 3						
Compliance with rules						
Baseline	41.57 (30–55)	9.00				0.09
Intervention	47.50 (40–55)	6.45	5.93	NS	0	−0.65
Maintenance	63.20 (50–75)	8.92	21.63	S	70	0.03
Follow-up	70.75 (67–75)	3.30	29.18	S	100	−0.37
Frustration tolerance						
Baseline	21.82 (0–28)	12.99				−0.11
Intervention	32.67 (25–40)	7.51	10.85	NS	33	−0.01
Maintenance	43.56 (25–60)	13.45	21.74	S	71	0.48
Follow-up	63.00 (50–75)	10.61	41.18	S	100	−0.60
Prosocial behaviors						
Baseline	53.57 (33–67)	11.19				0.15
Intervention	54.00 (45–67)	11.53	1.57	NS	0	−0.20
Maintenance	72.50 (60–87)	8.66	18.93	NS	75	−0.47
Follow-up	69.25 (60–75)	7.23	15.68	NS	50	0.01
Cooperative play						
Baseline	62.41 (50–75)	11.45				−0.25
Intervention	91.25 (75–100)	11.81	28.84	S	75	−0.32
Follow-up	87.50 (75–100)	14.43	23.09	S	50	0.25

*$p < .05$

phase for compliance, and during the maintenance phase for frustration tolerance, and prosocial behaviors, respectively (*ps* < .01).

Preplanned comparison confirmed the presence of a significant linear trend from intervention-maintenance for compliance, $t(12) = 3.64$, $p < .01$ depicted in Fig. 5.1, and in the same phase for prosocial behaviors, $t(4) = 2.44$, $p < .05$, as can be seen in Fig. 5.3. No significant trends were detected for frustration tolerance and cooperative play (*ps* > .05). However, based on significant level and variability changes for cooperative play, there is evidence supporting the notion that the intervention was effective for cooperative play behaviors in the intervention phase as presented in Fig. 5.4.

Table 5.4 *Z* scores derived from the *C* statistic and its standard deviations for observed classroom behaviors

	BL	*BL+INT*	*MAINT*	*INT+MAINT*	*MAINT+FU*
Participant 1					
Compliance with rules	4 observations	4 + 4 observations	9 observations	4 + 9 observations	9 + 4 observations
Z_C		0.60	−0.33	4.71**	8.85**
C		0.06	−0.03	0.33	0.62
SD		0.10	0.09	0.07	0.07
Frustration tolerance	8 observations	8+3 observations	6 observations	3+6 observations	6+4 observations
Z_C	4.00**	3.63**	3.00**	6.00**	3.25**
C	0.40	0.29	0.33	0.48	0.26
SD	0.10	0.08	0.11	0.08	0.08
Prosocial behaviors	11 observations	11+3 observations	3 observations	3+3 observations	3+4 observations
Z_C	6.00**	5.17**		4.36**	4.20**
C	0.42	0.31		0.48	0.42
SD	0.07	0.06		0.11	0.10
	BL	*BL+INT*	*INT+FU*		
Cooperative play	14 observations	14+3 observations	3+4 observations		
Z_C	7.26**	8.56**	−2.12		
C	0.45	0.45	−0.22		
SD	0.06	0.05	0.10		
	BL	*BL + INT*	*MAINT*	*INT + MAINT*	*MAINT + FU*
Participant 2					
Compliance with rules	5 observations	5 + 3 observations	9 observations	3 + 9 observations	9 + 3 observations
ZC		4.60**	−5.88	−5.25	−7.75
C		0.46	−0.53	−0.42	−0.62
SD		0.10	0.09	0.08	0.08

(*continued*)

Table 5.4 (continued)

	BL	*BL+INT*	*MAINT*	*INT+MAINT*	*MAINT+FU*
Frustration tolerance	8 observations	8 + 3 observations	6 observations	3 + 6 observations	6 + 3 observations
ZC	0.78	−0.86	5.10**	4.00**	6.25**
C	0.07	−0.06	0.51	0.32	0.50
SD	0.09	0.07	0.10	0.08	0.08
Prosocial behavior	11 observations	11 + 3 observations	4 observations	3 + 4 observations	4 + 3 observations
ZC	−0.63	0.17		5.08**	2.10
C	−0.05	0.01		0.66	0.21
SD	0.08	0.06		0.13	0.10

	BL	*BL + INT*	*INT + FU*
Cooperative play	14 observations	14 + 4 observations	4 + 3 observations
ZC	1.20	0.75	6.50**
C	0.06	0.03	0.65
SD	0.05	0.04	0.10

	BL	*BL + INT*	*MAINT*	*INT + MAINT*	*MAINT + FU*
Participant 3					
Compliance with rules	7 observations	7 + 4 observations	10 observations	4 + 10 observations	10 + 4 observations
ZC	2.80**	3.75**	3.88**	9.00**	2.83**
C	0.28	0.30	0.31	0.54	0.17
SD	0.10	0.08	0.08	0.06	0.06
Frustration tolerance	11 observations	11+3 observations	7 observations	3+7 observations	7+4 observations
ZC	1.00	3.57**	4.38**	5.63**	5.63**
C	0.08	0.25	0.57	0.45	0.45
SD	0.08	0.07	0.13	0.08	0.08

Prosocial behavior	14 observations	14 + 3 observations	3 observations	3 + 3 observations	3 + 4 observations
ZC	4.67**	5.40**		5.50**	−2.10
C	0.28	0.27		0.55	−0.22
SD	0.06	0.05		0.10	0.10
	BL	*BL + INT*	*INT + FU*		
Cooperative play	17 observations	17 + 3 observations	3 + 4 observations		
ZC	−4.20	−6.75	−0.30		
C	−0.21	−0.27	−0.03		
SD	0.05	0.04	0.10		

Note: *BL* = baseline, *INT* = intervention, *MAINT* = maintenance, *FU* = follow-up
** $p < .01$

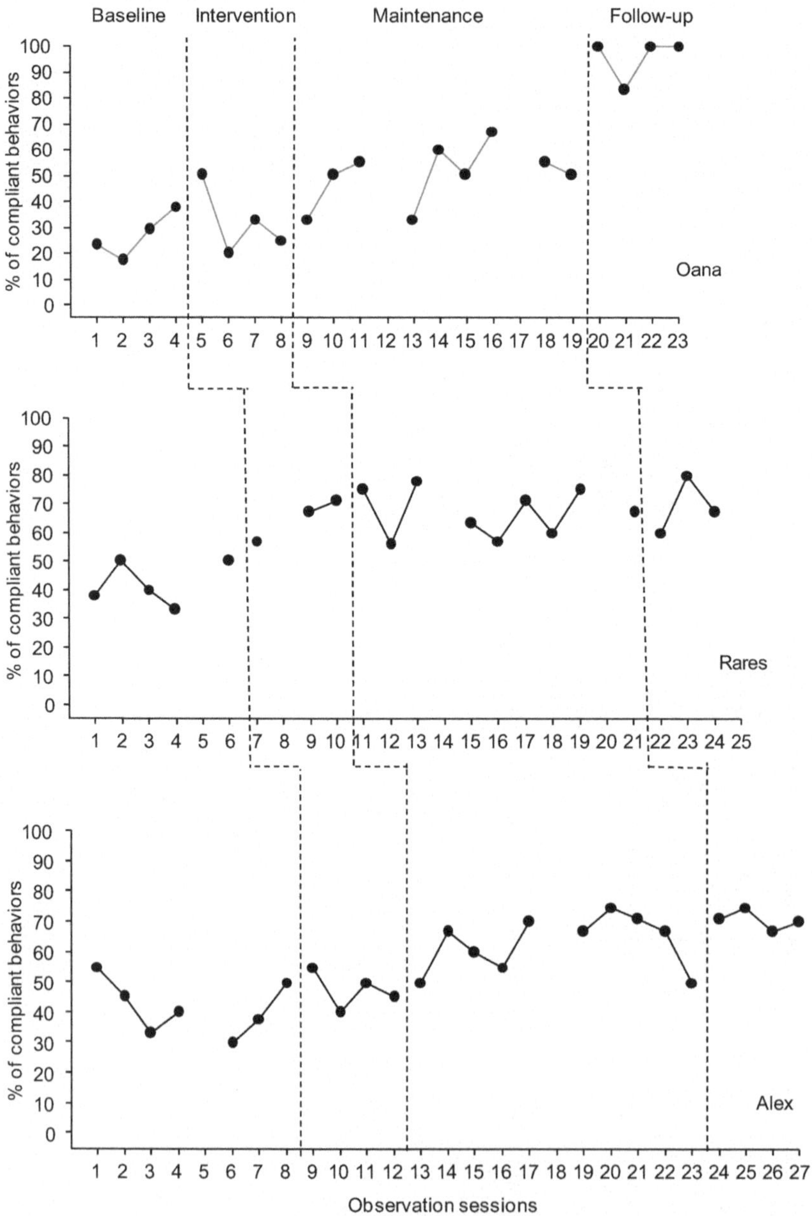

Fig. 5.1 Observation of compliance across 3 participants in a non-concurrent MBD

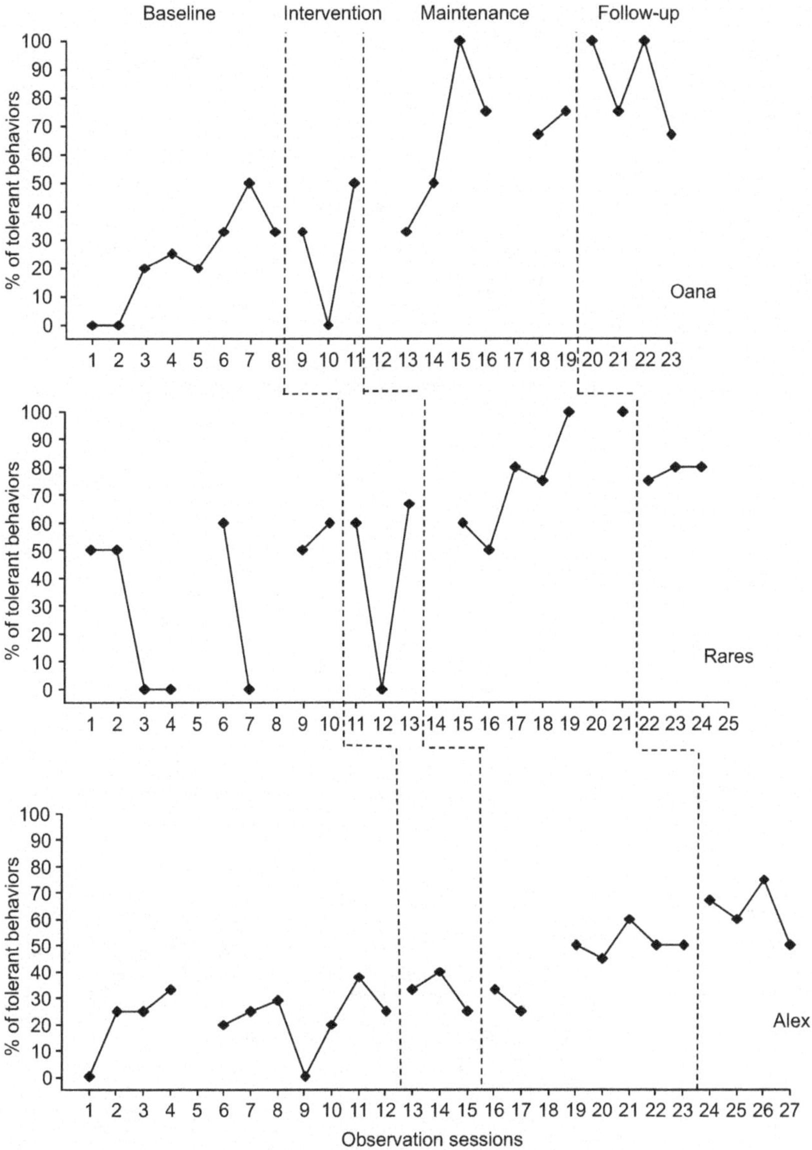

Fig. 5.2 Observation of frustration tolerance across 3 participants in a non-concurrent MBD

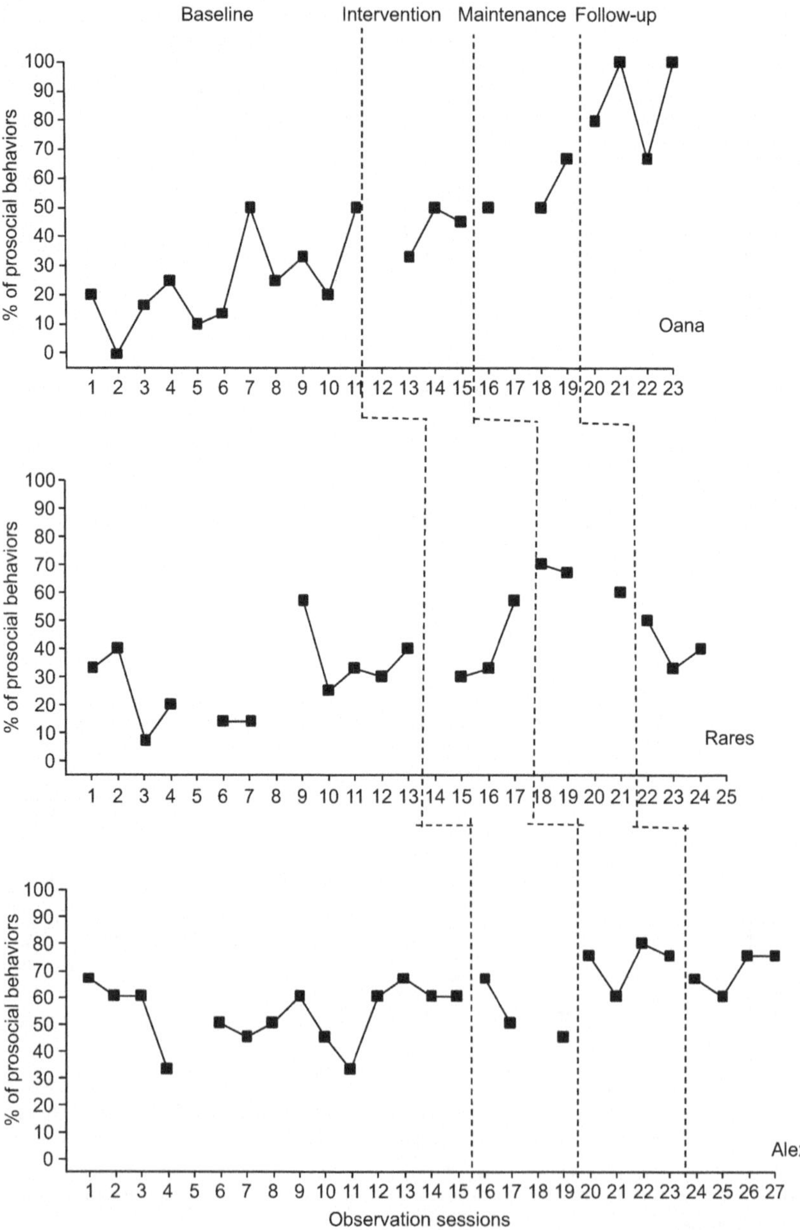

Fig. 5.3 Observation of prosocial behaviors across 3 participants in a non-concurrent MBD

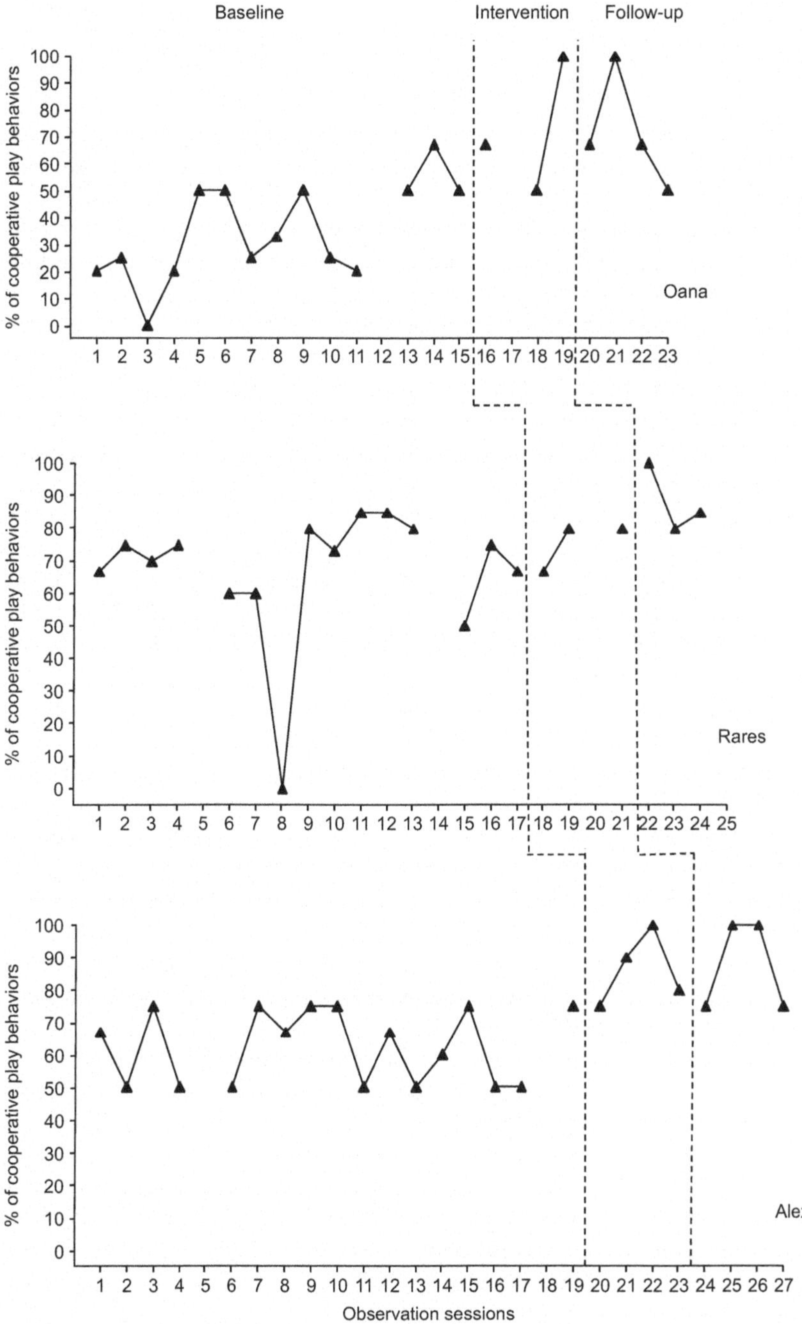

Fig. 5.4 Observation of cooperative behaviors across 3 participants in a non-concurrent MBD

Discussion

While in most community-based settings preventive interventions have been consistently evaluated using group comparison designs, the first aim of the current study was to examine SEP efficacy on at risk children's classroom behaviors using a single-subject design methodology. Only the efficacy of the Incredible Years community-based intervention for children with ADHD was previously investigated employing a similar methodology to the one used in this study (Lees and Ronan 2008).

Data gathered from classroom observations suggest that SEP elicited consistent changes in children's classroom behaviors in the expected directions. These findings indicate that similar mechanisms to those employed in individualized interventions for clinically referred children are responsible for eliciting intervention effects for at-risk children in community-based settings. For instance, a combination of antecedent-based (i.e., rules, limit setting) and consequence-based strategies (i.e., response-cost procedures, logical consequences), which were found effective for clinically referred children (Chandler et al. 1999; Conroy et al. 2005; McGoey and DuPaul 2000), was associated with children's increased compliance after SEP implementation.

Also, this study is among the first to define behavioral outcomes for intervention strategies related to emotion regulation abilities. The results suggest that intervention strategies for improving responses to frustrating situations can be positively influenced by supporting the development of anger management techniques through role-play, feedback, as well as behavioral management strategies for reinforcing appropriate anger management during conflict situations (Blum 2001). Interestingly, these results also provide indirect support to the notion that the "turtle technique", is an effective strategy for anger management not only for children who are clinically referred for conduct problems, but also for at risk children (Robin et al. 1976).

Previous studies showed that increased use of prosocial strategies (i.e., sharing, turn-taking, waiting, cooperating) are the result of problem-solving training, as well as modeling and reinforcing positive solutions in conflict situations in individualized interventions (DuPaul et al. 2001; Matthys et al. 1999; Mayer 1995). Evidence obtained from the current study on SEP efficacy suggests that children's training during the classroom curriculum in problem-solving, as well as teacher training in coaching and supporting the development of these skills, provides the context for improved management of potential conflicts.

And finally, there was some evidence suggesting that cooperative play was more consistently employed by children after participating in the social skills training focused on developing friendships coupled with teachers' emphasis on modeling and praising such behaviors. These results mimic those obtained for clinically referred children, who showed improvements in play cooperation after exposure to social skills training (Chen 2006; Klein et al. 2003).

Results indicate that all significant SEP related changes in at risk children's classroom behaviors were also maintained at follow-up. Also, these results provide additional support for the fact that programs delivered in community-based settings for this category of children elicit significant changes not only at the group level, but also at the individual level (Lees and Ronan 2008). Therefore, it is possible that group interventions might be a valuable strategy for ensuring positive outcomes for at risk children, which have been consistently cited as results of research using partially randomized controlled trials (CPPRG 2002; Domitrovich et al. 2007; Webster-Stratton et al. 2001). Furthermore, these results indirectly support the notion that, at the indicated intervention level, it is important to link children's learning from the classroom curriculum to adults' use of coaching and behavior management strategies. Furthermore, in this study classroom behaviors were observed for children whose caregivers attended more than half of the parent training sessions, and therefore, it is possible to some extent that these outcomes are also related to parents' involvement. Future studies, contrasting changes in behaviors for children of participating vs. non-participating parents could provide a more specific perspective on the extent to which parental training influences child related outcomes over and beyond classroom curriculum and teacher training.

The second aim of the current study was to investigate the extent to which there were differences between group and individualized interventions concerning the patterns of behavioral change. Besides similarities among clinically referred children and at risk children with respect to the intervention strategies that proved effective, the results also suggest some particularities of intervention patterns for at-risk children. More precisely, most of the significant changes found in children's classroom behaviors occurred in the maintenance phase of SEP, not immediately postintervention as in the case of individualized interventions (Fenstermacher et al. 2006; Loftin et al. 2008). Although this finding must be replicated, it could be argued that possibly where group interventions are concerned, more time is needed to elicit observable changes requiring more teach and practice sequences than in individualized interventions (Lewis and Sugai 1999). Another potential explanation for this effect might be the fact that intervention outcomes were the result of interactions between different intervention modules. Support for this assumption comes from data which showed some carry-over effects between different intervention phases. This is not surprising because the dependent variables of this study were highly correlated constructs. For example, the results showed that cooperative play patterns were improved for one participant before the module on cooperative play was implemented. These changes occurred concurrently with those on prosocial behaviors. It might be that an increase in prosocial behaviors such as sharing, turn-taking, or offering help might lead to more positive group interactions, and implicitly, a more obvious preference for cooperative play (Marion 2003; Sheridan et al. 1999).

It is also noteworthy that some intervention effects occurred immediately postintervention for compliance with adults' requests and cooperative play. Potential explanations for these intervention patterns might be related to the children's age. Such effects were found for children who were 4 years old at the beginning of the intervention. Research on children's compliance and play strategies shows that there is a consistent age-related increase mostly influenced by children's prior exposure to rules (Lee et al. 2004, 2008), or group play strategies (Cutting and Dunn 2006; Howe et al. 2002).

As indicated in the results section, some of the participants showed no intervention effects across some observed behaviors. This lack of effect seemed to be related to high baseline scores. Such baselines would suggest that unlike the case of clinically referred children, who exhibit considerable difficulties regarding all behaviors associated with externalizing problems, at risk children might not show these generalized deficits across all externalizing type behaviors. Therefore, this raises the possibility that for an at risk child some behaviors might require intervention, while others might not.

Conclusions and Implications for Practice

The current study provided an in-depth assessment of individual level changes associated with SEP implementation in at risk children. As most current evidence-based interventions implemented in schools rely on comparing group effects based on teacher and/or parent ratings of broadly defined behavioral outcomes, this approach was among the few to take a closer look at observed classroom behaviors. As such, these results offer practitioners several potentially useful insights into how community-based interventions elicit changes in at risk children's behaviors.

First, it seems that children who are rated as at risk by adults might exhibit different types of difficulties. For instance, whereas some children perceived as at risk exhibit difficulties with all observed classroom behaviors (e.g., compliance, frustration tolerance, prosocial behaviors, and play cooperation), for others such problems can be observable only for some behaviors. Screening practices rely on perceptions about children's behaviors, not actual observations of such behaviors. Thus, it is important to conduct in schools, classroom observations as well as questionnaire-based screening practices, in order to better understand the particular strengths and difficulties of each at risk child. In particular, acknowledging children's strengths is an important part of a skill building approach, which encourages teachers to rely in developing new skills upon children's already existing abilities. This would be a welcome emphasis, given that teachers often label children, and such preconceived ideas affect the quality of teacher-child interactions, which can act as a catalyst for reinforced patterns of negative behaviors (Baker et al. 2008; Buyse et al. 2008).

Second, related to the earlier point that children's strengths should be considered when implementing preventive measures, it is apparent that at least in some cases previous knowledge and/or exposure to certain behaviors in the classroom, such as setting rules, cooperative games, and problem-solving as teaching methods, could provide an excellent scaffold for learning positive behaviors. Therefore, it could be that good teaching practices employed by teachers in the classroom can boost the development of children's protective factors against conduct problems, as well as indirectly supporting behavioral changes during implementation of classroom interventions.

And finally, not only children's individual responses to intervention might differ, but it is also plausible that especially in the case of interventions aiming to develop different types of social-emotional skills, changes in children's behaviors are not always observable, as in clinical settings, immediately after a treatment is implemented. More specifically, interventions for all children could require more time to exert effects compared to individualized interventions. Furthermore, data from this study suggested that prolonged timelines could be needed due to the fact that different intervention modules might actually have a combined effect on a given behavior. Understanding and considering these differences between classroom and clinical settings could be important for understanding that group learning might occur more slowly than individual learning, but with similar benefits for children. Hence, both teachers and parents should be aware of these differences, and understand that high expectations of overnight changes could be counterproductive in terms of children's progress.

Note

1. Text and tables in the Results and Discussion sections in the current chapter were previously published in: Ştefan, C.A., & Miclea, M. (2014). Effectiveness of the Social-Emotional Prevention Program as a function of children's baseline risk status. *European Early Childhood Education Research Journal, 22*, 14–44, doi: https://doi.org/10.1080/1350293X.2013.865359 by ©Springer, and their permission as copyright holders was obtained for the reuse of the material.

References

Baker, J. A., Sycarah, G., & Morlock, L. (2008). The teacher-student relationship as a developmental context for children with internalizing or externalizing behavior problems. *School Psychology Quarterly, 23*, 3–15. https://doi.org/10.1037/1045-3830.23.1.3.

Blum, P. (2001). *A teacher's guide to anger management*. London: Routledge Falmer.

Borckhardt, J. J., Nash, M. R., Murphy, M. D., Moore, M., Shaw, D., & O'Neil, P. (2008). Clinical practice as natural laboratory for psychotherapy research: A guide to case-based time-series analysis. *American Psychologist, 63*, 77–95. https://doi.org/10.1037/0003-066X.63.2.77.

Buyse, E., Verschueren, K., Doumen, S., Van Damme, J., & Maes, F. (2008). Classroom problem behavior and teacher-child relationships in kindergarten: The moderating role of classroom climate. *Journal of School Psychology, 46*, 367–391. https://doi.org/10.1016/j.jsp.2007.06.009.

Carr, J. (2005). Recommendations for reporting multiple-baseline designs across participants. *Behavioral Interventions, 20*, 219–224. https://doi.org/10.1002/bin.191.

Chandler, L. K., Dahlquist, C. M., Repp, A. C., & Feltz, C. (1999). The effects of team-based functional assessment on the behavior of students in classroom settings. *Exceptional Children, 66*, 101–122.

Chen, K. (2006). Social skills intervention for students with emotional/behavioral disorders: A literature review from the American perspective. *Educational Research and Reviews, 1*, 143–149.

Christ, T. J. (2007). Experimental control and threats to internal validity of concurrent and nonconcurrent multiple baseline designs. *Psychology in the Schools, 44*, 451–459. https://doi.org/10.1002/pits.20237.

Conduct Problems Prevention Research Group. (1999a). Initial impact of the Fast Track prevention trial for conduct problems: I. The high risk sample. *Journal of Consulting and Clinical Psychology, 67*, 631–647. https://doi.org/10.1037/0022-006X.67.5.648.

Conduct Problems Prevention Research Group. (1999b). Initial impact of the Fast Track prevention trial for conduct problems: II. Classroom effects. *Journal of Consulting and Clinical Psychology, 67*, 648–657. https://doi.org/10.1037/0022-006X.67.5.648.

Conduct Problems Prevention Research Group. (2002). Evaluation of the first 3 years of the Fast Track prevention trial with children at high risk for adolescent conduct problems. *Journal of Abnormal Child Psychology, 30*, 19–35. https://doi.org/10.1023/A:1014274914287.

Conroy, M. A., Dunlap, G., Clarke, S., & Alter, P. J. (2005). A descriptive analysis of behavioral intervention research with young children with challenging behavior. *Topics in Early Childhood Special Education, 25*, 157–166. https://doi.org/10.1177/02711214050250030301.

Conroy, M. A., Stichter, J. P., Daunic, A., & Haydon, T. (2008). Classroom-based research in the field of emotional and behavioral disorders: Methodological issues and future research directions. *Journal of Special Education, 41*, 209–222. https://doi.org/10.1177/0022466907310369.

Cutting, A. L., & Dunn, J. (2006). Conversations with siblings and with friends: Links between relationship quality and social understanding. *British Journal of Developmental Psychology, 24*, 73–87. https://doi.org/10.1348/026151005X70337.

Denham, S. A., Mason, T., Caverly, S., Schmidt, M., Hackney, R., Caswell, C., & DeMulder, E. (2001). Preschoolers at play: Co-socializers of emotional and social competence. *International Journal of Behavioral Development, 25*, 90–101. https://doi.org/10.1080/016502501143000067.

Dennis, T. (2006). Emotional self-regulation in preschoolers: The interplay of child approach reactivity, parenting, and control capacities. *Developmental Psychology, 42*, 84–97. https://doi.org/10.1037/0012-1649.42.1.84.

Domitrovich, C. E., Cortes, R. C., & Greenberg, M. T. (2007). Improving young children's social and emotional competence: A randomized trial of the preschool "PATHS" curriculum. *The Journal of Primary Prevention, 28*, 67–91. https://doi.org/10.1007/s10935-007-0081-0.

Domitrovich, C. E., Gest, S. D., Gill, S., Jones, D. J., & DeRouise, R. S. (2009). Teacher factors related to the professional development process of the Head Start REDI intervention. *Early Education and Development, 20*, 402–430. https://doi.org/10.1080/10409289.2013.825565.

Ducharme, J. M., & DiAdamo, C. (2005). An errorless approach to management of child noncompliance in a special education setting. *School Psychology Review, 34*, 107–115.

Ducharme, J. M., Spencer, T., Davidson, A., & Rushford, N. (2002). Errorless compliance training: Building a cooperative relationship between parents with brain injury and their oppositional children. *American Journal of Ortopsychiatry, 72*, 585–595. https://doi.org/10.1037/0002-9432.72.4.585.

Ducharme, J. M., Padova, T. D., & Ashworth, M. (2010). Errorless compliance training to reduce extreme conduct problems and intrusive control strategies in home and school settings. *Clinical Case Studies, 9*, 167–180. https://doi.org/10.1177/1534650110370714.

Dunlap, G., Strain, P. S., Fox, L., Carta, J. J., Conroy, B., et al. (2006). Prevention and intervention with young children's challenging behavior: Perspectives regarding current knowledge. *Behavioral Disorders, 32*, 29–45.

DuPaul, G. J., McGoey, K. E., Eckert, T. L., & VanBrakle, J. (2001). Preschool children with attention-deficit/hyperactivity disorder: Impairments in behavioral, social, and school functioning. *Journal of the American Academy of Child and Adolescent Psychiatry, 40*, 508–515. https://doi.org/10.1097/00004583-200105000-00009.

Eisenberg, N., Guthrie, I. K., Murphy, B. C., Shepard, S. A., Cumberland, A., & Carlo, G. (1999). Consistency and development of prosocial dispositions: A longitudinal study. *Child Development, 70*, 1360–1372. https://doi.org/10.1111/1467-8624.00100.

Eisenberg, N., Fabes, R. A., Guthrie, I. K., & Reiser, M. (2000). Dispositional emotionality and regulation: Their role in predicting quality of social functioning. *Journal of Personality and Social Psychology, 78*, 136–157. https://doi.org/10.1037/0022-3514.78.1.136.

Fabes, R. A., Gaertner, M. B., & Popp, T. K. (2006). Getting along with others: Social competence in early childhood. In K. M. D. Phillips (Ed.), *Handbook of early childhood development* (pp. 297–315). Malden: Blackwell Publishing.

Fairbanks, S., Sugai, G., Guardino, D., & Lathrop, M. (2007). Response to intervention: Examining classroom behavior support in second grade. *Exceptional Children, 73*, 288–310.

Fenstermacher, K., Olympia, D., & Sheridan, S. M. (2006). Effectiveness of a computer-facilitated, interactive social skills training program for boys with attention deficit hyperactivity disorder. *School Psychology Quarterly, 21*, 197–224. https://doi.org/10.1521/scpq.2006.21.2.197.

Filcheck, H. A., McNeil, C. B., Greco, L. A., & Bernard, R. S. (2004). Using a whole-class token economy and coaching of teacher skills in a preschool classroom to manage disruptive behavior. *Psychology in the Schools, 4*, 351–361. https://doi.org/10.1002/pits.10168.

Freeman, K. A., & Mash, E. J. (2007). Single-case research designs. In M. Hersen & A. M. Gross (Eds.), *Handbook of clinical psychology, volume II: Children and adolescents* (pp. 322–351). New York: Wiley.

Gibson, G., & Ottenbacher, K. J. (1988). Characteristics influencing the visual analysis of single subject data: An empirical analysis. *Journal of Applied Behavioral Science, 24*, 298–314. https://doi.org/10.1177/0021886388243007.

Gmeider, K. L., & Kratochwill, T. R. (1998). Short-term, home-based intervention for child noncompliance using behavioral consultation and a self-help manual. *Journal of Educational and Psychological Consultation, 9*, 91–117. https://doi.org/10.1207/s1532768xjepc0902_1.

Gunter, P. L., Hummel, J. H., & Conroy, M. A. (1998). Increasing incorrect academic responding: An effective intervention strategy to decrease behavior problems. *Effective School Practices, 17*, 55–62.

Hastings, P. D., Zahn-Waxler, C., Robinson, J., Usher, B., & Bridges, D. (2000). The development of concern for others in children with behavior problems. *Developmental Psychology, 36*, 531–546. https://doi.org/10.1037/0012-1649.36.5.531.

Howe, N., Rinaldi, C. M., Jennings, M., & Petrakos, H. (2002). "No! The lambs can stay out because they got cozies": Constructive and destructive sibling conflict, pretend play, and social understanding. *Child Development, 75*, 1460–1473. https://doi.org/10.1111/1467-8624.00483.

Hughes, J. N., Cavell, T. M., Meehan, B. T., Zhang, D., & Collie, C. (2005). Adverse school context moderates the outcomes of selective interventions for aggressive children. *Journal of Consulting and Clinical Psychology, 73*, 731–736. https://doi.org/10.1037/0022-006X.73.4.731.

Kam, C.-M., Greenberg, M. T., & Walls, C. T. (2003). Examining the role of implementation quality in school-based prevention using the PATHS curriculum. *Prevention Science, 4*, 55–63. https://doi.org/10.1023/A:1021786811186.

Kazdin, A. E. (1982). *Single-case research designs: Methods for clinical and applied settings*. New York: Oxford University Press.

Klein, T., Wirth, D., & Linas, K. (2003). Play: Children's context for development. *Young Children, 58*, 38–45.

LaFreniere, P. J., & Dumas, J. E. (1995). *Social competence and behavior evaluation* (Preschool ed.). Los Angeles: Western Psychological Services.

Lane, K. L., Wehby, J., Menzies, H. M., Doukas, G. L., Munton, S. M., & Gregg, R. M. (2003). Social skills instruction for students at risk for antisocial behavior: The effects of small-group instruction. *Behavioral Disorders, 28*, 229–248.

Lee, D. L., Belfiore, P. J., Scheeler, M. C., Hua, Y., & Smith, R. (2004). Behavioral momentum in academics: Using embedded high-p sequence to increase academic productivity. *Psychology in the Schools, 41*, 789–801. https://doi.org/10.1002/pits.20014.

Lee, D. L., Belfiore, P. J., & Gormley, S. (2008). Riding the wave: Creating a momentum of school success. *Teaching Exceptional Children, 40*, 65–70.

Lees, D. G., & Ronan, K. R. (2008). Engagement and effectiveness of parent management training (Incredible Years) for solo high-risk mothers: A multiple baseline evaluation. *Behaviour Change, 25*, 109–128. https://doi.org/10.1375/bech.25.2.109.

Lewis, T. J., & Sugai, G. (1999). Effective behavior support: A system approach to proactive schoolwide management. *Focus on Exceptional Children, 31*, 1–24.

Loftin, R. L., Odom, S. L., & Lantz, J. F. (2008). Social interaction and repetitive motor behaviors. *Journal of Autism and Developmental Disorders, 38*, 1124–1135. https://doi.org/10.1007/s10803-007-0499-5.

Mantzicopoulos, P. Y., & Neurath-Pritchett, S. (1998). Transitional first-grade referrals: An analysis of school-related factors and children's characteristics. *Journal of Educational Psychology, 90*, 122–133. https://doi.org/10.1037/0022-0663.90.1.122.

Marchant, M., Young, K. R., & West, R. P. (2004). The effects of parental teaching on compliance behavior of children. *Psychology in the Schools, 41*, 337–350. https://doi.org/10.1002/pits.10165.

Marion, M. (2003). *Guidance of young children*. Columbus: Merrill Prentice Hall.

Matthys, W., Cuperus, J. M., & Van Engeland, H. (1999). Deficient social problem solving in boys with OCD/CD, with ADHD, and with both disorders. *Journal of the American Academy of Child and Adolescent Psychiatry, 38*, 311–321. https://doi.org/10.1097/00004583-199903000-00019.

Mayer, G. R. (1995). Preventing antisocial behavior in the schools. *Journal of Applied Behavior Analysis, 28*, 467–478. https://doi.org/10.1901/jaba.1995.28-467.

McGoey, K. E., & DuPaul, G. J. (2000). Token reinforcement and response cost procedures: Reducing the disruptive behavior of preschool children with attention-deficit/hyperactivity disorder. *School Psychology Quarterly, 15*, 330–343. https://doi.org/10.1037/h0088790.

Mendez, J. L., McDermott, P., & Fantuzzo, J. (2002). Identifying and promoting social competence with African American preschool children: Developmental and contextual considerations. *Psychology in the Schools, 39*, 111–123. https://doi.org/10.1002/pits.10039.

Miclea, M., Bălaj, A., Porumb, M., Porumb, D., & Porumb, S. (2010). *PEDa: The developmental assessment platform for 3–6/7 year old children*. Cluj-Napoca: ASCR Publishing.

Morgan, D. L., & Morgan, R. K. (2008). *Single case research methods for the behavioral and health sciences* (pp. 159–125). Thousand Oaks: Sage Publications.

Nation, M., Crusto, C., Wandersman, A., Kumpfer, A., Seybolt, D., Morrissey-Kane, E., & Davino, K. (2003). What works in prevention – Principles of effective prevention programs. *American Psychologist, 58*, 449–456. https://doi.org/10.1037/0003-066X.58.6-7.449.

Nelson, G., Westhues, A., & MacLeod, J. (2003). A meta-analysis of longitudinal research on preschool prevention programs for children. *Prevention and Treatment, 6*, 1–25.

Nourbakhsh, M. R., & Ottenbacher, K. J. (1994). The statistical analysis of single-subject data: A comparative examination. *Physical Therapy, 74*, 768–776.

Raver, C. C., Jones, S. M., Li-Grining, C., Zhai, F., Metzger, M. W., & Solomon, B. (2009). Targeting children's behavior problems in preschool classrooms: A cluster-randomized controlled trial. *Journal of Consulting and Clinical Psychology, 77*, 302–316. https://doi.org/10.1037/a0015302.

Robin, A., Schneider, M., & Dolnick, M. (1976). The turtle technique: An extended case study of self-control in the classroom. *Psychology in the Schools, 13*, 449–453. https://doi.org/10.1002/1520-6807(197610).

Scruggs, T. E., Mastropieri, M. A., & Casto, G. (1987). The quantitative synthesis of single-subject research: Methodology and validation. *Remedial and Special Education, 8*, 24–33. https://doi.org/10.1177/074193258700800206.

Sheridan, S. M., Hungelman, A., & Maughan, P. D. (1999). A contextualized framework for social skills assessment, intervention, and generalization. *School Psychology Review, 28*, 84–103.

Ştefan, C. A., & Miclea, M. (2010). Prevention programs targeting emotional and social development in preschoolers: Current status and future directions. *Early Child Development and Care, 180*, 1103–1128. https://doi.org/10.1080/03004430902830263.

Stichter, J. P., Lewis, T. J., Johnson, N., & Trussell, R. (2004). Toward a structural assessment: Analyzing the merits of an assessment tool for a student with E/BD. *Assessment for Effective Intervention, 30*, 25–40. https://doi.org/10.1177/073724770403000103.

Trentacosta, C. J., Izard, C. E., Mostow, A. J., & Fine, S. E. (2006). Children's emotional competence and attentional competence in early elementary school. *School Psychology Quarterly, 21*, 148–170. https://doi.org/10.1037/t31163-000.

Tryon, W. W. (1982). A simplified time-series analysis for evaluating treatment interventions. *Journal of Applied Behavior Analysis, 15*, 423–429. https://doi.org/10.1901/jaba.1982.15-423.

Wahler, R. G. (1997). On the origins of children's compliance and opposition: Family context, reinforcement, and rules. *Journal of Child and Family Studies, 6*, 191–208. https://doi.org/10.1023/A:1025050724559.

Watson, P. J., & Workman, E. A. (1981). The non-concurrent multiple baseline across-individuals design: An extension of the traditional multiple baseline design. *Journal of Behavior Therapy and Experimental Psychiatry, 12*, 257–259. https://doi.org/10.1016/0005-7916(81)90055-0.

Webster-Stratton, C., & Taylor, T. (2001). Nipping early risk factors in the bud: Preventing substance abuse, delinquency, and violence in adolescence through interventions targeted at young children (0–8 years). *Prevention Science, 2*, 165–192. https://doi.org/10.1023/A:1011510923900.

Webster-Stratton, C., Reid, J. M., & Hammond, M. (2001). Preventing conduct problems, promoting social competence: A parent-teacher training partnership in Head Start. *Journal of Clinical Child Psychology, 30*, 283–302.

Webster-Stratton, C., Reid, J. M., & Hammond, M. (2004). Treating children with early-onset conduct problems: Intervention outcomes for parent, child, and teacher training. *Journal of Clinical Child and Adolescent Psychology, 33*, 105–124. https://doi.org/10.1207/S15374424JCCP3301_11.

Webster-Stratton, C., Reid, M. J., & Stoolmiller, M. (2008). Preventing conduct problems and improving school readiness: Evaluation of the Incredible Years teacher and child training programs in high-risk schools. *The Journal of Child Psychology and Psychiatry, 49*, 471–488. https://doi.org/10.1111/j.1469-7610.2007.01861.x.

CHAPTER 6

Conclusion: Contributions of Research on SEP Efficacy to the Field of Early Education Programs, Limitations, and Future Directions

Theoretical, Methodological and Empirical Contributions to Advancing Knowledge About Preventive Programs for Preschoolers

Results presented in the previous chapters focus on a wide range of themes, from establishing principles related to the development of early education programs to testing their efficacy. Consequently, it is important to establish the extent to which this undertaking contributes to the field by advancing knowledge in terms of theoretical, methodological, and empirical evidence. These contributions are outlined in Table 6.1.

From a theoretical point of view, the first chapter offers an in-depth analysis of the protective and risk factors involved in enhancing children's risk of developing and maintaining behavior problems. Understanding the mechanisms related to the early onset of behavior problems constitutes an important prerequisite for developing and effectively implementing interventions aimed at reducing children's risk of behavior problems (Webster-Stratton and Taylor 2001; Nelson et al. 2003). As suggested by the research summarized and analyzed in Chap. 1, knowledge concerning risk factors is translated into specific intervention strategies which aim to address multiple risk sources for the development and

C. A. Ştefan, *Social-Emotional Prevention Programs for Preschool Children's Behavior Problems*,
https://doi.org/10.1007/978-3-319-74751-4_6

Table 6.1 Theoretical, methodological, and empirical contributions

Theoretical and practical contributions		
Analysis of relevant literature	Systematic description of skills associated with preschoolers' emotional competencies and their social competencies Proposing a revised model of interaction between child, parent, and educational environment risk factors responsible for early onset conduct problems Analyzing the features of evidence-based interventions, which can inform effective program development	
Intervention program development	Developing the first multi-focused (children, teachers, parents) early education program in Romania Adapting the hybrid universal and indicated intervention Fast Track model for preschoolers Developing a theory-driven intervention for preventing preschoolers' behavior problems, and employing innovative approaches for each intervention component (a) **Child-focused program** Supporting high-risk children through teacher training, instead of added small group child training (b) **Teacher training** Providing consultations and support for teachers in implementing the program and enhancing children's social-emotional competencies (c) **Parent training** Combining information providing strategies with discipline strategies and coaching for children's emotional and social development/delivering a short 4-session training format Linking the SEP intervention to a universal screening system	
Methodological contributions		
Classroom level effects	*Group level effects*	*Individual level effects*
Employing a partially randomized controlled trial to gather evidence of SEP efficacy as a hybrid prevention program	Employing a 2-stage screening method for identifying at risk preschoolers Differentiating between the moderate- vs. low-risk children as target groups of the universal intervention	Employing a single-subject design methodology for testing the efficacy of the intervention on high-risk children
Gathering evidence for SEP efficacy from parent and teacher rated social-emotional competencies and behavior problems, as well as child reported emotion knowledge and problem-solving		Developing observation tools for children's classroom behaviors

(*continued*)

Table 6.1 (continued)

Empirical contributions		
Classroom level effects	*Group level effects*	*Individual level effects*
Providing evidence that SEP is an effective intervention for enhancing children's social-emotional skills, and reducing behavior problems from a multi-rater perspective (teacher, parent, and child report measures) Obtaining evidence supporting the claim that a short parent training program can sustain children's skill transfer and appropriate levels of involvement in a community-based setting	Providing evidence for the sustainability of a single intervention program for both universal and indicated intervention purposes Comparing outcomes for 2 intervention levels: High-risk children benefit to the largest extent (except for children's behaviors at home) (*indicated intervention*) Moderate-risk children make the most consistent gains (*universal intervention*) Providing a comparative analysis of results based on emotional and social competencies screening	Supporting the notion that classroom interventions are effective in eliciting changes in high-risk children's behaviors in the classroom Identifying similarities between at risk and clinically referred children in terms of effective intervention strategies Identifying differences between at risk and clinically referred children in terms of the time needed for effects to take place Establishing the presence of carry-over effects in the context of group, multi-focused interventions

maintenance of behavior problems. The analysis of the current literature in the field of developmental psychology was used to first identify a working definition of social-emotional competencies. One potential contribution is that children's competencies are conceptualized by emphasizing the relative independence of social and emotional skills. Although shown to be highly related (Blair et al. 2004; Denham et al. 2003a, b; Eisenberg et al. 2002), these types of competencies refer to different behavioral markers as described in Chap. 1. This view is supported by recent theoretical perspectives emphasizing the role of emotions as multi-component systems related to adaptation, and not as an isolated consequence of cognitive and brain maturation processes (Izard 2001; Witherington and Crichton 2007). Also, a recent theory of social stimuli processing proposed by Lemerise and Arsenio (2000), establishes the independent role that emotions associated with previous socializing experiences play in selecting and implementing certain behavioral responses.

Therefore, from a theoretical perspective Chap. 1 also proposed a revised version of the Webster-Stratton and Taylor (2001) model concerning children's risk of early onset behavioral problems, and suggested several types of interactions between child, parent, and educational environment, which could lead to difficulties in social-emotional development and increased risk of behavior problems. In turn, such knowledge allows researchers to develop theory-driven interventions, which are more likely to maximize the intervention's efficacy. Consequently, Chap. 2 addressed the way successful prevention approaches and empirically supported intervention strategies can inform the development of new interventions. Thus, the Social-Emotional Prevention Program (SEP) was developed considering the *Fast Track* model which employs a hybrid approach to concomitantly delivering both a universal and an indicated intervention for school aged children (Conduct Problems Prevention Research Group [CPPRG] 1999a, b). Hence, to our knowledge, SEP is the first program to employ a dual delivery model in the context of preventing behavior problems in preschoolers, and it also constitutes the first prevention program developed in Romania aimed at reducing behavior problems in this age range.

As suggested in Chap. 2, the development of SEP was grounded in previous research about intervention programs' efficacy. First, drawing from research suggesting that a combination of child, parent, and teacher related factors increases the risk of maladjustment, SEP was developed as a multi-focused intervention. The first component, the *classroom curriculum*, includes separate intervention modules for the development of emotional competencies (e.g., emotion recognition, emotion regulation), and social competencies (e.g., problem-solving, play cooperation), thus emphasizing a separate conceptualization of the 2 types of competencies (Domitrovich et al. 2007; Kellam et al. 1998; Webster-Stratton 2000). Moreover, SEP rationale supports the notion that both low- and high-risk children benefit to the same extent from participating in classroom activities, rather than adding pullout intervention strategies for high-risk children (Lochman and Wells 2002; van Lier et al. 2005). The second component, *teacher training*, was developed considering the intervention needs of low-risk children by emphasizing preventive discipline strategies, whereas at risk children's needs were considered by focusing on positive discipline strategies aimed at managing misbehaviors. Moreover, children's needs irrespective of their risk status were addressed through strategies aimed at coaching social-emotional development, as a strategy for complementing the implementation of the classroom curriculum. Hence, from this point of view the classroom curriculum represents a stand-alone intervention with specific activities taught in a predetermined sequence, but also an embedded intervention which aims to offer children the opportunity of ample practice under teacher supervision. This latter approach further develops the role of consultations in teacher training, which were previously considered only as strategies aimed at familiarizing teachers with the classroom curriculum (Domitrovich et al. 2007; Kam et al. 2003), to include more emphasis on preparing teachers to use social interactions in the classroom as a teaching opportunity for social-emotional learning. The third component of SEP, *parent training*, emphasized different levels of intervention ranging from strategies meant to inform parents to strategies intended to address behavior management and coaching children's social-emotional development (Sanders and Morawska 2005; Turner and Sanders 2006). Similar to teacher training, parent training was therefore intended to address the intervention needs of both low- and high-risk parents. Also, considering empirical evidence suggesting that interventions aimed only at targeting parents of high-risk children might be detrimental to the implementation quality and participation of parents (Turner and Sanders 2006), the SEP aimed at including all parents in a short 4-session training format. This strategy of employing fewer parent training sessions had been previously implemented successfully in preventive programs in community-based settings, which targeted reductions in children's risk of anxiety (Dadds and Roth 2008; Rapee et al. 2005).

A second major innovation associated with the development of SEP was related to the fact that it is linked to a specific screening system (Essex et al. 2009; Severson et al. 2007). The screening system proposes the use of a universal screener assessing separately children's emotional and social development from both teachers' and parents' perspectives. The specific cutoff points allow the identification of 3 risk categories: (1) high-risk children (below the 10th percentile), who are the recipients of the indicated intervention actions; (2) moderate-risk (between the 11th and 33rd percentiles) children; and low-risk children (above the 34th percentile), who are the recipients of the universal intervention (Miclea et al. 2010). This is a highly innovative approach to screening, which considers evidence suggesting that up to one-third of preschoolers could, at some point, be at risk of behavior problems (Prinz and Sanders 2007).

In terms of methodological contributions, there were 2 major approaches to SEP efficacy testing: (1) a partially randomized controlled trial; and (2) a single-subject design. The first strategy was used to evaluate SEP efficacy by comparing outcomes for the intervention and the control groups (i.e., nomothetic approach), whereas the latter strategy allowed for an in-depth analysis of the intervention's effects at the individual level (i.e., idiographic approach). The intervention's effects employing group comparisons were further performed by assessing classroom-level outcomes using HLM analyses; conversely, in the second approach based on the 2-stage screening procedure previously outlined, outcomes were evaluated separately for 3 risk categories (high, moderate, and low). Moreover, these studies are among the few to employ screening of children's competencies rather than relying exclusively on measures of behavior problems to establish risk status (Durlak and Wells 1998).

Additionally, the measures employed for testing the efficacy of SEP included both teacher and parent evaluations of children's social-emotional competencies and behavior problems (Ştefan et al. 2009). Such a multirater perspective was thought to offer a more nuanced perspective on SEP efficacy both in terms of classroom related outcomes, and changes in children's behaviors at home. Also, this was among the few efficacy studies to report outcomes on child-reported measures of emotion knowledge and problem-solving in the context of a hybrid universal and indicated intervention, as the previous results mostly stem from research performed on children with clinical intensity behavior problems (Webster-Stratton and Hammond 1997; Webster-Stratton and Reid 2003). Conversely, for the individual level approach, behavioral codes were developed and observations were carried out with the aim of providing data on specific classroom behaviors targeted by SEP: compliance, frustration tolerance, prosocial behaviors, and play cooperation.

The research data presented in Chap. 3 described SEP related outcomes at the classroom level. These results provide some initial evidence of SEP efficacy, supporting the notion that SEP participation was associated with consistent gains in terms of increased social-emotional skills and reduced behavior problems for intervention group children in comparison with children from the control group. These findings were relatively consistent across 3 types of measures: child, teacher, and parent report. Hence, these results provide evidence that SEP as a hybrid prevention strategy seems to result in promising outcomes in terms of children's knowledge, classroom behaviors, and skill transfer from classroom to children's behaviors at home. Furthermore, SEP would be the first hybrid preventive intervention designed for preventing preschoolers' behavior problems which elicits such outcomes, as previously such results were reported in the context of a similar type of approach to preventing behavioral problems for school age children (Bierman 2002; CPPRG 1999a, b).

Concerning SEP components, it is noteworthy that as expected outcomes related to children's behavior problems indicated the presence of significant reductions in non-compliance and aggression in the absence of pullout intervention sessions. These findings indirectly support the claim that maladaptive interaction patterns are more likely to arise in homogenous play groups comprised of children with behavior problems, and consequently aggression is less likely to appear when children are exposed to positive peer models (Lochman and Wells 2002; van Lier et al. 2005). On a similar note, the results from this study indicated that children from the intervention group not only showed reduced levels of behavior problems, but also increased social-emotional competencies. Such results in the context of a hybrid prevention program point to the fact that one potential contributor to these effects could be the guiding principles underlying the development of teacher training. Unlike previous preventive programs which implemented teacher consultations aimed at enhancing their ability to reliably and effectively deliver the classroom activities (Domitrovich et al. 2007), the rationale of SEP teacher consultations as previously emphasized was to train adults to support children's social-emotional development in the daily classroom context, which could contribute to their learning about emotions, emotion regulation, problem-solving, or play cooperation. Another source of potential contribution to the aforementioned outcomes is related to the fact that not only teachers, but also parents, were trained in emphasizing the importance of coaching children's skill development. These findings could be relevant for supporting the idea that skill transfer between the classroom and the context of parent-child interactions at home might be largely the consequence of not only promoting parental involvement, but also of actively promoting skill coaching during teacher consultations and parent training. Additionally, in the parents' case, this effect might have been potentiated by the relatively high levels of parental attendance for this type of intervention, which included on average 54% of children's caregivers, which is relatively within the range reported by previous research with non-risk populations (Prinz and Sanders 2007). Therefore, this efficacy study also provided evidence that short-format parent training previously employed in the context of anxiety prevention for preschoolers, could be effectively used to attract parental involvement in the context of preventing behavior problems (Dadds and Roth 2008; Rapee et al. 2005).

The results presented in Chap. 4 provided an analysis of SEP efficacy at the group level. More precisely, this data was obtained for different categories of risk, which were established based on the 2-stage screening procedure described previously in this chapter, combining the assessment of children's social-emotional development with the assessment of externalizing problems (Durlak and Wells 1998). Based on this screening procedure, risk categories were established in correspondence with the SEP prevention levels: (1) the high-risk level corresponding to the indicated intervention; and (2) the moderate- and low-risk levels corresponding to the universal intervention. According to the data concerning SEP effects on children's classroom behaviors, it was apparent that the intervention's effects increased as a function of higher-risk status, meaning that the most consistent gains in terms of social-emotional development and reduced levels of behavior problems were reported for children from the high-risk group, who were the beneficiaries of the indicated intervention. These findings were largely similar to those reported in the literature for children identified as at risk of behavior problems (Stoolmiller et al. 2000). Interestingly, although previous studies failed to identify consistent changes in children targeted by universal interventions, the results reported in this study suggested that there is a category of children, namely moderate-risk children who were overlooked in previous research, but who seem to exhibit significant changes in their behaviors as a result of SEP participation. Therefore, it is possible that marginally at risk children might actually be the group targeted by universal interventions; although effect sizes for outcomes were not as large as for the high-risk group, children who are marginally at risk might respond best to universal interventions. On the other hand, the pattern of results indicated a somewhat different situation for children's behaviors at home. Moderate-risk children as recipients of the universal intervention showed more consistent gains than high-risk children, the risk category targeted by the indicated intervention. This could suggest that observing changes in children's behaviors at home might take longer to occur than in the case of children who do not exhibit behavioral difficulties. However, the results for externalizing problems showed that in fact when parental involvement in the intervention was considered, reductions in behavior problems were more likely to be observed in high-risk children. Such findings might be informative for variations in reports concerning skill transfer from classroom to home, and could also indicate that designing interventions which include parental involvement might be essential for mental health programs delivered in community-based settings.

Furthermore, data from 2 screening strategies which established different risk categories for emotional and social competencies suggested that results stemming from social competence screening were aligned with findings reported in the literature; however, gains in emotional competencies were not necessarily followed by improved social competencies. This raises the interesting possibility that improved emotional competence might need more time to be translated in effective social interaction patterns.

Chapter 5 provided an extensive presentation of SEP efficacy assessment at the individual level. While single-subject designs were traditionally used for determining the efficiency of interventions for clinically referred children (Gmeider and Kratochwill 1998; Fenstermacher et al. 2006; Loftin et al. 2008), this undertaking was among the few to use this approach in the context of assessing the efficacy of a community-based intervention (Lees and Ronan 2008). The results emphasized that SEP participation was associated with a boost in children's social-emotional competencies in the classroom. Furthermore, most of the effects found in the context of this group intervention suggested that positive effects for high-risk children were detectable in the maintenance phase rather than the intervention phase, as is usually reported for clinically referred children. Moreover, changes occurring in the intervention phase could be associated either with the child's previous knowledge or skills, or to intervention carry-over effects. These effects highlight the fact that when interventions aim to target behaviors which are highly associated, it is possible that gains in one domain become more salient when the intervention begins to target another behavior. Therefore, such findings would suggest that group interventions require more time for their effects to be visible. Also, findings that these SEP effects were obtained for children whose parents attended at least 3 out of 4 parent training sessions add to empirical evidence which suggest that parental involvement is paramount for the success of any intervention strategy for this age category, and particularly for children at risk of behavior problems (Prinz and Sanders 2007; Turner and Sanders 2006).

Limitations and Future Directions of Research

There are several limitations of the studies presented in Chaps. 3, 4, and 5, which need to be acknowledged. For each limitation, corresponding future directions of research are suggested. The first limitation is related to requirements of the American Psychological Association (APA) which need to be fulfilled in order to consider an intervention as evidence based. One main criterion is that results concerning a preventive program's efficacy should include replication studies made by the developers of the program, as well as independent ones made by other research groups (Chambless and Hollon 1998). Consequently, where SEP is concerned, one of the following steps should include further replication of the data obtained in these studies, including research performed by independent researchers.

It is also noteworthy that the research on SEP efficacy was conducted in a predominantly urban community, with parents from low-SES background underrepresented in the final sample. One major risk factor of children's behavior problems is associated with low-SES status (Curtner-Smith et al. 2006; Schultz et al. 2001), and this raises the question of whether implementation of SEP in a more diverse sample would yield similar effects. Consequently, replication of these results in the context of a more diverse socio-economic parental background could provide added information about SEP efficacy.

The SEP was developed in Romania, and therefore data on this prevention program's validity were obtained from a sample of Romanian children. This means that the generalizability of the reported findings is limited, and data about SEP efficacy should be gathered in different cultural contexts in order to draw more specific conclusions about the program's efficacy. However, because SEP development was theoretically driven by research on early education preventive programs, it is plausible that in cultures which share similar expectations about children's social-emotional skills such an undertaking could prove equally efficient.

The SEP version tested in this study included age-appropriate activities for developing children's social-emotional competencies. These skills were previously shown to be related not only to children's mental health, but also to increased school readiness and children's ability to adapt to school requirements (Denham 2006; Snow 2006). Given these findings, some preventive programs such as the *The Incredible Years* contain specific modules targeting the development of mathematical and literacy prerequisites in older preschoolers (Webster-Stratton 2000). Hence, one potential avenue of research that could be considered is related to extending the SEP classroom curriculum to include both age-appropriate activities for social-emotional development for older preschoolers than those included in the previously discussed efficacy studies, as well as activities designed to enhance children's school readiness. Hence, such an extended curriculum could be tested in a sample of preschoolers before being enrolled in school.

In a similar vein, another direction for testing SEP efficacy is the development of additional intervention modules which would allow a broader range of behavioral problems, including those manifested by clinically referred children, to be effectively targeted. The current approach included participants who were at risk of behavior problems but with no clinical diagnosis. Some previous studies suggest that community-based interventions can sustain psychotherapeutic approaches when used as complementary strategies (Hinshaw et al. 2000). Also, other studies suggest that children with clinical intensity symptoms might benefit from more individualized intervention plans, which can be implemented in community-based settings (Reid et al. 2004; Webster-Stratton and Reid 2003). Hence, it is possible that SEP efficacy could be tested as a complementary intervention in the context of psychotherapeutic interventions for children's behavior problems.

Another potential direction for developing SEP could be to implement activities from the classroom curriculum through computer-based applications. Some data concerning computer- assisted interventions suggested that preschool children benefited in terms of improved social problem-solving skills (Buckleitner 2004; Fenstermacher et al. 2006). However, empirical data also indicated that although computer-assisted components can in fact support development of social behavior (Anderson 2000; Crook 1998), generalization and performance are related to children's classroom experiences, and the methods teachers use for facilitating their social-emotional development (Lau et al. 2005). Hence, a potential avenue for future research might consider comparing the efficacy of different delivery formats of the classroom curriculum on children's social-emotional competencies.

Results specifically presented in Chaps. 3 and 4 included data concerning SEP efficacy at follow-up, with results generally supporting the notion that the program maintained its effects on most of the assessed outcomes. However, as pointed out in the literature, it is desirable for future studies, including those related to SEP efficacy, to employ longer follow-up intervals, mostly due to the limited data on preventive intervention's long-term outcomes (Nelson et al. 2003). These follow-up studies might include testing outcomes associated with mental health indicators, as well as school adjustment records, as it is known that social-emotional competencies are core components of school readiness and children's school performance in the 1st grade (Snow 2006; Ramey and Ramey 2004). Moreover, these studies should attempt to gather objective data on school attendance and drop-out rates in adolescence, since these problems have a high rate of cooccurrence in children with diagnosed conduct disorders (Caldarella and Merrell 1997; Fabes et al. 2003; Linares et al. 2005).

Assessment tools employed for testing classroom and group level effects relied predominantly on teacher- and parent-rated questionnaires. Hence, some concerns can be raised about the social desirability of the answers provided by parents and teachers. However, it is noteworthy that in the efficacy studies concerning classroom and group level effects, child-reported measures of emotion knowledge and problem-solving strategies were employed, whereas in the efficacy studies for the individual level effects, a small number of children were assessed through direct observation of their behaviors. Therefore, it could be that future studies might consider conducting observations of children's classroom behaviors, especially for evaluating changes in at risk children. Given that teacher ratings of child behaviors are moderately correlated with independent observations (Hinshaw et al. 1992), it could be inferred that obtaining such measures should lead to uncovering similar results, but not necessarily consistent with the findings reported in this study. On the other hand, similar observations of children's behaviors could be conducted at home. However, because SEP was implemented in a community-based setting, it is unlikely that home observations could be carried out, because such strategies are mainly employed for clinically referred children (Webster-Stratton and Hammond 1997; Webster-Stratton and Reid 2003), but it is possible that laboratory type observations of parent-child interactions could be employed as measures of child and parent related outcomes.

On a related note, the fact that teachers were also in charge of implementing the classroom intervention and were not blinded to the expected outcomes of SEP might have acted as a potential bias in their estimates of change in children's classroom behaviors. Also, the results reported in the previous chapters were obtained in the context of high levels of teacher-led curriculum implementation. More than 90% of classroom activities were implemented with high accuracy, and teachers received extensive support and feedback throughout implementation, especially during consultations preceding each classroom intervention unit. Due to the fact that consultations are known to positively affect intervention outcomes (Domitrovich et al. 2007), it would be interesting to compare interventions with high levels of implementation support to those with lower involvement from program developers. This is particularly relevant for effectiveness studies, which permit a more nuanced interpretation of the intervention's sustainability, considering that in less-controlled circumstances teachers might implement the activities from the classroom curriculum to a lesser extent. This in turn, could indirectly affect the outcomes of SEP implementation, and future studies might take a closer look at outcomes resulting in less-controlled intervention circumstances.

Also, it is noteworthy that the teachers' training was designed to support their ability to manage children's classroom behaviors, as well as to implement the classroom curriculum of activities for social-emotional development. However, no direct measures of the training's efficacy were obtained for teachers, due to the relatively small sample size. Hence, another potential avenue for future research might include an evaluation of the training effects on teacher's beliefs, attitudes, and behaviors concerning children's skill development and behavior management strategies. On a related note, parent ratings of children's behaviors and self-reported discipline practices were obtained predominantly from mothers. More researchers have called for including fathers in parent training, because of their increased involvement in child rearing (Pollack 1995). In turn, fathers' presence is seen as relevant for obtaining a more comprehensive perspective on the intervention's effects, although such effects were shown to be more difficult to achieve when fathers were involved (Helfenbaum-Kun and Ortiz 2007; Morawska and Sanders 2006). However, one possible future direction would be to include fathers in the intervention, and evaluate the outcomes from both parents' perspective.

Given that SEP was designed as a multi-focused prevention program, the results reported were the result of a combination of intervention strategies. For instance, effects on children's classroom behaviors could be the consequence of implementing the classroom curriculum, teacher training, parent training, or the interactions between these components. Conversely, changes in children's behaviors at home could be the result of parental involvement with the intervention, but also participation in the classroom curriculum. Therefore, it is difficult to make any inferences concerning which intervention components have the most significant contributions in terms of changing children's behaviors. It would be interesting for future studies to compare the effects of the classroom curriculum, teacher and parent training, as well as the combined effect of the 3 strategies on children's social-emotional competencies and behavior problems (Webster-Stratton et al. 2001). Additionally, results stemming from screening of social and emotional competencies could be compared in order to more clearly articulate potential differences in response to intervention between children with different risk profiles.

Particularly, in the last SEP efficacy study when individual level effects of SEP were investigated, some carry-over effects were found due to the intercorrelations between the dependent variables. These suggested that in some cases behavioral changes occurred during the baseline observations. Although changes in baseline trends are considered threats to the internal validity of the multiple baseline designs (Christ 2007), acknowledging the possibility of such effects could provide valuable information for disseminating classroom delivered interventions, and understanding how group intervention elicit changes as opposed to individualized interventions. From a methodological point of view, a potential solution would be the use of a "latin square" design, which counterbalances the order of intervention modules (Carr 2005). Such a design would allow drawing conclusions with respect to which SEP intervention module's interactions affect children's target behaviors, but such strategies are relatively difficult to implement. This is due to the rationale underlying the sequence of modules from the classroom curriculum, which supports the following order: (1) teaching children about rules and responsibility allows for an improved classroom climate and facilitates learning; (2) compliance fosters improved ability to regulate emotions (Stifter et al. 1999), and emotion knowledge is also associated with improved ability to regulate emotions (Eisenberg et al. 2005); (3) emotion regulation ability sustains problem-solving, and provide a means of preventing aggressive behaviors (Romano et al. 2005); and (4) development of prosocial behaviors sustains the process of acquiring cooperative play strategies (Sheridan et al. 1999).

And finally, SEP efficacy was tested across several types of child or parent related variables, but no specific analyses were carried out on potential moderators or mediators of the intervention. Moreover, most of the reported results in the literature are provided by research focused on clinically referred children. For instance, boys, younger children, and those with depressed mothers tended to exhibit greater improvement after participating in an intervention for conduct problems (Gardner et al. 2010). Consequently, the current line of research could be extended by investigating child and parent associated characteristics which might account for the improved efficacy of preventive programs for children at risk of behavior problems. The presence of such risk factors can be a source of moderation of the intervention's effects on both children's behaviors and parental discipline strategies (Frick et al. 1992; Snyder 2007). Furthermore, some research also suggested that changes in positive parenting and harsh parenting mediate the relationship between the intervention and changes in children's conduct problems (Beauchaine et al. 2005; Gardner et al. 2006). It is therefore possible that similar intervention mechanisms operate in the context of reductions in behavior problems for children who are at risk.

Implications for Practice and Policy Makers in the Field of Early Education

Besides the implications of SEP efficacy studies for implementing social-emotional interventions in schools, which were discussed throughout Chaps. 3, 4 and 5, it is important to understand how interventions such as SEP could inform policy makers. In order to do this, early education programs fostering social-emotional development need to be considered within the broader context of extant policies for children aged 0–8. Recent developments in policies concerning young children include incorporating the Early Childhood Care and Education in the Education for all (EFA) policy (UNESCO 2000), which marked the beginning of a rapid expansion of early education programs throughout the world aiming to ensure young children's access to high-quality educational programs. Advocacy for these initiatives is supported by empirical evidence. First, factors such as poverty, parent stress, exposure to trauma, and environmental toxins can have a damaging effect on children's brain development and on their ability to learn (Grantham-McGregor et al. 2007). Second, especially for children who are exposed to such risk, participation in early education practices are more cost effective than interventions taking place at later developmental stages, suggesting that early intervention is preferable and more beneficial than delayed interventions (Heckman 2006). And third, early intervention is associated with improved individual outcomes such as increased school performance, increased income levels in adulthood

(Schweinhart et al. 2005; Walker et al. 2006), as well as reduced social costs usually associated with school dropout, delinquency, or unemployment (Barnett 2008a, b).

One particularly important direction for developing early education programs concerns children's social-emotional learning (SEL). The origins of the SEL movement date to the mid-1990s, when Goleman (1995) coined the term emotional intelligence and the concept quickly became of interest to educators. Briefly stated, social-emotional competencies refer to a set of skills which allow individuals to monitor their emotions and regulate them in order to become more skilled at navigating interpersonal relationships (Denham et al. 2003a, b). This concept has gained increasing popularity as a reaction to the excessive emphasis placed in the United States by the No Child Left Behind Act on academic skills to the detriment of other equally important abilities such as social-emotional skills. This is especially relevant as these competencies were shown to be important contributing factors to school success (Denham 2006; Snow 2006), and many social-emotional skills develop predominantly within the classroom context (Denham and Burton 2003). Social-emotional skills are interwoven with children's cognitive skills, for example improved ability to manage negative emotions is associated with increased executive functioning (Diamond et al. 2007; Shonkoff et al. 2009). Moreover, the relationship between social-emotional competencies and learning is not uni-directional, with research suggesting that low skills in these domains are not only predictors of difficulties in school, but also a consequence of children's inability to adjust to school expectations (Arnold et al. 1999; Raver and Knitzer 2002). Furthermore, as pointed out consistently throughout the previous chapters social-emotional skills' relevance is not limited to academic achievement, but has important implications for mental health, as a protective factor against development of emotional and behavior problems (Raver 2002), thus increasing children's resilience and ability to face life's challenges.

In spite of a plethora of research concerning positive effects of SEL in schools, implementation of such programs is often fragmented and lacks a coherent approach to skill development, because schools do not always have access to research driven interventions supported by empirical evidence. In this context, a better articulated connection between research outcomes and advances in educational policies needs to be formed so that effective, evidence-based interventions become best practice recommendations for schools. Current findings from recently conducted quantitative meta-analyses generally support the notion that social-emotional learning programs can be recommended based on data indicating that SEL participation was associated with effect sizes varying from .22 to .57, meaning that changes in social-emotional competencies and school performance can be as large as one-half of a standard deviation (Durlak et al. 2011; Jones et al. 2008).

However, as pointed out by Durlak et al. (2011) such effects are usually associated with high-quality implementation of a given program, and therefore, such recommendations need to be considered in developing educational policies for children: (1) the program should contain a coordinated set of sequenced activities; (2) the program should include active forms of learning; (3) at least one component of the program should be focused specifically on the development of social skills; and (4) the program should explicitly target specific social-emotional skills rather than positive development in general. As it can be inferred from the description in Chap. 2, SEP is similar to other evidence-based interventions which include a sequenced set of activities, provide children, parents and teachers with active learning situations in which skills can be exercised, and are specifically oriented towards teaching social-emotional skills. Furthermore, in accordance with other effective interventions, SEP complements classroom activities with teacher and parent training, aimed at supporting adult-child interactions that promote skill development, thus including a multi-component approach to SEL. Besides the recommendations of Durlak et al. (2011), the experience of SEP implementation in schools suggests that there are several additional conditions which could be considered as relevant for appropriate implementation of such practices in early education:

- *Integrating SEL in the classroom.* While acknowledging the importance of SEL, many educators are reluctant to implement such strategies due to the overly busy classroom schedule. Therefore, specifically in the context of preschool education, programs should include not only curricula of activities, but also a set of learning principles which can be implemented in the classroom as routine strategies with minimal interference with other activities, that can become an integrative part of classroom learning. From this perspective SEP combines formal teaching during prescheduled classroom activities (stand-alone intervention), with activities aimed at supporting social-emotional development during daily activities (embedded intervention).

- *Providing training and support to teachers.* Research supports the notion that teachers who are themselves more emotionally and socially skilled are in fact more competent in delivering classroom strategies aimed at enhancing children's social-emotional development (Jennings and Greenberg 2009). Therefore, training teachers in SEL development and providing support for implementing such programs should become a priority, which could maximize outcomes of such school-based practices.
- *Fostering parental involvement.* High-quality SEL programs also approach and seek parental involvement. Interventions in which teachers or mental health professionals interact with parents, educate them about child development, and teach them about ways to develop social-emotional competencies, were found to elicit better intervention outcomes especially for children at risk of mental health problems or from low-SES backgrounds (Raver et al. 2009; Webster-Stratton et al. 2004).
- *Enhancing school involvement in the assessment and implementation of SEL interventions.* Although research groups have a key role in developing and implementing SEL programs, as well as gathering evidence to support program efficacy, wide-scale implementation of such practices can be achieved when school heads, teachers, and school psychologists/counselors take on the responsibility of disseminating these practices in school settings with the explicit focus on fidelity of implementation and assessment of outcomes.
- *Developing school mental health services that respond to different categories of children.* As described previously, SEL interventions are recognized as fostering positive effects for children's mental health. Thus, school-based interventions need to consider the needs of at least 2 categories of children: the majority who are not at risk, and those who are at risk. Universal and indicated intervention principles should guide SEL implementation with the emphasis on non-discriminative and non-segregation practices. As noted in the discussions about SEP efficacy, focus on developing social-emotional competencies in the classroom rather than during separate sessions with at risk children, and training all parents not only those whose children were at risk, probably had a positive impact on the overall efficacy of the intervention.

The above described criteria can become a starting point for policy makers in developing standards for including SEL programs in the school curricula. Implicitly, such standards would support an integrated, systematic approach to SEL rather than the fragmented, inconsistent approaches which seem to characterize a relatively large proportion of undertakings regarding school-based interventions (Nadeem et al. 2010; Pianta et al. 2009). These standards should be associated with the provision of funding for school personnel training and implementation of such activities.

Specifically within the Romanian educational system, SEP together with other empirically supported interventions for preschoolers, could become an example of sound educational practices suggested as a model for integrating SEL in the classroom. Such practices could result in several positive consequences: (1) providing mental health services in the form of preventive interventions for children; (2) supporting teachers in developing a positive classroom climate conducive to learning in both the social-emotional and academic domains; (3) fostering parental learning and involvement in children's education; and (4) providing school psychologists with step-by-step standards for implementing and assessing SEL in schools.

References

Anderson, G. T. (2000). Computers in a developmentally appropriate curriculum. *Young Children, 55*, 90–93.

Arnold, D. H., Ortiz, C., Curry, J. C., Stowe, R. M., Goldstein, N. E., Fisher, P. H., & Yershova, K. (1999). Promoting academic success and preventing disruptive behavior disorders through community partnership. *Journal of Community Psychology, 27*, 589–598. https://doi.org/10.1002/(SICI)1520-6629(199909)27:5%3C589:AID-JCOP6%3E3.0.CO;2-Y.

Barnett, W. S. (2008a). *Preschool education and its lasting effects: Research and policy implications* (EPRU policy brief). Boulder and Tempe: Education and the Public Interest Center & Education and Policy Research Unit.

Barnett, W. S. (2008b). Why governments should invest in early education. *CESifo DICE Report, 6*, 9–14.

Beauchaine, T. P., Webster-Stratton, C., & Reid, M. J. (2005). Mediators, moderators, and predictors of 1-year outcomes among children treated for early-onset conduct problems: A latent growth curve analysis. *Journal of Consulting and Clinical Psychology, 73*, 371–388. https://doi.org/10.1037/0022-006X.73.3.371.

Bierman, K. (2002). Evaluation of the first 3 years of the Fast Track prevention trial with children at high risk for adolescent conduct problems. *Journal of Abnormal Child Psychology, 30*, 19–35. https://doi.org/10.1023/A:1014274914287.

Blair, K. A., Denham, S. A., Kochanoff, A., & Whipple, B. (2004). Playing it cool: Temperament, emotion regulation, and social behavior in preschoolers. *Journal of School Psychology, 42*, 419–443. https://doi.org/10.1016/j.jsp.2004.10.002.

Buckleitner, W. (2004). *The relationship between software interface instructional style and the engagement of young children*. Unpublished doctoral dissertation. Retrieved July 26, 2006, from http://www.childrenssoftware.com/dis/dis.menu.htm

Caldarella, P., & Merrell, K. W. (1997). Common dimensions of social skills of children and adolescents: A taxonomy of positive behaviors. *School Psychology Review, 26*, 264–278.

Carr, J. (2005). Recommendations for reporting multiple-baseline designs across participants. *Behavioral Interventions, 20*, 219–224. https://doi.org/10.1002/bin.191.

Chambless, D. L., & Hollon, S. D. (1998). Defining empirically supported psychotherapies. *Journal of Consulting and Clinical Psychology, 66*, 7–18. https://doi.org/10.1037/0022-006X.66.1.7.

Christ, T. J. (2007). Experimental control and threats to internal validity of concurrent and nonconcurrent multiple baseline designs. *Psychology in the Schools, 44*, 451–459. https://doi.org/10.1002/pits.20237.

Conduct Problems Prevention Research Group. (1999a). Initial impact of the Fast Track prevention trial for conduct problems: I. The high risk sample. *Journal of Consulting and Clinical Psychology, 67*, 631–647. https://doi.org/10.1037/0022-006X.67.5.648.

Conduct Problems Prevention Research Group. (1999b). Initial impact of the Fast Track prevention trial for conduct problems: II. Classroom effects. *Journal of Consulting and Clinical Psychology, 67*, 648–657. https://doi.org/10.1037/0022-006X.67.5.648.

Crook, C. (1998). Children as computer users: The case of collaborative learning. *Computers and Education, 30*, 237–247.

Curtner-Smith, M. E., Culp, A. M., Culp, R., Scheib, C., Owen, K., Tilley, A., et al. (2006). Mothers' parenting and young economically disadvantaged children's relational and overt bullying. *Journal of Child and Family Studies, 15*, 181–193. https://doi.org/10.1007/s10826-005-9016-7.

Dadds, M. R., & Roth, J. H. (2008). Prevention of anxiety disorders: Results of a universal trial with young children. *Journal of Child and Family Studies, 17*, 320–335. https://doi.org/10.1007/s10826-007-9144-3.

Denham, S. A. (2006). Social-emotional competence as support for school readiness: What is it and how do we assess it? *Early Education and Development, 17*, 57–89. https://doi.org/10.1207/s15566935eed1701_4.

Denham, S. A., & Burton, R. (2003). *Social and emotional prevention and intervention programming for preschoolers*. New York: Kluwer Academic/Plenum Press.

Denham, S. A., Blair, K. A., DeMulder, E., Levitas, J., Sawyer, K., Auerbach-Major, S., & Quinnan, P. (2003a). Preschool emotional competence: Pathway to social competence? *Child Development, 74*, 238–256. https://doi.org/10.1111/1467-8624.00533.

Denham, S. A., Blair, K. A., Schmidt, M. S., Blair, K., DeMulder, E., Caal, S., et al. (2003b). Preschool understanding of emotions: Contributions to classroom anger and aggression. *Journal of Child Psychology and Psychiatry, 43*, 901–916. https://doi.org/10.1111/1469-7610.00139.

Diamond, A., Barnett, W. S., Thomas, J., & Munro, S. (2007). Preschool program improves cognitive control. *Science, 30*, 1387–1388. https://doi.org/10.1126/science.1151148.

Domitrovich, C. E., Cortes, R. C., & Greenberg, M. T. (2007). Improving young children's social and emotional competence: A randomized trial of the preschool "PATHS" curriculum. *The Journal of Primary Prevention, 28*, 67–91. https://doi.org/10.1007/s10935-007-0081-0.

Durlak, J. A., & Wells, A. M. (1998). Evaluation of indicated preventive intervention (secondary prevention) mental health programs for children and adolescents. *American Journal of Community Psychology, 26*, 775–802. https://doi.org/10.1023/A:1022162015815.

Durlak, J. A., Weissberg, R. P., Dymnicki, A. B., Taylor, R. D., & Schellinger, K. B. (2011). The impact of enhancing students' social and emotional learning: A meta-analysis of school-based universal interventions. *Child Development, 82*, 405–432. https://doi.org/10.1111/j.1467-8624.2010.01564.x.

Eisenberg, N., Fabes, R. A., Guthrie, I. K., & Reiser, M. (2002). The role of emotionality and regulation in children's social competence and adjustment. In L. Pulkinnen & A. Caspi (Eds.), *Paths to successful development: Personality in the life course* (pp. 46–70). Cambridge: Cambridge University Press.

Eisenberg, N., Sadovsky, A., & Spinrad, T. L. (2005). Associations of emotion-related regulation with language skills, emotion knowledge, and academic outcomes. *New Directions for Child and Adolescent Development, 2005*(109), 109–118. https://doi.org/10.1002/cd.143.

Essex, M. J., Kraemer, H. C., Slattery, M. J., Burk, L. R., Boyce, W. T., Woodward, H. R., & Kupfer, D. J. (2009). Screening for childhood mental health problems: Outcomes and early identification. *Journal of Child Psychology and Psychiatry, 50*, 562–570. https://doi.org/10.1111/j.1469-7610.2008.02015.x.

Fabes, R. A., Martin, C. L., & Hanish, L. D. (2003). Young children's play qualities in same-, other-, and mixed-sex peer groups. *Child Development, 74*, 921–932. https://doi.org/10.1111/1467-8624.00576.

Fenstermacher, K., Olympia, D., & Sheridan, S. M. (2006). Effectiveness of a computer-facilitated, interactive social skills training program for boys with attention deficit hyperactivity disorder. *School Psychology Quarterly, 21*, 197–224. https://doi.org/10.1521/scpq.2006.21.2.197.

Frick, P. J., Lahey, B. B., Loeber, R., Stouthamer-Loeber, M., Christ, M. A. G., & Hanson, K. (1992). Familial risk factors to oppositional defiant disorder and conduct disorder: Parental psychopathology and maternal parenting. *Journal of Consulting and Clinical Psychology, 60*, 49–55. https://doi.org/10.1037/0022-006X.60.1.49.

Gardner, F., Burton, J., & Klimes, I. (2006). Randomised controlled trial of a parenting intervention in the voluntary sector for reducing child conduct problems: Outcomes and mechanisms of change. *Journal of Child Psychology and Psychiatry, 47*, 1123–1132. https://doi.org/10.1111/j.1469-7610.2006.01668.x.

Gardner, F., Hutchings, J., Bywater, T., & Whitaker, C. (2010). Who benefits and how does it work? Moderators and mediators of outcomes in a randomised trial of parenting interventions in multiple "Sure Start" services. *Journal of Clinical Child and Adolescent Psychology, 39*, 568–580. https://doi.org/10.1080/15374416.2010.486315.

Gmeider, K. L., & Kratochwill, T. R. (1998). Short-term, home-based intervention for child noncompliance using behavioral consultation and a self-help manual. *Journal of Educational and Psychological Consultation, 9*, 91–117. https://doi.org/10.1207/s1532768xjepc0902_1.

Goleman, D. (1995). *Emotional intelligence: Why it can matter more than IQ*. New York: Bantam Books.

Grantham-McGregor, S., Cheung, Y. B., Cueto, S., Glewwe, P., Richter, L., Strupp, B., & The International Child Development Steering Group. (2007). Developmental potential in the first 5 years for children in developing countries. *Lancet, 369*, 60–70. https://doi.org/10.1016/S0140-6736(07)60032-4.

Heckman, J. J. (2006). Skill formation and the economics of investing in disadvantaged children. *Science, 312*, 1900–1902. https://doi.org/10.1126/science.1128898.

Helfenbaum-Kun, E. D., & Ortiz, C. (2007). Parent-training groups for fathers of Head Start children: A pilot study of their feasibility and impact on child behavior and intra-familial relationships. *Child and Family Behavior Therapy, 29*, 47–64. https://doi.org/10.1080/15374416.2016.1266648.

Hinshaw, S. P., Han, S. S., Erhardt, D., & Huber, A. (1992). Internalizing and externalizing behavior problems in preschool children: Correspondence among parent and teacher ratings and behavior observations. *Journal of Clinical Child Psychology, 21*, 143–150. https://doi.org/10.1207/s15374424jccp2102_6.

Hinshaw, S. P., Owens, E. B., Wells, K. C., Kraemer, H. C., Abikoff, H. B., Arnold, E., et al. (2000). Family processes and treatment outcome in the MTA: Negative/ineffective parenting practices in relation to multimodal treatment. *Journal of Abnormal Child Psychology, 28*, 555–568. https://doi.org/10.1023/A:1005183115230.

Izard, C. E. (2001). Emotional intelligence or adaptive emotions? *Emotion, 1*, 249–257. https://doi.org/10.1037/1528-3542.1.3.249.

Jennings, P. A., & Greenberg, M. T. (2009). The prosaically classroom: Teacher social and emotional competence in relation to student and classroom outcomes. *Review of Education Research, 79*, 491–525. https://doi.org/10.3109/0034654308325693.

Jones, S. M., Brown, J. L., & Aber, J. L. (2008). The longitudinal impact of a universal school-based social-emotional and literacy intervention: An experiment in translational developmental research. *Child Development, 82*, 533–554. https://doi.org/10.1111/j.1467-8624.2010.01560.x.

Kam, C.-M., Greenberg, M. T., & Walls, C. T. (2003). Examining the role of implementation quality in school-based prevention using the PATHS curriculum. *Prevention Science, 4*, 55–63. https://doi.org/10.1023/A:1021786811186.

Kellam, S. G., Ling, X., Merisca, R., Brown, C. H., & Ialongo, N. (1998). The effect of the level of aggression in the first grade classroom on the course and malleability of aggressive behavior into middle school. *Development and Psychopathology, 10*, 165–185. https://doi.org/10.1017/S0954579498001564.

Lau, C., Higgins, K., Gelfer, J., Hong, E., & Miller, S. (2005). The effects of teacher facilitation on the social interactions of young children during computer activities. *Topics in Early Childhood Special Education, 25*, 208–217. https://doi.org/10.1177/02711214050250040201.

Lees, D. G., & Ronan, K. R. (2008). Engagement and effectiveness of parent management training (Incredible Years) for solo high-risk mothers: A multiple baseline evaluation. *Behaviour Change, 25*, 109–128. https://doi.org/10.1375/bech.25.2.109.

Lemerise, A. E., & Arsenio, C. R. (2000). An integrated model of emotion processes and cognition in social information processing. *Child Development, 71*, 107–118. https://doi.org/10.1111/1467-8624.00124.

Linares, L. O., Rosbruch, N., Stern, M. B., Edwards, M. E., Walker, G., Abikoff, H. B., & Alvir, J. M. I. (2005). Developing cognitive-social-emotional competencies to enhance academic learning. *Psychology in the Schools, 42*, 405–418. https://doi.org/10.1002/pits.20066.

Lochman, J. E., & Wells, K. C. (2002). The Coping Power program at the middle-school transition: Universal and indicated prevention effects. *Psychology of Addictive Behaviors, 16*, S40–S54. https://doi.org/10.1037/0893-164X.16.4S.S40.

Loftin, R. L., Odom, S. L., & Lantz, J. F. (2008). Social interaction and repetitive motor behaviors. *Journal of Autism and Developmental Disorders, 38*, 1124–1135. https://doi.org/10.1007/s10803-007-0499-5.

Miclea, M., Bălaj, A., Porumb, M., Porumb, D., & Porumb, S. (2010). *PEDa: The developmental assessment platform for 3–6/7 year old children*. Cluj-Napoca: ASCR Publishing.

Morawska, A., & Sanders, M. R. (2006). Self-administered behavioural family intervention for parents of toddlers: Part I – Efficacy. *Journal of Consulting and Clinical Psychology, 74*, 10–19. https://doi.org/10.1037/0022-006X.74.1.10.

Nadeem, E., Maslak, K., Chacko, A., & Hoagwood, K. E. (2010). Aligning research and policy on social-emotional and academic competence for young children. *Early Education and Development, 21*, 765–779. https://doi.org/10.1080/10409289.2010.497452.

Nelson, G., Westhues, A., & MacLeod, J. (2003). A meta-analysis of longitudinal research on preschool prevention programs for children. *Prevention and Treatment, 6*, 1–25.

Pianta, R. C., Barnett, W. S., Burchinal, M., & Thornburg, K. R. (2009). The effects of preschool education: What we know, how public policy is or is not aligned with the evidence base, and what we need to know. *Psychological Science in the Public Interest, 10*, 49–88. https://doi.org/10.1177/1529100610381908.

Pollack, W. S. (1995). A delicate balance: Fatherhood and psychological transformation—a psychotherapeutic perspective. In J. L. Shapiro, M. H. Diamond, & M. Greenberg (Eds.), *Becoming a father* (pp. 316–331). New York: Springer.

Prinz, R. J., & Sanders, M. R. (2007). Adopting a population-level approach to parenting and family support interventions. *Clinical Psychology Review, 27*, 739–749. https://doi.org/10.1016/j.cpr.2007.01.005.

Ramey, C. T., & Ramey, S. L. (2004). Early learning and school readiness: Can early intervention make a difference? *Merrill-Palmer Quarterly, 50*, 471–491. https://doi.org/10.1353/mpq.2004.0034.

Rapee, R. M., Kennedy, S., Ingram, M., Edwards, S., & Sweeney, L. (2005). Prevention and early intervention of anxiety disorders in inhibited preschool children. *Journal of Consulting Clinical Psychology, 73*, 488–497. https://doi.org/10.1037/0022-006X.73.3.488.

Raver, C. C. (2002). Emotions matter: Making the case for the role of young children's emotional development for early school readiness. *Social Policy Report, 16*, 3–18.

Raver, C. C., & Knitzer, J. (2002). *Ready to enter: What research tells policymakers about strategies to promote social and emotional school readiness among three- and four-year-old children*. New York: National Center for Children in Poverty, Columbia University Mailman School of Public Health.

Raver, C. C., Jones, S. M., Li-Grining, C., Zhai, F., Metzger, M. W., & Solomon, B. (2009). Targeting children's behavior problems in preschool classrooms: A cluster-randomized controlled trial. *Journal of Consulting and Clinical Psychology, 77*, 302–316. https://doi.org/10.1037/a0015302.

Reid, J. M., Webster-Stratton, C., & Hammond, M. (2004). Follow-up of children who received the Incredible Years intervention for oppositional defiant disorder: Maintenance and prediction of 2-year outcome. *Behavior Therapy, 34*, 471–491. https://doi.org/10.1016/S0005-7894(03)80031-X.

Romano, E., Tremblay, R. E., Boulerice, B., & Swisher, R. (2005). Multilevel correlates of childhood physical aggression and prosocial behavior. *Journal of*

Abnormal Child Psychology, 33, 565–578. https://doi.org/10.1007/s10802-005-6738-3.

Sanders, M. R., & Morawska, A. (2005). Can changing parental knowledge, dysfunctional expectations and attributions, and emotion regulation improve outcomes for children? In R. E. Tremblay, R. G. Barr, & R. V. De Peters (Eds.), *Encyclopedia on early childhood development.* Retrieved March 13, 2010, from www.excellence-earlychildhood.ca

Schultz, D., Izard, C. E., Ackerman, B. P., & Youngstrom, E. A. (2001). Emotion knowledge in economically disadvantaged children: Self-regulatory antecedents and relations to social difficulties and withdrawal. *Development and Psychopathology, 13*, 53–67. https://doi.org/10.1017/S0954579401001043.

Schweinhart, L. J., Montie, J., Xiang, Z., Barnett, W. S., Belfield, C. R., & Nores, M. (2005). *Lifetime effects: The High/Scope Perry preschool study through age 40.* Ypsilanti: High Scope Press.

Severson, H. H., Walker, H. M., Hope-Doolittle, J., Kratochwill, T. R., & Gresham, F. M. (2007). Proactive, early screening to detect behaviorally at-risk students: Issues, approaches, emerging innovations, and professional practices. *Journal of School Psychology, 45*, 193–223. https://doi.org/10.1016/j.jsp.2006.11.003.

Sheridan, S. M., Hungelman, A., & Maughan, P. D. (1999). A contextualized framework for social skills assessment, intervention, and generalization. *School Psychology Review, 28*, 84–103.

Shonkoff, J. P., Boyce, W. T., & McEwen, B. S. (2009). Neuroscience, molecular biology, and the childhood roots of health disparities: Building a new framework for health promotion and disease prevention. *JAMA, 301*, 2252–2259. https://doi.org/10.1001/jama.2009.754.

Snow, K. L. (2006). Measuring school readiness: Conceptual and practical considerations. *Early Education and Development, 17*, 7–41. https://doi.org/10.1207/s15566935eed1701_2.

Snyder, K. A. (2007). A vocabulary of motives: Understanding how parents define quality time. *Journal of Marriage and Family, 69*, 320–340. https://doi.org/10.1111/j.1741-3737.2007.00368.x.

Ştefan, C. A., Bălaj, A., Porumb, M., Albu, M., & Miclea, M. (2009). Preschool screening for social and emotional competencies – Development and psychometric properties. *Cognition, Brain, Behavior. An Interdisciplinary Journal, 13*, 121–146.

Stifter, C. A., Spinrad, T., & Braungart-Rieker, J. (1999). Toward a developmental model of child compliance: The role of emotion regulation in infancy. *Child Development, 70*, 21–32. https://doi.org/10.1111/1467–8624.00003.

Stoolmiller, M., Eddy, M., & Reid, J. B. (2000). Detecting and describing preventive intervention effects in a universal school-based randomized trial targeting delinquent and violent behavior. *Journal of Consulting and Clinical Psychology, 68*, 296–306. https://doi.org/10.1037//0022-006X.68.2.296.

Turner, K. M. T., & Sanders, M. R. (2006). Dissemination of evidence-based parenting and family support strategies: Learning from the Triple P – Positive Parenting Program system approach. *Aggression and Violent Behavior, 11*, 176–193. https://doi.org/10.1016/j.avb.2005.07.005.

UNESCO. (2000, April). *Dakkar framework for education: Education for all.* Meeting of our collective commitments adopted by the World Education Forum, Dakkar. Document retrieved from http://www.unesco.org/education/efa/ed_for_all/dakfram_eng.html. Accessed July 2009.

van Lier, P. A. C., Vuijk, P., & Crijnen, A. A. M. (2005). Understanding mechanisms of change and development of antisocial behavior: The impact of a universal intervention. *Journal of Abnormal Child Psychology, 33*, 521–535. https://doi.org/10.1007/s10802-005-6735-7.

Walker, S. P., Chang, S. M., Powell, C. A., Simonoff, E., & Grantham-McGregor, S. M. (2006). Effects of psychosocial stimulation and dietary supplementation in early childhood on psychosocial functioning in late adolescence: Follow-up of randomised controlled trial. *British Medical Journal, 333*, 472. https://doi.org/10.1136/bmj.38897.555208.2F.

Webster-Stratton, C. (2000). *The Incredible Years Training Series.* Washington, DC: Office of Juvenile Justice and Delinquency Prevention.

Webster-Stratton, C., & Hammond, M. (1997). Treating children with early-onset conduct problems: A comparison of child and parent training interventions. *Journal of Consulting and Clinical Psychology, 65*, 93–109. https://doi.org/10.1037/0022-006X.65.1.93.

Webster-Stratton, C., & Reid, J. M. (2003). Treating conduct problems and strengthening social and emotional competence in young children: The Dina Dinosaur Program. *Journal of Emotional and Behavioral Disorders, 2*, 130–143. https://doi.org/10.1177/10634266030110030101.

Webster-Stratton, C., & Taylor, T. (2001). Nipping early risk factors in the bud: Preventing substance abuse, delinquency, and violence in adolescence through interventions targeted at young children (0–8 years). *Prevention Science, 2*, 165–192. https://doi.org/10.1023/A:1011510923900.

Webster-Stratton, C., Reid, J. M., & Hammond, M. (2001). Preventing conduct problems, promoting social competence: A parent-teacher training partnership in Head Start. *Journal of Clinical Child Psychology, 30*, 283–302.

Webster-Stratton, C., Reid, J. M., & Hammond, M. (2004). Treating children with early-onset conduct problems: Intervention outcomes for parent, child, and teacher training. *Journal of Clinical Child and Adolescent Psychology, 33*, 105–124. https://doi.org/10.1207/S15374424JCCP3301_11.

Witherington, D. C., & Crichton, J. A. (2007). Frameworks for understanding emotions and their development: Functionalist and dynamic systems approaches. *Emotion, 7*, 628–637. https://doi.org/10.1037/1528-3542.7.3.628.

Appendix 1

Treatment Planner for the Classroom Curriculum

The classroom activities curriculum contains 5 intervention modules. A description of general and specific objectives for each intervention phase, as well as the corresponding activities from each intervention module, is provided below.

C. A. Ştefan, *Social-Emotional Prevention Programs for Preschool Children's Behavior Problems*,
https://doi.org/10.1007/978-3-319-74751-4

Module	*General objectives (G.O.)*	*Specific objectives (S.O.)*
Compliance with rules	Increasing children's compliance with rules and teacher's requests (G.O. 1);	Recognizing and naming classroom rules (S.O. 1); Practicing behaviors associated with classroom rules (S.O. 2); Naming the consequences of rule appropriate and inappropriate behaviors (S.O. 3);
Emotion recognition	Increasing children's ability to name correctly their own and others' emotions (e.g., happiness, anger, sadness, fear) (G.O. 2);	Identifying and correctly naming emotions in different contexts (e.g., stories, pictures, daily interactions with adults and other children) (S.O. 1); Associating the label of an emotion with specific facial cues (S.O. 2); Identifying multiple emotions for similar contexts (S.O. 3); Identifying associations between emotions and behavioral consequences (S.O. 4); Promoting perspective-taking as foundation for empathic behaviors (S.O. 5);
Emotion regulation	Increasing children's ability to use anger regulation strategies (G.O. 3);	Differentiating between appropriate and inappropriate behaviors in anger-eliciting situations (S.O. 1); Introducing and exercising the steps of the "turtle technique" (S.O. 2); Exercising other anger management strategies (e.g., reorienting attention, distancing, asking for adult assistance) (S.O. 3); Implementing anger management strategies during daily interactions with or without the teacher's assistance (S. O. 4);
Problem-solving	Increasing children's ability to problem-solve (G.O. 4);	Acquiring problem-solving language (S.O. 1); Identifying problems and offering multiple solutions to those problems (S.O. 2); Evaluating the adequacy of a solution (S.O. 3); Identifying the consequences of one's behavior on other people's emotions (S.O. 4)
	Increasing the frequency of prosocial behaviors (e.g., turn-taking, sharing, waiting, help offering) (G.O. 5);	Acquiring and exercising prosocial behaviors as aggression preventing strategies (S.O. 5); Applying problem-solving during daily interactions with or without the teacher's assistance (S.O. 6);
Play cooperation	Increasing the frequency of children's group play and use of cooperative play strategies (G.O. 6);	Differentiating between friendly and unfriendly behaviors (S.O. 1); Acquiring and exercising cooperative play strategies (e.g., offering help, sharing, inviting someone to come and play) (S.O. 2); Acquiring and exercising group entry skills (e.g., asking for permission to play with others, suggesting a strategy for continuing a game, imitating other children's play activities) (S.O. 3); Implementing cooperative play behaviors with or without the teacher's assistance (S.O. 4).

Module 1—Compliance with rules

Duration: 1 + 3 weeks; 2–3 activities/week; 15–20 minutes/activity

Objective G.O. 1	*Activity description*	*Strategies/methods*
S.O. 1	The teacher introduces children to their new classroom friend, Ami, who is going to help them find out how to behave in the classroom. The teacher reads a story, in which the main character is Ami. For each behavior of the characters from the story, the children in the classroom are prompted to identify whether it was an appropriate or an inappropriate behavior. In the end, children are presented with visual cues depicting classroom rules, and each child is asked to name one of them.	Games: Puppet-play Didactic methods: Story telling Think aloud Comprehension questions Behavioral strategies (antecedent-based) Visual cues
S.O. 1 & S.O. 2	The teacher reminds children about Ami, and asks them to name the classroom rules using the visual cues introduced in the previous activity. With Ami's help, the teacher introduces games designed to assist children in understanding the behaviors associated with each rule, and expected behaviors are modeled through these games. Afterwards, the behaviors are practiced through role-play by the children.	Games: Puppet-play Behavioral strategies (antecedent-based) Visual cues Social learning strategies: Modeling Role-play
S.O. 1 & S.O. 3	Again the teacher reads the story from the first activity and children are asked to recognize the rules. Then, the teacher introduces them to the consequences of rule appropriate and inappropriate behaviors. Each child receives from Ami a token economy sheet, which is going to be placed on a poster. The teacher explains to the children that for each day, in which they behave according to the rules, they are going to receive a stamp. At the end of every week, children with more than 3 stamps for each behavior will trade their stamps for extra privileges (e.g., bringing to the classroom a favorite toy, picking the bedtime story, choosing a game for the whole classroom, etc.).	Games: Puppet-play Story telling Didactic methods: Story telling Comprehension questions Puppet-play Behavioral strategies (consequence-based) Token economy

(*continued*)

(continued)

Module 1—Compliance with rules		
Duration: 1 + 3 weeks; 2–3 activities/week; 15–20 minutes/activity		
Objective G.O. 1	***Activity description***	***Strategies/methods***
S.O. 1 & S.O. 3	During the second week of the intervention, each day during circle time the teacher discusses with the children the rules and each child is asked to evaluate his/her own behavior. If the behavior was according to the rules, then the child is given a stamp on his/her token economy sheet and praised. If not, the child is asked to identify an appropriate behavior and is encouraged to behave accordingly. This process is repeated each day for approximately 2 weeks, after which the classroom teachers decide whether to continue with the same reward interval, or switch to a 2-day interval for the delivery of the same rewards. After another 2 weeks, the teachers have to decide whether to administer the rewards once a week, or substitute the rewards system with praise. At the end of implementing the token economy system, if most of the children earned a previously established number of stamps, the entire classroom receives a group reward (e.g., a party, going to the zoo, an extended visit to the park, etc.).	Behavioral strategies (consequence-based) Token economy Praise Individual and group rewards

Module 2—Emotion recognition

Duration: 3 weeks; 2–3 activities/week; 15–20 minutes/activity

Objective G.O. 2	*Activity description*	*Strategies/methods*
S.O. 1 & S.O. 2	The teacher chooses a story children are familiar with. During the story reading the teacher shows the children the pictures and asks them to recognize the character's emotions. After the story is read, the children are asked to tell the story in their own words. The teacher also asks the children about the character's emotions, and uses an "emotion map" consisting of sketch-like human faces expressing emotions such as happiness, anger, sadness, and fear. This strategy is used in order to assist them in identifying the emotions.	Didactic methods Story telling Comprehension questions Visual aids Behavioral strategies (consequence-based) Praise
S.O. 1 & S.O. 2	The teacher places pictures depicting people expressing different emotions (happy, angry, sad, and fearful) in a box. The teacher models children's behavior by extracting a card, identifying the emotion, and a context in which she/he felt that particular emotion. Each child is asked to take out a card from the box, present the card to the other children and name the emotion depicted on the card. The teacher assists each child in identifying the emotion by emphasizing how people's faces change according to the emotions they feel.	Didactic methods Association Visual aids Social learning strategies: Modeling Behavioral strategies (consequence-based) Praise
S.O. 1, S.O. 2 & S.O. 3	The children are asked to draw a picture depicting a situation in which they were happy, angry, sad, or afraid. During the activity the teacher uses the "emotion map", and reminds children which are the facial cues for each emotion. At the end of the activity the children present their drawing and tell others how they felt and why.	Didactic methods Drawing Comprehension questions Association Visual aids Behavioral strategies (consequence-based) Praise

(*continued*)

(continued)

Module 2—Emotion recognition

Duration: 3 weeks; 2–3 activities/week; 15–20 minutes/activity

Objective G.O. 2	*Activity description*	*Strategies/methods*
S.O. 1, S.O. 2, S.O. 3 & S.O. 4	The children are presented the "emotion map". Each child in the classroom is asked to identify an emotion and to give an example of a situation, in which they felt happy, angry, sad, or afraid. Then, the teacher asks children to think and describe their behaviors in those contexts.	Didactic methods Visual aids Comprehension questions Association Behavioral strategies (consequence-based) Praise
S.O. 3 & S.O. 4	The teachers are provided with a list of situations, which are presented to the children. They are asked to think about various emotions elicited by those situations. The "emotion map" can be used to assist children in naming the emotions. Then, the children are asked to identify the behavioral consequences of the emotions they have identified.	Didatic methods Anticipation Comprehension questions Visual aids Association Behavioral strategies (consequence-based) Praise
S.O. 1, S.O. 2 & S.O. 3	The teacher places in a small sack cards depicting people with different emotional expressions. Children are blind-folded and asked to extract a card. Then, each child is paired with a classmate. They show their cards to each other and each has to recognize the emotion on the other child's card. The children are asked by their teacher to identify situations in which they experienced similar emotions to those depicted in the cards. Then, children are asked to sort the cards according to the type of emotion at Ami's request.	Didactic methods Association Rehearsal Guided questions Visual aids Behavioral strategies (consequence-based) Praise

S.O. 1 & S.O. 4	Children are presented with a set of vignettes depicting situations, in which a child is treated unkindly by a peer/has an accident. The teacher requests children to identify the emotions of the child, as well as possible behaviors the child might exhibit as a consequence of a particular emotion. Children are then asked to identify the adequate behaviors. Also, teachers assist children in role-playing possible reactions, which they might have towards a classmate in a similar situation as those depicted in the vignettes.	Games
		  Puppet-play
		Didactic methods
		  Comprehension questions
		  Alternative scenarios
		Social learning strategies
		  Role-play
		Behavioral strategies (consequence-based)
		  Praise

S.O. 1 & S.O. 2	The teacher selects a familiar story. The children are divided into 2 groups. The children from one group are expected to pay attention to the teacher and identify the emotions of the characters. The children from the second group are asked to mime each emotion identified by the children from the other group. Then, a second story is read, and children from the 2 groups switch their roles.	Didactic methods
		  Story telling
		Games
		  Mime game
		  Group play
		Behavioral strategies (consequence-based)
		  Praise

S.O. 1 & S.O. 4	The scenarios are interpreted by the teacher using puppets. For each scenario the teacher asks the children to identify the emotion of the character, and provide some possible behavioral consequences of the identified emotion. Then, the scenario is continued and children are presented with both appropriate and inappropriate solutions. Consequently, the teacher asks them to identify appropriate solutions and to exercise them through role-play.	Didactic methods
		  Puppet-play
		  Comprehension questions
		  Alternative scenarios
		  Association
		Behavioral strategies (consequence-based)
		  Praise

S.O. 1 & S.O. 2	The children are reminded about the emotions they learned using the "emotion map". Then, each child has to pay attention to Ami, who asks them to mime a certain emotion. The teacher can provide children with mirrors in order to see their facial reactions and reminds them, with Ami's help, of the facial cues characteristic of each emotion.	Didactic methods
		  Visual aids
		  Puppet-play
		  Comprehensive questions
		Games
		  Mime game

Module 3—Emotion regulation

Duration: 3 weeks; 2–3 activities/week; 15–20 minutes/activity

Objective G.O. 3	*Activity description*	*Strategies/methods*
S.O. 1 & S.O. 3	The teacher introduces with Ami's help 2 new friends, the 2 bears Bruno and Bruni. After the children get acquainted with their new friends, teachers use puppet-play for interpreting a set of scenarios depicting anger-eliciting situations. Each scenario provides 2 possible endings: one with an appropriate behavior, and the other with an inappropriate behavior. The teacher and the children discuss the emotions, and establish which character behaved appropriately, and which one did not. The exercise is continued by role-playing adequate behaviors.	Didactic methods Puppet-play Alternative evaluation Comprehensive questions Social learning strategies Role-play Behavioral strategies (consequence-based) Praise
S.O. 2	The activity encompasses 2 sections. During the first stage of the activity the teacher introduces Tobias, the tiny turtle. Children are asked to tell the teacher where they have seen turtles, and why they have shells. Then, the children color a work sheet with a drawing of Tobias, the tiny turtle. The second part of the activity requires the teacher to read the story of the turtle. During the story the teacher asks children to recognize the characters' emotions, and establish whether the characters' behavior was appropriate or inappropriate. When the story depicts the steps of the "turtle technique", the teacher demonstrates it to the children. At the end of the story, children are presented with a chart depicting the steps of the "turtle technique", which is exercised together with the teacher.	Didactic methods Drawing Comprehension questions Story telling Evaluating alternatives Social learning strategies Modeling Role-play Behavioral strategies (antecedent-based) Visual cues

S.O. 1, S.O. 2. & S.O. 3	The teacher uses the chart with the "turtle technique" steps in order to help remind children about the steps. The teacher presents the children with a set of scenarios using puppet-play and they are asked to identify the character's emotions and whether the character's behavior was appropriate or not. Then, the teacher pairs up children in the classroom and guides them in role-playing adequate solutions to the scenarios by reminding them about using the steps of the "turtle technique".	Didactic methods Puppet-play Comprehension questions Social learning strategies Role-play Behavioral strategies (antecedent-based) Visual cues Behavioral strategies (consequence-based) Praise
S.O. 4	During the last 2 weeks of the intervention for developing children's emotion regulation skills, teachers are asked to coach children in using the "turtle technique" or any other strategy exercised during the activities from this module. The teacher reminds children about the "turtle technique", provides children with help during emotionally arousing situations by discussing about emotions, and directs children's behavior toward choosing appropriate strategies for managing their emotions. Also, the teacher uses praise and encourages children to use these strategies. At the end of the module, each child in the classroom receives a "tiny turtle diploma" as a reward for learning the technique.	Behavioral strategies (antecedent-based) Visual cues Prompting Behavioral strategies (consequence-based) Praise Classroom reward

Module 4—Problem-solving

Duration: 4 weeks; 2–3 activities/week; 15–20 minutes/activity

Objective G.O. 4 & G.O.5	*Activity description*	*Strategies/methods*
G.O. 4–S.O. 1	The teacher uses the Bruno and Bruni puppets to interpret several scenarios designed to help children with understanding similarities and dissimilarities between the 2 characters. The game can be continued using a similar strategy in order to compare children, objects or other story characters, until all children have participated in it.	Didactic methods Puppet-play Association
G.O. 4–S.O. 1	This activity is also based on a set of scenarios which are interpreted using puppets. The teacher establishes similarities among different characters. Then, the game is continued using similar scenarios that allow all the children to be involved.	Didactic methods Puppet-play Association
G.O. 4–S.O. 1	The teacher reads the story, while showing children the accompanying pictures. The teacher asks questions regarding the emotions of the story's main characters, Bruno and Bruni. After reading the story, the children are asked to arrange the pictures in the order of the story's events. Then, children are asked to remember which events took place before or after another event.	Didactic methods Story telling Comprehensive questions
G.O. 4–S.O. 2	The teacher reads the children a story with the same characters as the previous one. During the story, Bruno and Bruni ask the children to help them find solutions to their problems. The solutions suggested by the children are then compared to those found by the 2 characters from the story.	Didactic methods Story telling Alternative scenarios Comprehensive questions
G.O. 4–S.O. 2 & S.O. 3	The teacher introduces the activity by telling children that Bruno and Bruni will share their secrets about how to be patient. The teacher uses puppet-play for interpreting scenarios in which Bruno and Bruni have to be patient and wait for the right moment to get what they want. Then, the teacher asks the children to think why it would be a good idea to wait. Similar situations are presented, and children are encouraged to role-play adequate solutions.	Didactic methods Puppet-play Comprehensive questions Anticipation
G.O. 4 – S.O. 2 & S.O. 3	Bruno and Bruni present the children with a set of vignettes depicting conflict situations. For each situation children are asked to identify the character's emotions, as well as possible behaviors associated with that emotion and their consequences. For each consequence, the teacher guides the discussion towards evaluating the solutions provided by the children. Then, adequate solutions are role-played by the children.	Didactic methods Puppet-play Comprehensive questions Anticipation Association Social learning strategies Role-play

G.O. 4–S.O. 2, S.O. 3 & **G.O. 5**–S.O. 5	The scenarios depicting conflict situations are interpreted using puppets. The teacher helps children identify as many solutions as it is possible. Each solution and its consequences are evaluated. Adequate solutions are role-played by the children with the teacher's guidance.	Didactic methods Puppet-play Comprehensive questions Social learning strategies Role-play Behavioral strategies (consequence-based) Praise
G.O. 4–S.O. 2, S.O. 3, S.O. 4 & **G.O. 5**–S.O. 5	The teacher introduces Bruno and Bruni who bring a present for all the children in the classroom, a magic hat that helps them find a problem's best solutions. The teacher uses puppet-play to enact the scenarios. During each puppet-play, the teacher asks children about the character's emotions and how their behaviors affect the other character's emotions. Each scenario is discussed and children are prompted to put on their magic hats, and find as many adequate alternatives as possible. These alternatives are role-played.	Didactic methods Puppet-play Comprehensive questions Anticipation Social learning strategies Role-play Behavioral strategies (consequence-based) Praise
G.O. 4–S.O. 2, S.O. 3, S.O. 4 & **G.O. 5**–S.O. 5	Each scenario constitutes a discussion between the teacher and one of the characters of the program (Ami, Bruno, or Bruni). The teacher discusses their problems by identifying their emotions, and their problems, as well as how appropriate or inappropriate were their behaviors. For each situation, children are asked to help their friends by identifying as many solutions as they can. Each solution is evaluated in terms of their consequences. Then, adequate solutions are role-played.	Didactic methods Puppet-play Comprehension questions Anticipation Alternative scenarios Social learning strategies Role-play Behavioral strategies (consequence-based) Praise

(*continued*)

(continued)

Module 4—Problem-solving		
Duration: 4 weeks; 2–3 activities/week; 15–20 minutes/activity		
Objective G.O. 4 & G.O.5	***Activity description***	***Strategies/methods***
G.O. 4–S.O. 2, S.O. 3, S.O. 4 & **G.O. 5**–S.O. 5	The teacher presents vignettes in which the characters employ an appropriate problem-solving strategy, but the strategy fails to produce a positive outcome. Children are asked to assess these situations in terms of elicited emotions and possible behaviors. Then, the teacher asks them to provide possible solutions to these situations. These alternatives are discussed, and if appropriate, they are role-played.	Didactic methods Puppet-play Anticipation Alternative scenarios Social learning strategies Role-play Behavioral strategies (consequence-based) Praise
G.O. 5–S.O. 6	During the last 2 weeks of this module, the teachers implement problem-solving strategies in the classroom during real conflict situations. They guide children in identifying their emotions, evaluating their own behavior, and how that behavior affects the other child's emotions. Possible solutions are discussed and, if possible, implemented in order to solve the conflict. Children are also reminded about the "turtle technique" and provided with support in implementing it in anger-eliciting situations. Moreover, children are praised for finding and implementing appropriate solutions in conflict situations.	Social learning strategies Problem-solving Behavioral strategies (antecendent-based) Verbal prompting Visual cues Behavioral strategies (consequence-based) Praise

Module 5—Cooperative play

Duration: 4 weeks; 2–3 activities/week; 15–20 minutes/activity

Objective G.O. 6	*Activity description*	*Strategies/methods*
S.O. 1	The teacher reads the story, in which the main characters are Ami and her new friends Alfi, Pusu, and Pufi. The children's task is to identify friendly, as well as unfriendly, behaviors. Friendly behaviors are then role-played with the teacher's guidance.	Didactic methods Story telling Comprehension questions Social learning strategies Role-play
S.O. 1 & S.O. 2	The teacher reminds children about the story from the previous activity. With the teacher's assistance children identify the friendly behaviors, and discuss the positive consequences of these behaviors. The teacher organizes a free play activity at his/her choosing, in which children are reminded about the friendly behaviors. The teacher participates in their play session in order to model those behaviors and praise children for their friendly attitudes.	Didactic methods Story telling Comprehensive questions Social learning Group play Modeling Behavioral strategies (antecendent-based) Prompting Behavioral strategies (consequence-based) Praise
S.O. 2	The teacher with the help of the children creates an obstacle track in the classroom. Then, the teacher demonstrates with the help of a child how to guide someone through the obstacle track. Children are paired, and one of the children is blindfolded, while the other guides him/her through the track. The game ends when all the children participated in both roles – the child who helps and the child who was provided with help.	Games Track Social learning strategies Modeling

(*continued*)

(continued)

Module 5—Cooperative play

Duration: 4 weeks; 2–3 activities/week; 15–20 minutes/activity

Objective G.O. 6	*Activity description*	*Strategies/methods*
S.O. 2	The teacher selects a "mystery object" or a "mystery person" from the classroom. The children must ask the teacher questions to find clues regarding that object or person. After the teacher exemplifies the task, each child selects an object or a classmate and answers the other children's questions.	Games "Mystery object/person" Didactic methods Comprehension questions Social learning strategies Modeling
S.O. 2	The teacher provides children with playing dough. The children are paired and are given a task to make together an object made from playing dough. The teacher guides each pair of children in cooperating in their task. Also, the children who demonstrate cooperative skills are praised. The objects are then displayed for all the children to see.	Social learning strategies Group play Modeling Behavioral strategies (antecedent-based) Prompting Behavioral strategies (consequence-based) Praise
S.O. 2	This activity resembles the previous one in terms of including a cooperative play project. The teacher draws a picture of a tower made of Lego-type pieces. The children are paired and are asked to build a similar tower with their play partner. The teacher guides the children, and praises those who cooperate. The towers are then displayed for all the children to see.	Social learning strategies Group play Modeling Behavioral strategies (antecedent-based) Prompting Behavioral strategies (consequence-based) Praise
S.O. 2	The teacher establishes teams of 3 or 4 children. Each team receives a task, to build a part of a larger project (e.g., a train station, a city, a playground, a castle). Each team receives a limited number of Lego pieces. Children are encouraged to cooperate, and the teacher demonstrates cooperative play strategies for each team. The teacher also praises children for cooperating and the final product of the classroom project is displayed.	Social learning strategies Group play Modeling Behavioral strategies (antecedent-based) Prompting Behavioral strategies (consequence-based) Praise

S.O. 2	The teacher, based on the weekly learning theme, selects a classroom project. Groups of 3 or 4 children are provided with colored paper and pencils, photos, glue, etc. Children are encouraged to cooperate, and the teacher demonstrates cooperative play strategies for each team. The teacher praises children for their cooperation strategies.	Social learning strategies Group play Modeling Behavioral strategies (antecedent-based) Prompting Behavioral strategies (consequence-based) Praise
S.O. 3	The teacher pairs up children and asks one child to talk to the other child about a favorite toy, a favorite game, or a special friend. Then, the teacher asks children from each pair questions about what they heard, to help them identify similarities and differences between their preferences.	Didactic methods Comprehension questions
S.O. 3	The teacher uses puppet-play to interpret a series of scenarios, which contain strategies that children can use in order to join an ongoing game. Then, the children are asked to role-play the strategies with guidance from their teacher.	Didactic methods Puppet-play Social learning strategies Role-play Behavioral strategies (consequence-based) Praise
S.O. 2 & S.O. 3	The teacher interprets puppet-play scenarios, which contain a dialogue between the teacher and the characters of Alfi, Pusu, and Pufi. Each scenario contains a possible problem, which children might be faced with during cooperative play. The children's task is to find as many solutions as possible, and evaluate the solutions based on their consequences on maintaining friendships. Then, adequate solutions are role-played by the children.	Didactic methods Puppet-play Comprehension questions Anticipation Social learning strategies Role-play Behavioral strategies (consequence-based) Praise
S.O. 4	Beginning with the first intervention week, the teachers are asked to promote cooperative games by involving themselves in children's play in order to model behaviors such as toy sharing, waiting, turn-taking, offering help. Also, teachers are encouraged to promote cooperation games on a daily basis, to monitor children's behaviors, and to praise them for friendly behaviors.	Social learning strategies Modeling Cooperative play Behavioral strategies (antecedent-based) Prompting Behavioral strategies (consequence-based) Praise

Appendix 2

Treatment Planner for the Teacher Training

The teacher training contains 3 intervention modules. A description of general and specific objectives for each intervention phase, as well as the corresponding activities is provided below.

C. A. Ştefan, *Social-Emotional Prevention Programs for Preschool Children's Behavior Problems*,
https://doi.org/10.1007/978-3-319-74751-4

Module	*General objectives (G.O.)*	*Specific objectives (S.O.)*
Positive discipline strategies	Increasing the frequency of preventive strategies for children's negative behaviors (G.O. 1);	Identifying and implementing age-appropriate classroom rules (S.O. 1); Acquiring high probability commands for increasing children's compliance in the classroom (S.O. 2); Understanding the psychological relevance of routines and implementing them (S.O. 3);
	Increasing the frequency of praise and reward use for children's positive behaviors (G.O. 2);	Understanding the relevance of reinforcements in increasing children's motivation for positive behaviors (S.O. 4); Acquiring and using praise and token economy systems for increasing children's motivation (S.O. 5); Identifying and preventing possible inappropriate ways of using token economy systems (S.O. 6);
	Increasing the frequency of positive discipline strategies for children's negative behaviors (G.O. 3);	Identifying negative consequences of using harsh and/or inconsistent discipline strategies in the classroom (S.O. 7); Identifying negative behaviors which can undergo extinction, implementing positive discipline strategies (e.g., ignoring, withdrawing privileges, timeout) (S.O. 8); Acquiring and exercising positive discipline strategies (S.O. 9); Identifying and preventing possible inappropriate ways of implementing positive discipline strategies (S.O. 10);
Communication and teacher-parent partnership	Increasing the frequency of adequate teacher-child communication strategies (G.O. 4);	Acquiring effective teacher-child communication strategies (e.g., "I" statements, discussions about emotions, problem-solving) (S.O. 1); Developing strategies for involving teacher's in children's play (S.O. 2);
	Increasing the frequency of activities which promote teacher-parent partnership (G.O. 5);	Identifying effective strategies for improving teacher-parent communication (S.O. 3); Identifying and implementing strategies for improving teacher-parent partnership (S.O. 4);
Consultations for implementing the classroom curriculum	Increasing teacher's ability to implement and use strategies for promoting children's emotional and social development (G.O. 6);	Familiarizing teachers with the contents of the classroom activities (S.O. 1); Developing age-appropriate expectations for each targeted behavior (S.O. 2); Identifying and implementing coaching strategies for supporting children's emotional and social competence development (S.O. 3).

Module 1—Positive discipline strategies

Duration: 4 sessions; 5 hours/day

Objective	*Activity description*	*Strategies/methods*
Session 1		
Normalizing/discussing participant's expectations about the intervention	The trainer introduces him/herself and asks the participants to do the same. Then, the content of the training program is presented, as well as its objectives. The participants together with the trainer brainstorm about their expectations, and these answers are discussed in the context of what the program provides at the 3 intervention levels (child, teacher, and parent). The trainer emphasizes that changes do not occur rapidly, that it is an ongoing process highly reliant on teacher and parental involvement, and their consistency in applying the strategies and methods taught during the training sessions the intervention program.	Brainstorming
Acquiring adequate and up-to-date information about the need for early education and its positive effects on children's long-term outcomes	The trainer reviews information from the literature regarding the importance of early education programs and identifies positive consequences of children's adequate emotional and social development. Then, the participants are required to brainstorm examples of behavior problems they often encounter in their practice. The examples are discussed, and the trainer emphasizes the extent to which behavior problems are in fact associated with poor emotional and social competencies development (e.g., aggression, non-compliance, anger tantrums). Also, difficulties with later school adjustment are discussed in terms of the relationship between poor social-emotional competencies, and deficient deployment of attentional resources and difficulties related to school performance.	Direct instruction Brainstorming Deductive reasoning Exemplifying

(*continued*)

(continued)

Module 1—Positive discipline strategies

Duration: 4 sessions; 5 hours/day

Objective	*Activity description*	*Strategies/methods*
Familiarizing teachers with the rationale of prevention programs and the risk sources associated with behavior problems	The teachers are introduced to the rationale of preventive interventions (universal, indicated, and early intervention). For each level of intervention the teachers identify the intervention needs of children, teachers, and parents. Based on the identified intervention needs the main risk factors for behavior problems are defined (e.g., child-related, parent-related, and school-related). This information is also provided on a handout. Then, the teachers together with the trainer reconstruct the interactions between these risk factors using a work sheet, in order to understand the need for added intervention strategies as the number of risk factors increases.	Direct instruction Brainstorming Deductive reasoning
Identifying the main preconceived ideas about "difficult" children and ineffective adult strategies for managing such behaviors	The teachers are asked to provide examples of possible reactions towards children's inappropriate behaviors. The examples are written on a flip-chart, and the trainer and teachers brainstorm examples of attitudes towards inappropriate behaviors, which might lead to counterproductive behaviors (e.g., excessive criticizing, yelling, lecturing, being overly permissive/overly strict, etc.). Teachers are encouraged to take a positive perspective on discipline, and focus on means of preventing misbehaviors rather than intervening when it actually occurs.	Brainstorming
Session 2 G.O. 1		
S.O. 1—formulating a positive discipline system based on classroom rules, and clear expectations	Handouts are provided in order to discuss the main principles of establishing classroom rules. The teachers are then asked to identify, using a work sheet, if the rules are adequately formulated (e.g., age-appropriate, include positive and clear expectations regarding children's behaviors). Then, the teachers are asked to brainstorm appropriate rules for their own classroom (e.g., "Put away toys after playing with them"; "Stay in seat during activities"; "Eyes to the teacher", "Listen to others when they speak", etc.).	Exercise Brainstorming

S.O. 1—promoting rule appropriate and responsible behaviors in children	Based on the previous discussion, the trainer directs the teachers to list a series of logical consequences, derived from not complying with the rules. The "if-then" strategy is exercised for each of the classroom rules proposed by the teachers during the previous activity (e.g., "If you don't put away the toys, you will not play with the other children"; "If you speak when not asked, we will not listen to what you have to say", etc.). Teachers are also required to brainstorm strategies, which reward rule appropriate behaviors. They are asked to list a set of privileges for appropriate behaviors (e.g., new crayons, balloons, choosing a story or a play activity). For these privileges, they are required to role-play situations, in which they use them for rewarding children's appropriate behaviors.	Exercise Role-play Brainstorming
S.O. 1—promoting consistency in rule implementation	The trainer emphasizes the benefits of being consistent in implementing rules and their consequences. Teachers are asked to brainstorm strategies which promote children's compliance with rules (e.g., visual cues, verbal prompting, modeling, rewards, logical consequences), and think about possible negative outcomes, when the strategy is used inconsistently.	Brainstorming
S.O. 2 Implementing limit-setting strategies and verbalizing adequate commands Supporting children's compliance through strategies designed to reduce power struggles	The trainer provides examples of commands, which encourage children's non-compliance (e.g., verbalizing more than one command at a time, unrealistic, unclear). The work sheet provides a few examples of inappropriate commands, and teachers are asked to identify the mistake, and role-play an appropriate way of eliciting children's compliance. Then, the trainer suggests strategies for ensuring children's increased willingness to adhere to adults' requests such as allowing time to comply, giving warnings, redirecting children's behavior, providing options, establishing consequences, rewarding positive behaviors.	Exercise Role-play

(*continued*)

(continued)

Module 1—Positive discipline strategies

Duration: 4 sessions; 5 hours/day

Objective	*Activity description*	*Strategies/methods*
S.O. 3—establishing a safe and predictable environment for children	The trainer emphasizes the importance of routines for developing children's sense of control and predictability over their own environment. The trainer asks the teachers to indicate the routines they use in their classrooms (e.g., daily schedule, going to the bathroom, going to lunch, eating), as well as the methods for implementing them (e.g., visual cues, songs, rhymes). The teachers are also taught how to prepare transitions between activities by drawing children's attention to the fact that a certain activity will end and another will begin. Also, teachers are requested to think about reasons why monitoring children during classroom activities is important for preventing inadequate child behaviors.	Brainstorming Group discussion Modeling
Session 3 G.O. 2		
S.O. 4 Understanding the principle of providing children with positive attention	Teachers are requested to think back to the examples of misbehaviors they provided in the end of the first intervention session. The trainer emphasizes that all behaviors have a social purpose and that providing children with positive attention motivates them to behave adequately, rather than misbehave. The trainer also encourages teachers to focus on positive behaviors, which they wish to reinforce (e.g., sharing, persistence, paying attention, etc.), rather than negative behaviors (e.g., aggressive, giving up, not paying attention, etc.). Teachers are asked to brainstorm about their use of rewards for children's adequate behaviors. Based on teacher's examples, the trainer establishes the different types of rewards (e.g., symbolic, activities, objects, social/praise).	Brainstorming Deductive reasoning

S.O. 4 & S.O. 5 Promoting children's adequate behaviors by positive attention and praise	The teachers are provided with a work sheet containing a series of statements about praise use. Each statement is discussed and possible myths are identified. Next, the trainer asks the teachers to find arguments, which sustain the use of praise in the classroom compared to other types of rewards. The trainer offers examples of how to deliver effective praises (e.g., being specific, showing enthusiasm, praising efforts to improve, contingent praise, group praise), which motivate children to learn or repeat an appropriate behavior. The teachers role-play praising different behaviors suggested by the trainer.	Deductive reasoning Role-play
S.O. 5 & S.O. 6 – familiarizing teachers with the principles of a token economy and preventing inappropriate use	The trainer identifies positive behaviors which might require added intervention for increasing motivation. The trainer models step by step implementing of a reward system. The main point of the presentation is emphasizing the token economy principle, which allows children to convert symbolic rewards into objects or activities. Teachers are also taught to extend the number of behaviors a child performs in order to obtain a similar reward, to prevent children's dependence on reinforcements to produce a certain behavior. The teachers are asked to role-play the steps for motivating children to gather their toys after play. The teachers are provided with a work sheet describing possible scenarios for implementing reward systems. The exercise is intended to detect mistakes in the use of rewards (e.g., using the same type of rewards, using rewards that are not perceived accordingly by the child, rewarding before the adequate behavior), and discussing their negative effects on children's motivation to exhibit positive behaviors in the classroom.	Modeling Role-play Case study
Session 4 G.O. 4		
S.O. 7—increasing awareness concerning the fact that children's misbehavior is goal- oriented	The trainer provides teachers with a work sheet and asks them to list inappropriate child behaviors, as well as their own response to the child's behavior. Based on these examples, the trainer and teachers discuss the possible causes of these behaviors (e.g., getting adult attention, testing the limits, curiosity, lack of appropriate skills, etc.).	Brainstorming Deductive reasoning

(*continued*)

(continued)

Module 1—Positive discipline strategies

Duration: 4 sessions; 5 hours/day

Objective	*Activity description*	*Strategies/methods*
S.O. 8, S.O. 9 & S.O. 10 Utilizing ignoring for behaviors reinforced by the teacher's attention Practicing the use of ignoring and identifying possible pitfalls	Using the examples provided in the handout, the trainer explains the rationale of ignoring behaviors, which are directed at obtaining the adults' attention. The trainer emphasizes that attention is a negative reinforcement, responsible for children's repeated attempts to gain attention through misbehavior. The trainer and the teachers brainstorm to identify behaviors which can be ignored (e.g., anger tantrums, yelling, whining, etc.). The trainer introduces a case study, and the teachers are asked to role-play the strategy. During the role-play the trainer introduces some pitfalls, which might suggest to the teachers that the strategy is ineffective (e.g., increased misbehavior in response to ignoring, offering attention before the child calms down). These problems are discussed and solutions are provided.	Direct instruction Case study Modeling Role-play
S.O. 8, S.O. 9 & S.O. 10 Utilizing response cost strategy for children's misbehaviors Practicing the use of response cost strategy and identifying possible pitfalls	The trainer introduces a case study, and the teachers are asked to identify the problem and propose a strategy for reducing the frequency of the child's misbehavior. The trainer explains the rationale of response cost procedures, namely withdrawing privileges in order to reduce children's misbehaviors (e.g., not being allowed to play with a toy, if he/she does not want to share it; not being allowed to play on the computer, if he/she refuses to participate in the activities). As in the case of ignoring, behaviors which respond to such strategies are identified. Then, the trainer and the teachers role-play the strategy. During role-play possible errors in implementing the strategy are identified and discussed (e.g., lack of warning before withdrawing a privilege, threats, inconsistency, excessive punishments). For each inadequate strategy the trainer offers an adequate solution.	Direct instruction Case study Modeling Role-play

S.O. 8, S.O. 9 & S.O. 10 Utilizing timeout for highly disruptive behaviors Practicing the use of timeout and identifying possible pitfalls	The trainer describes the timeout procedure and provides guidelines for implementing timeout depending on the age of the child, and the type of misbehavior (e.g., repeated aggression and non-compliance). The trainer also identifies the circumstances under which the use of timeout is effective. Both the trainer and the teachers role-play situations which require the use of timeout. Possible difficulties are discussed (e.g., refusing to accept timeout, consistency, expecting children to be ashamed, lack of warning before applying timeout). For each pitfall, adequate strategies are provided by the trainer.	Direct instruction Case study Modeling Role-play
S.O. 1, S.O. 2, S.O. 3, S.O. 5, S.O. 8 & S.O. 9—establishing homework assignment	At the end of Module 1 the teachers and trainer review the main ideas discussed and emphasize the new information provided during the training. The teachers receive a homework assignment consisting of reading material regarding positive discipline strategies. Teachers are also asked to implement the learned strategies and monitor the outcomes, as well as report their difficulties during the next meeting.	Homework

Module 2—Communication and teacher-parent partnership

Duration: 2 sessions; 2 hours/day

Objective	*Activity description*	*Strategies/methods*
Session 1 G.O. 4		
Discussing possible problems encountered in implementing the classroom management strategies	The trainer welcomes the teachers to the second training session. Also, the trainer reviews the discussion topics from the previous training session. Then, the homework assignments are discussed. Teachers are invited to ask questions about the reading material. The next step is discussing observations made during implementing classroom management strategies. Difficulties are discussed and teachers are assisted in finding solutions to their problems.	Homework Group discussion
S.O. 1—identifying attitudes which block communication	The teachers are asked to provide a definition of communication. The trainer explains the principles of communication and establishes possible sender or receiver attitudes, which block communication (e.g., criticizing, lecturing, focusing excessively on own emotions). Each blocker is discussed separately, an example is provided, and teachers are asked to propose an alternative strategy, which enhances communication efficacy. The teachers are also asked to provide personal examples of failure to communicate adequately, and proposed remedial strategies are discussed.	Direct instruction Exemplifying Role-play Group discussion Brainstorming
S.O. 1—promoting communication strategies designed to improve the quality of the teacher-child relationship	The teachers are asked to provide metaphors, which they think best describe the teacher-child relationship (e.g., planting seeds, growing a flower, investing money in a business). Based on these metaphors the trainer and the teachers identify adult behaviors, which promote a positive teacher-child relationship (e.g., taking about emotions, talking about the children's preferences, criticizing the child's behavior and not the child). For each strategy an example is provided, and then teachers are asked to role-play these strategies.	Metaphors Role-play Exemplifying

S.O. 2—identifying adequate ways to get involved in children's play	The trainer identifies with the teachers' assistance the main errors adults make when they get involved in children's play (e.g., imposing their own opinions, competing, projecting adult logic). For each inadequate strategy, negative consequences are discussed. Then, the trainer asks the teachers to identify their own strategies for play involvement. The teachers are asked to reflect on how often they use these strategies, and why it is important for them as adults to get involved in children's play.	Brainstorming Deductive reasoning Self-reflection
Session 2 G.O. 5		
S.O. 3—applying effective communication principles in relation to parents	The trainer provides teachers with a work sheet. The exercises' aim is for the teachers to identify the communication errors from the examples and provide alternative strategies. The effects of both the inappropriate and appropriate strategies on the teacher-parent relationship are discussed. Then, the trainer suggests a typical parent-teacher communication scenario, and teachers are invited to role-play managing the situation.	Role-play
S.O. 4—familiarizing teachers with methods, which promote improved teacher-parent partnership	The trainer asks the teachers to think of some advantages of having a positive teacher-parent relationship (e.g., easier implementing of behavior interventions, involving parents in children's activities, reducing mistrust and defensive reactions). Teachers are also encouraged to provide examples of how they promoted parental involvement in children's activities in the past. The trainer also suggests methods which optimize teacher-parent partnership (e.g., informing the parents about the progress, suggesting parent-child activities, inviting parents to attend outings and classroom activities).	Brainstorming Exemplifying
S.O. 1, S.O. 2, S.O. 3 & S.O. 4 Discussing the homework assignment	The trainer reviews the main ideas discussed and emphasizes the new information provided during the training. The teachers receive a homework assignment, which requires them to implement communication strategies in the classroom and in the context of teacher-parent interactions. Also, the teachers are provided with reading materials regarding effective communication strategies.	Homework

Module 3—Consultations for implementing the classroom curriculum

Duration: 5 sessions; 1 hour/session

Objective G.O. 6	*Activity description*	*Strategies/methods*
Session 1		
Establishing the rationale of consultations	The trainer introduces the teachers to the concept of consultations, which are provided in the beginning of each module of the children-focused curriculum. The trainer and teachers establish a consultation schedule.	Direct instruction
S.O. 2 & S.O. 3 Establishing and implementing rules for each classroom	Teachers are reminded about developmental milestones for rule compliance. Each group of teachers is required to select a maximum of 4 classroom rules. Then, they select 1 or 2 rules, which most children have difficulty in complying with, in order to be reinforced through a classroom reward system. The next step is to remind teachers about the rationale of the token economy strategy and discuss how to implement this strategy in the context of the selected classroom rules. Then, the trainer models the implementation of the reward system for a set of proposed classroom rules. Afterwards, each teacher proposes an individualized plan for implementing rules in the classroom and using a token economy.	Direct instruction Modeling
S.O. 1—promoting adequate implementation of activities designed to increase compliance	Each activity from the curriculum for rule compliance is discussed. Teachers are familiarized with the content of the activity, the materials, and the strategies required for implementing them. Teachers are encouraged to think about possible problems, which could arise during the classroom curriculum's implementation and to discuss them. They are also asked to make suggestions and observations regarding the activities from the classroom curriculum. Teachers are provided with a fidelity checklist as a reminder of the sequence in which the activities must be implemented, as well as a handout containing a description of the methods for supporting children's compliance with rules development. The teachers are reminded about the positive discipline strategies discussed in Module 1 and they are encouraged to employ them consistently in the classroom. The trainer establishes the date of the next consultation session.	Group discussion Fidelity checklists

Session 2		
Discussing problems and suggestions related to the classroom activities	The trainer asks the teachers about their experience with implementing the first module. The trainer suggests solutions in case difficulties were identified by the teachers. Also, teachers are encouraged to provide feedback on the quality and feasibility of the activities from the classroom curriculum. The trainer introduces the activities for developing emotion recognition.	Feedback
S.O. 2 & S.O. 3—establishing and implementing strategies for supporting children's emotion recognition	The trainer discusses developmental milestones for emotion recognition. The teachers and trainer discuss strategies for developing children's emotion vocabulary (e.g., discussions about emotions, providing a safe environment for expressing emotions, providing support for manifesting empathy). Each strategy is role-played with the trainer's assistance.	Direct instruction Role-play
S.O. 1—promoting adequate implementation of activities	Each activity from the curriculum for emotion recognition is discussed. Teachers are familiarized with the content of the activity, the materials, and the strategies required for implementing them. Teachers are encouraged to think about possible problems, which could arise during the implementation of this module and to discuss them. They are also asked to make suggestions and observations regarding the activities from the classroom curriculum. Teachers are provided with a fidelity checklist as a reminder of the sequence in which the activities must be implemented, as well as a handout containing the description of the methods for supporting children's emotion knowledge development. The trainer establishes the date of the next consultation session.	Group discussion Fidelity checklists
Session 3		
Discussing problems and suggestions related to the classroom activities	The trainer asks the teachers about their experience with implementing the second module from the child-focused curriculum. The trainer suggests solutions in case difficulties were identified by the teachers. Also, teachers are encouraged to provide feedback on the quality and feasibility of the activities from the classroom curriculum. The trainer introduces the activities for developing emotion regulation.	Feedback

(*continued*)

(continued)

Module 3—Consultations for implementing the classroom curriculum

Duration: 5 sessions; 1 hour/session

Objective G.O. 6	*Activity description*	*Strategies/methods*
S.O. 2 & S.O. 3—establishing and implementing strategies for supporting children's emotion regulation	The trainer discusses the developmental milestones for emotion regulation. The teachers and trainer discuss strategies for developing children's emotion regulation (e.g., the "turtle technique", modeling, role-playing). For each strategy the trainer presents the rationale, and the steps required for implementing it when working with children in the classroom. Teachers are encouraged to use these strategies for coaching children during daily classroom interactions, and therefore supporting the development of their emotion regulatory strategies.	Direct instruction Role-play
S.O. 1—promoting adequate implementation of the activities	Each activity from the curriculum for emotion regulation is discussed. Teachers are familiarized with the content of the activity, the materials, and the strategies required for implementing them. Teachers are encouraged to think about possible problems, which could arise during the implementation of this module and to discuss them. They are also asked to make suggestions and observations regarding the activities from the classroom curriculum. Teachers are provided with a fidelity checklist as a reminder of the sequence in which the activities must be implemented, as well as a handout containing the description of the methods for supporting children's emotion regulation development. The trainer establishes the date of the next consultation session.	Group discussion Fidelity checklists
Session 4		
Discussing problems and suggestions related to the classroom activities	The trainer asks the teachers about their experience with implementing the third module from the child-focused curriculum. The trainer suggests solutions in case difficulties were identified by the teachers. Teachers are also encouraged to provide feedback on the quality and feasibility of the activities from the classroom curriculum. The trainer introduces the activities for developing problem-solving.	Feedback

S.O. 2 & S.O. 3—establishing and implementing Strategies for supporting children's problem-solving	The trainer discusses the developmental milestones for problem-solving. The teachers and trainer discuss strategies for developing children's problem-solving (e.g., implementing problem-solving strategies, modeling and prompting prosocial behaviors, praising adequate problem-solving). For each strategy the trainer presents the rationale, and the steps required for implementing it when working with children in the classroom. Teachers are encouraged to use these strategies for coaching children, and supporting the development of their problem-solving strategies during daily classroom interactions.	Direct instruction Role-play
S.O. 1—promoting adequate implementation of the activities	Each activity from the curriculum for problem-solving is discussed. Teachers are familiarized with the content of the activity, the materials, and the strategies required for implementing them. Teachers are encouraged to think about possible problems, which could arise during the implementation of this module and to discuss them. Teachers are provided with a fidelity checklist as a reminder of the sequence in which the activities must be implemented, as well as a handout containing a description of the methods for supporting the children's problem-solving skills. The trainer establishes the date of the next consultation session.	Group discussion Fidelity checklists
Session 5		
Discussing problems and suggestions related to the classroom activities	The trainer asks the teachers about their experience with implementing the fourth module from the child-focused curriculum. The trainer suggests solutions in case difficulties were identified by the teachers. Teachers are also encouraged to provide feedback on the quality and feasibility of the activities. The trainer introduces the activities for developing cooperative play skills.	Feedback
S.O. 2 & S.O. 3—establishing and implementing strategies for supporting children's cooperative play strategies	The trainer discusses the developmental milestones for play cooperation. The teachers and trainer discuss strategies for developing children's cooperative play (e.g., modeling and prompting cooperative behaviors, providing children with group activities, praising cooperation between children). For each strategy the trainer presents the rationale, and the steps required for implementing it when working with children in the classroom. Teachers are encouraged to use these strategies for coaching children, and supporting the development of their cooperative play strategies during daily classroom interactions.	Direct instruction Role-play

(*continued*)

(continued)

Module 3—Consultations for implementing the classroom curriculum		
Duration: 5 sessions; 1 hour/session		
Objective G.O. 6	***Activity description***	***Strategies/methods***
S.O. 1—promoting adequate implementation of the activities	Each activity from the curriculum for play cooperation is discussed. Teachers are familiarized with the content of the activity, the materials, and the strategies required for implementing them. Teachers are encouraged to think about possible problems, which could arise during the implementation of this module and to discuss them. Also, teachers are provided with a fidelity checklist as a reminder of the sequence in which the activities must be implemented, as well as a handout containing a description of the methods for supporting the development of children's cooperative play strategies.	Group discussion Fidelity checklists
Debriefing		
Evaluating the content of the intervention and the trainer	The trainer asks the teachers about their experience with implementing the fifth module from the child-focused curriculum. The trainer suggests solutions in case difficulties were identified by teachers. Teachers are also encouraged to provide feedback on the quality and feasibility of the activities. The trainer asks the teachers to provide written feedback on the utility of the teacher training and the classroom curriculum. Also, the teachers evaluate the trainer. Participants are thanked for their involvement.	Feedback

Appendix 3

Treatment Planner for the Parent Training

The parent training contains 4 *group training sessions* and *individual training sessions* conducted at the parents' request. A description of general and specific objectives for each intervention phase, as well as corresponding activities, is provided below.

C. A. Ştefan, *Social-Emotional Prevention Programs for Preschool Children's Behavior Problems*,
https://doi.org/10.1007/978-3-319-74751-4

Group training	*General objectives (G.O.)*	*Specific objectives (S.O.)*
Compliance with rules	Increasing the frequency of parental use of positive discipline strategies (G.O. 1);	Understanding the benefits of limit setting and identifying age-appropriate rules (S.O. 1); Acquiring high probability commands for increasing children's compliance at home (S.O. 2); Understanding the psychological relevance of routines and implementing them (S.O. 3);
	Increasing parental knowledge about children's developmental milestones (G.O. 2);	Discussing developmental milestones for compliance and normalizing parental expectations regarding this behavior (S.O. 4);
	Increasing the frequency of coaching strategies used by parents for supporting the development of children's competencies (G.O. 3);	Acquiring and implementing strategies for enhancing children's compliance (S.O. 5); Acquiring and implementing strategies for managing children's non-compliance (S.O. 6);
Praise and rewards. Emotional development	Increasing the frequency of parental use of positive discipline strategies (G.O. 1);	Understanding the relevance of reinforcements in increasing children's motivation for positive behaviors (S.O. 1); Acquiring and using praise and token economy systems for increasing children's motivation (S.O. 2); Identifying and preventing possible inappropriate ways of using token economy systems (S.O. 3);
	Increasing parental knowledge about children's developmental milestones (G.O. 2);	Discussing developmental milestones for emotion recognition, and normalizing parental expectations regarding this behavior (S.O. 4); Discussing developmental milestones for emotion regulation, and normalizing parental expectations regarding this behavior (S.O. 5);
	Increasing the frequency of coaching strategies used by parents for supporting the development of children's competencies (G.O. 3);	Acquiring and implementing strategies for enhancing children's emotion literacy and emotion regulation strategies (S.O. 6); Acquiring and implementing strategies for managing children's anger tantrums (S.O. 7);

Positive discipline strategies. Problem-solving for children	Increasing the frequency of parental use of positive discipline strategies (G.O. 1);	Identifying negative consequences of using harsh and/or inconsistent discipline strategies in the classroom (S.O. 1); Identifying negative behaviors which can undergo extinction, implementing positive discipline strategies (e.g., ignoring, withdrawing privileges, timeout) (S.O. 2); Acquiring and exercising positive disciple strategies (S.O. 3); Identifying possible inappropriate ways of implementing positive discipline strategies (S.O. 4);
	Increasing parental knowledge about children's developmental milestones (G.O. 2);	Discussing developmental milestones for problem-solving and normalizing parental expectations regarding this behavior (S.O. 5);
	Increasing the frequency of coaching strategies used by parents for supporting the development of children's competencies (G.O. 3);	Acquiring and implementing strategies for enhancing children's problem-solving strategies (S.O. 6); Acquiring and implementing strategies for managing children's aggression (S.O. 7);
Play cooperation and adult-child communication	Increasing parental knowledge about children's developmental milestones (G.O. 2); Increasing the frequency of appropriate parent-child interactions (G.O. 4);	Discussing developmental milestones for problem-solving and normalizing parental expectations regarding this behavior (S.O. 1); Understanding the relevance of play for children's development (S.O. 2); Developing strategies for parental involvement in children's play (S.O. 3); Developing and exercising strategies for improving parent-child communication strategies ("I" statements, discussions about emotions, how to say "no" to a child, etc.) (S.O. 4).
Individual training		
	Providing additional assistance to parents in managing children's behavior problems through positive discipline strategies and coaching social-emotional development (G.O. 1).	Identifying negative behaviors and providing parents with a behavioral analysis (S.O. 1); Developing an intervention plan for the problem behavior (S.O. 2); Evaluating the outcomes of the intervention and suggesting alternative steps if necessary (S.O. 3).

I. Group training sessions		
Duration: 4 sessions; 1½–2 hours/session		
1. Compliance with rules		
Objective G.O. 1, G.O. 2 & G.O. 3	***Activity description***	***Strategies/methods***
Informing parents about the benefits of attending the parenting sessions	The trainer introduces him/herself and asks the participants to do the same. Parents are provided with information about the importance of emotional and social development for children's future adjustment. The need for parental involvement is emphasized, as well as the positive outcomes for parent-child interactions (e.g., improved understanding of children's developmental stages, providing a positive environment for children's development, acquiring strategies to manage inappropriate behaviors).	Direct instruction Brainstorming
G.O 2 – S.O. 4 Identifying the developmental milestones for compliance with rules	The trainer provides parents with handouts and introduces the developmental milestones for children's compliance with rules. The trainer assists parents in determining whether their children's behaviors are age-appropriate. The trainer establishes the relationship between parents' age-appropriate expectations and children's behaviors. Also, they discuss the negative consequences of being overprotective (e.g., relying excessively on parental help, lack of autonomy, resistance to new), or extremely harsh (e.g., lack of self-esteem, non-compliance, feelings of sadness and inadequacy).	Direct instruction Guided discovery Brainstorming

G.O. 1 – S.O. 1 & **G.O. 3** – S.O. 5, S.O. 6 Promoting strategies for limit setting, establishing rules, and implementing them at home	The trainer and parents brainstorm the importance of implementing rules (e.g., providing structure, setting limits, and clear expectations, teaching children to be independent and responsible). The trainer asks parents to provide examples of rules they established at home, or encourages them to provide examples of rules they think would be appropriate. The examples are discussed, and based on the handouts the trainer suggests adequate strategies for establishing rules (e.g., clear, positive, age-appropriate). The trainer teaches parents to model children's rule-appropriate behaviors, and these strategies are exercised through role-play (e.g., "When I leave the table, I put my plate in the sink. Next time I would like you to do the same"). Parents are also taught to provide reminders using verbal prompting in a polite, adequate manner ("Please go to your room and put away the toys"), to monitor their children, and to assist in gaining their compliance (e.g., proposing games, story telling). Parents are also provided with drawings, which can help children to behave according to the rules.	Brainstorming Modeling Role-play Visual cues
G.O. 1 – S.O. 2 & **G.O. 3** – S.O. 5, S.O. 6 Exercising and implementing appropriate strategies for delivering commands	The trainer asks parents to identify possible parent behaviors which might be responsible for children's non-compliance (e.g., lecturing, shouting, criticizing). The trainer suggests strategies for formulating appropriate commands such as establishing eye contact, monitoring the child's behavior, delivering one command at a time, clear, positive, in terms of "do", etc. The parents are asked to complete an exercise, which requires them to identify errors in formulating instructions, and proposing alternative adequate commands. Parents are also asked to role-play the appropriate versions. The parents are also instructed to use controlled choices that allow children to develop a sense of autonomy and control (e.g., "Would you like to go to the park or go on a bicycle ride?").	Deductive reasoning Modeling Role-play

(*continued*)

(continued)

I. Group training sessions		
Duration: 4 sessions; 1½–2 hours/session		
1. Compliance with rules		
Objective G.O. 1, G.O. 2 & G.O. 3	***Activity description***	***Strategies/methods***
G.O. 1 – S.O. 3 & **G.O. 3** – S.O. 5, S.O. 6 Structuring the environment and implementing routines to increase children's compliance	Parents are directed towards using strategies to implement routines and schedules (e.g., eating, sleeping). The psychological benefits of routines are discussed and the trainer emphasizes their positive impact on children's sense of control and safety. Then, the trainer asks parents to think about previously experienced difficulties with setting routines for children's sleeping and eating habits. The parents are asked to provide strategies from their own experience regarding these routines. Possible strategies are brainstormed and discussed.	Brainstorming Modeling
G.O. 3 – S.O. 5, S.O. 6 Establishing the homework assignment Introducing the rationale of self-monitoring	Parents receive 2 homework assignments. The first requires them to implement rules at home, and practice appropriate instructions. The second homework includes a self-monitoring exercise for the use of praise and positive discipline strategies. The trainer introduces parents to the rationale of self-monitoring, and asks them to complete the exercise once a week. The trainer announces the date and time of the next group training session, and reminds parents that they can sign up for individual parent sessions.	Homework Self-monitoring sheets

I. Group training sessions		
Duration: 4 sessions; 1½–2 hours/session		
2. Praise and rewards. Emotional development		
Objective G.O. 1, G.O. 2 & G.O. 3	***Activity description***	***Strategies/methods***
Discussing problems and suggestions related to rule setting, commands and routines	The trainer asks the parents to describe their experience with establishing rules, commands, and routines. Possible difficulties and setbacks are discussed, and solutions are provided. The trainer introduces the topics of the second training session.	Feedback
G.O. 1 – S.O. 1 & S.O. 2 Understanding the relevance of praise for motivating children's positive behaviors Promoting the use of praise as reinforcement	The parents are provided with a work sheet containing a series of statements about praise. Each statement is discussed and possible myths are identified, as well as arguments for using praise (e.g., does not cost money, motivates children, develops children's sense of autonomy, encourages appropriate behaviors). The trainer offers examples of how to deliver effective praise, which motivates children to learn, or repeat an appropriate behavior. The parents are encouraged to role-play examples of praise for adequate behaviors. They are also reminded that praise should be contingent on the behavior, and should be associated with positive attitudes (e.g., smile, hug, high five, hand shake). Parents are encouraged to "catch" their children's positive behaviors, by monitoring them and providing feedback for appropriate attitudes.	Direct instruction Brainstorming Exercising Role-play Modeling

(*continued*)

(continued)

I. Group training sessions		
Duration: 4 sessions; 1½–2 hours/session		
2. Praise and rewards. Emotional development		
G.O. 1 – S.O. 2 & S.O. 3 Initiating reinforcement strategies to help the child develop appropriate behavior	The trainer identifies behaviors which require added intervention. The trainer also explains the steps involved in effectively implementing a reward system. The main point of the presentation is emphasizing the token economy principle, which allows children to convert symbolic rewards into objects or activities. Parents are also taught to extend the number of behaviors a child performs in order to obtain a similar reward, to prevent children's dependence on reinforcements. Parents are asked to role-play the steps of using a reward system. They are also provided with a work sheet describing possible scenarios for implementing reward systems. The exercise is intended to detect mistakes in the use of rewards (e.g., using the same type of rewards, using rewards that are not perceived accordingly by the child, rewarding before the adequate behavior), and discussing their negative effects, while identifying correct strategies for reward use.	Direct instruction Role-play Modeling Deductive reasoning
G.O. 2 – S.O. 4 & S.O. 5 – identifying developmental milestones for emotion recognition and emotion regulation	The trainer provides parents with handouts and introduces the developmental milestones for children's emotion recognition and emotion regulation. The trainer assists parents in determining whether their children's behavior is age-appropriate.	Direct instruction Guided discovery

G.O. 3 – S.O. 6 Introducing and implementing strategies for developing children's emotion recognition and emotion regulation	A set of strategies for developing children's emotion vocabulary is proposed such as: discussing emotions, providing a safe environment for expressing emotions, reading stories, etc. Parents are instructed to avoid the induction of negative perceptions about emotions. Parents are also asked to complete an exercise on their work sheets, which requires them to detect inappropriate attitudes towards emotions. The second set of strategies includes familiarizing parents with the "turtle technique". Parents are also provided with a poster describing the steps involved in implementing the "turtle technique". Parents are directed to model the "turtle technique", as well as prompt children to use it.	Direct instruction Modeling Visual cues
G.O. 3 – S.O. 6 & S.O. 7 Directing parents towards implementing strategies for managing behavior problems	The trainer asks the parents to think about previously experienced difficulties with children's anger tantrums. An intervention method directed at preventing this type of behaviors is discussed (e.g., the "turtle technique"), and also strategies which reduce such negative behaviors (e.g., ignoring, and withdrawing positive attention for negative behaviors). The trainer provides an example of how these strategies can be implemented. Parents are also given examples of other behavior problems which can be prevented by developing age-appropriate emotion regulation strategies, such as repetitive behaviors (e.g., nail biting, thumb sucking). Parents are asked to provide insights into how they handled these behaviors. Then, the trainer and parents brainstorm and discuss strategies for managing these behaviors.	Brainstorming Modeling
G.O. 3 – S.O. 6 & S.O. 7 Establishing the homework assignment	The parents receive 2 homework assignments. The first requires them to implement at home strategies for developing children's emotion recognition and emotion regulation. The second assignment includes continuing the self-monitoring exercise for the use of praise and positive discipline strategies. The trainer announces the date and time of the next group training session, and reminds parents that they can sign up for individual parent sessions.	Homework Self-monitoring sheets

(*continued*)

(continued)

I. Group training sessions		
Duration: 4 sessions; 1½–2 hours/session		
3. Positive discipline strategies. Problem-solving for children		
Objective G.O. 1, G.O. 2 & G.O. 3	***Activity description***	***Strategies/methods***
Discussing difficulties with using praise/reward systems	The trainer asks the parents to describe their experience with praising or rewarding children's adequate behaviors and discussing their observations regarding children's attitudes towards their parent's praise. Possible difficulties and setbacks are discussed, and solutions are provided. The trainer introduces the topics of the third training session.	Feedback
G.O. 1 – S.O. 1 Promoting parental awareness about the fact that misbehaviors are goal-oriented and maintained by their consequences	The parents are provided with a handout. The trainer clarifies the negative outcomes of using harsh and/or inconsistent discipline strategies. Parents are also familiarized with the rationale of extinction: sanctioning inappropriate behaviors, while praising or rewarding adequate behaviors. The trainer provides parents with a work sheet and asks them to list inappropriate child behaviors, as well as their own behavior. Based on the examples provided, the trainer and parents discuss the possible causes of these behaviors (e.g., getting adult attention, testing the limits, curiosity, lack of appropriate skills).	Direct instruction Deductive reasoning
G.O. 1 – S.O. 2, S.O. 3 & S.O. 4 Understanding the rationale of ignoring behaviors meant to get the parents' attention Practicing the use of ignoring and identifying possible pitfalls	Using the examples provided in the handout, the trainer explains the rationale of ignoring behaviors which are aimed at obtaining the adults' attention. The trainer emphasizes that attention is a negative reinforcement, responsible for children's repeated attempts to gain attention. The trainer and parents brainstorm to identify behaviors which can be ignored (e.g., anger tantrums, yelling, whining). The trainer warns parents about pitfalls, which might affect the efficacy of the strategy (e.g., increased misbehavior in response to ignoring, offering attention before the child calms down). These problems are discussed and solutions are offered. The trainer models the parental behavior regarding ignoring. Parents are required to brainstorm examples about ways in which children can receive positive attention from adults.	Direct instruction Modeling Brainstorming

G.O. 1 – S.O. 2, S.O. 3 & S.O. 4 Understanding the relevance of natural and logical consequences to redirect children's behaviors Practicing the use of privilege withdrawal and identifying possible pitfalls	The trainer exemplifies the difference between natural (e.g., losing a toy because the child did not put it away), and logical consequences (e.g., not playing the next day with a toy, because the child refused to put it away). The trainer and parents discuss situations in which parents can let their children experience logical consequences (e.g., refuses to share a toy, loses that toy till the next day; refusing to go to bed, loses the bedtime story). Parents are advised to redirect inappropriate behavior by warning children about the possible consequences, and enforcing them consistently. Parents are warned about possible pitfalls (e.g., lack of warning before withdrawing a privilege, threats, inconsistency, excessive punishments). For each inappropriate strategy the trainer offers an appropriate solution.	Direct instruction Modeling
G.O. 1 – S.O. 2, S.O. 3 & S.O. 4 Understanding the relevance of timeout as a logical consequence Practicing the use of timeout and identifying possible pitfalls	The timeout procedure is introduced by the trainer, who identifies behaviors which require implementing this strategy (e.g., repeated aggression and non-compliance). The trainer emphasizes the use of timeout as being dependent on the child's age and misbehavior frequency. The trainer models the timeout procedure. Possible difficulties in implementing timeout are identified (e.g., refusing to accept timeout, consistency, expecting children to be ashamed, lack of warning before applying timeout), and solutions are proposed.	Direct instruction Modeling
G.O. 2 – S.O. 5 Identifying developmental milestones for problem-solving abilities	The trainer provides parents with handouts and introduces developmental milestones for children's problem-solving abilities. The trainer assists the parents in determining whether their children's behavior is age-appropriate. The parents are directed towards supporting children's independent problem-solving either in social (e.g., cooperative play) or non-social situations (e.g., drawing, building, making puzzles).	Direct instruction Guided discovery

(*continued*)

(continued)

I. Group training sessions		
Duration: 4 sessions; 1½–2 hours/session		
3. Positive discipline strategies. Problem-solving for children		
G.O. 3 – S.O. 6 & S.O. 7 Introducing and implementing strategies for supporting children's problem-solving Developing strategies for managing children's aggression	Parents are introduced to problem-solving strategies as a way of preventing future aggressive behaviors. A problem-solving script from the handout is discussed with the trainer. The problem-solving strategies discussed include discussing emotions, establishing behaviors associated with particular emotions, evaluating these behaviors and establishing adequate future behaviors. These steps are role-played with the trainer's assistance. Then, the trainer asks the parents to think about previously experienced difficulties with their children's aggression, and fighting with siblings or other children. The parents are asked to share their strategies and these strategies are discussed.	Direct instruction Role-play Brainstorming Modeling
G.O. 3 – S.O. 6 & S.O. 7 Discussing the homework assignment	The parents receive 2 homework assignments. The first requires them to implement strategies for preventing children's aggression. The second assignment includes continuing the self-monitoring exercise for the use of praise and positive discipline strategies. The trainer announces the date and time of the next group training session, and reminds them that they can sign up for individual parent sessions.	Homework Self-monitoring sheets

I. Group training sessions

Duration: 4 sessions; 1½–2 hours/session

4. Play cooperation and adult-child communication

Objective G.O. 2 & G.O. 4	***Activity description***	***Strategies/methods***
Discussing difficulties with implementing positive discipline strategies	The trainer asks the parents to describe their experience with implementing positive discipline strategies and discusses their observations regarding children's attitudes towards their parents' consistency in implementing these methods. Possible difficulties and setbacks are discussed, and solutions are provided. The trainer introduces the topics of the fourth training session.	Feedback
G.O. 2 – S.O. 1 & S.O. 2 Identifying developmental milestones for children's play patterns Understanding the relevance of play for children's development	Parents are first introduced to developmental patterns of children's play. Subsequently, they are provided with a work sheet. The exercise includes identifying if the statements about children's play are true or false. Each statement is discussed and arguments are provided. Parents are familiarized with the positive effects of play on children's cognitive, emotional, social, and physical development. After indicating the positive outcomes of children's involvement in play activities, parents are introduced to the importance of adult involvement in children's play.	Direct instruction Deductive reasoning
G.O. 4 – S.O. 3 Promoting and modeling strategies for parental involvement in children's play	The trainer identifies, with parents' help, the main errors adults make when they get involved in children's play (e.g., imposing their own opinions, competing, projecting adult logic). For each inadequate strategy, negative consequences are discussed. Parents are also encouraged to role-play adequate involvement.	Role-play Modeling

(*continued*)

(continued)

I. Group training sessions		
Duration: 4 sessions; 1½–2 hours/session		
4. Play cooperation and adult-child communication		
G.O. 4 – S.O. 4 Promoting communication strategies and activities designed to improve the quality of parent-child relationship	Parents are provided with a work sheet containing examples of adequate and inadequate communication strategies. Parents are asked to identify the inadequate communication strategies and formulate adequate examples where necessary (e.g., taking about emotions, talking about the children's preferences, criticizing the child's behavior and not the child). For each strategy an example is provided, and then parents are asked to role-play. Parents are also encouraged to identify strategies which allow them to spend quality time with their children (e.g., reading, playing, watching a movie).	Direct instruction Brainstorming Role-play
G.O. 4 – S.O. 3 & S.O. 4 Discussing the homework assignment	The parents receive 2 homework assignments. The first requires them to implement strategies for parent-child play and adequate communication strategies. The second assignment includes continuing the self-monitoring exercise for the use of praise and positive discipline strategies. Parents are asked to attach the self-monitoring sheets to the questionnaires they would have to return at the end of the intervention program. The trainer thanks the parents for their involvement and asks them to provide feedback regarding the relevance of the training.	Homework Self-monitoring sheets Feedback

II. Individual parent training sessions

Objective G.O. 1	*Activity description*	*Strategies/methods*
S.O. 1 & S.O. 2 Assisting parents in identifying the causes and implementing strategies for managing their children's behavior problems	The trainer invites the parent to talk about his/her concerns. The problem is then identified and a behavior analysis is conducted as a means of educating the parent in understanding the child's misbehavior in terms of triggering antecedents and maintaining consequences. The parent is guided towards identifying and focusing on developing appropriate behaviors by reinforcement. Then, adequate response cost procedures are established for managing the inappropriate behavior. The parent is taught to monitor the outcomes, and focus on directing the child towards the appropriate behavior. Furthermore, strategies for supporting social-emotional skills' development are discussed in order to support changes in children's behaviors.	Direct instruction Problem-solving Role-play
S.O. 3 Evaluating the intervention outcomes	The parent is asked to attend a follow-up session designed to evaluate the outcomes of the intervention. If parents report expected changes in their children's behavior and no difficulties in implementing the previously discussed strategies, the intervention is discontinued. If parents report difficulties, these are discussed, and the problem-solving process is reiterated. In this case, another follow-up session is scheduled in order to evaluate the outcomes of the intervention.	Direct instruction Problem-solving Role-play

Index[1]

B

Behavior problems, 8, 11–13, 16, 17, 21, 24
See also Externalizing problems

C

Classroom curriculum, vi, vii, 45, 46, 48–53, 55, 68, 69, 73, 74, 86, 96, 105, 147, 164, 167, 169, 184, 185, 198, 199, 205, 207, 208, 221, 238, 248, 252
Classroom management, 11, 18, 19, 49, 52–54, 68, 69, 146, 147, 246

E

Early education, vii, 22–25, 41, 45–48, 67, 100, 195–213, 239
Efficacy, v–vii, 2, 9, 16, 17, 20–22, 24, 25, 42, 43, 45, 47, 67–89, 95–155, 163–188, 195–213, 246, 262
Evidence-based, vi, 1–25, 42, 45–48, 67, 88, 186, 196, 211
Externalizing problems, 1–5, 7–10, 12, 13, 16, 17, 20, 22, 25, 41–44, 46, 51, 52, 67, 68, 70, 77, 78, 80, 84–87, 98, 108, 109, 112, 117, 120, 123, 126, 130, 136, 141, 144, 146, 147, 149, 153, 167, 170, 186, 202
See also Behavior problems

H

Harsh discipline, 10, 12, 13, 106, 129, 130, 132, 135, 138, 140, 143

I

Implications for practice, 88–89, 154–155, 186–188, 209–213

[1] Note: Page number followed by 'n' refer to notes.

C. A. Ştefan, *Social-Emotional Prevention Programs for Preschool Children's Behavior Problems*,
https://doi.org/10.1007/978-3-319-74751-4

Inconsistent discipline, 10–14, 20, 48, 97, 104, 106, 126, 129, 130, 132, 135, 138, 140, 143, 167, 170, 238, 255, 262
Indicated interventions, 20–23, 42–44, 84, 95, 97–99, 109–112, 126–130, 144–147, 149–152, 185, 196–200, 202, 212

M
Mental health, v, vi, 1, 2, 8, 11, 13, 15, 16, 22, 24, 41, 44, 67, 68, 71, 88, 203, 204, 206, 210, 212, 213
Multifocused, vi, 19–22, 42, 47, 48, 68, 87, 89n1, 97, 105, 196–198, 207

P
Parent training, vi, vii, 17–20, 22, 23, 43, 47, 48, 55–58, 68–70, 72, 74, 86, 87, 96, 97, 105, 151–153, 155, 167, 173, 185, 196, 197, 199, 201, 203, 207, 208, 211, 253
Positive discipline, 10, 18–20, 22, 46, 54, 55, 57, 100, 147, 153, 165, 198, 238–240, 245, 248, 254, 255, 258, 261, 262, 264–266
Preschool children, 1, 2
  See also Preschoolers
Preschoolers, 1–25, 41, 42, 47, 50, 51, 55, 56, 68, 74, 75, 84, 86, 95, 96, 144, 146, 195–203, 205, 213
  See also Preschool children
Prevention programs, vi, 1–25, 42, 43, 45, 67, 69, 84, 86, 87, 95, 97, 105, 144, 147, 149–151, 154, 196, 198, 201, 204, 207, 240
Protective factor, 52, 151, 153, 187, 210

R
Risk factors, vi, 8–15, 20, 21, 23, 67, 86, 96, 108, 123, 147, 149, 151, 163, 164, 167, 195, 196, 204, 209, 240
Risk group, 25, 155

S
School, v, 1, 8, 11, 12, 22, 24, 44, 84, 154, 163, 198
Screening, vi, 42, 44, 76, 77, 98–104, 109, 126–130, 133, 151, 154, 170, 187, 196, 197, 199, 200, 202, 203, 208
SEP, *see* Social-Emotional Prevention Program
Social-emotional competencies, 2–8, 18–19, 41, 42, 44, 45, 48, 55, 67–89, 99, 100, 105, 109, 112, 133, 144, 147, 152–154, 163, 196, 197, 200, 201, 204–206, 208, 210–212, 239
Social-Emotional Prevention Program (SEP), vi, vii, 1–25, 41–58, 67–89, 95–155, 163–188, 195–213

T
Teacher training, vi, vii, 17, 21, 23, 45, 46, 48, 52–55, 57, 68–70, 96, 97, 105, 147, 164, 166, 184, 185, 196, 198, 199, 201, 207, 237

U
Universal interventions, vi, 16, 17, 68, 89, 95–155, 164, 196, 197, 199, 202

The manufacturer's authorised representative in the EU is Springer Nature Customer Service Centre GmbH, Europaplatz 3, 69115 Heidelberg, Germany. If you have any concerns regarding our products, please contact ProductSafety@springernature.com

Printed and bound by CPI Group (UK) Ltd, Croydon, CR0 4YY
30/09/2026
02225660-0011